OFFICIAL

Netscape
Beginner's Guide
TO THE Internet

2ND EDITION

FOR WINDOWS & MACINTOSH

SHELLEY O'HARA

Official Netscape Beginner's Guide To The Internet

Limits of Liability and Disclaimer of Warranty

Trademarks

The Coriolis Group, Inc.
An International Thomson Publishing Company
14455 N. Hayden Road, Suite 220
Scottsdale, Arizona 85260

602.483.0192
FAX 602.483.0193
http://www.coriolis.com

Library of Congress Cataloging-In-Publication Data
O'Hara, Shelley.
   Official Netscape beginner's guide to the Internet/by Shelley O'Hara. -- 2nd ed.
      p. cm.
   Includes index.
   ISBN 1-56604-859-1
   1. Internet (Computer network)   I. Title.
TK5105.875.I57048 1998
005.7'13769—dc21

                                                          98-5703
                                                          CIP

Printed in the United States of America
10 9 8 7 6 5 4 3 2 1

Publisher

Keith Weiskamp

Acquisitions

Jeff Duntemann
Stephanie Wall

Project Editor

Meredith Brittain

Production Coordinator

Kim Eoff

Cover Design

Anthony Stock

Layout Design

April Nielsen

 an International Thomson Publishing company I⊤P®

Albany, NY • Belmont, CA • Bonn • Boston • Cincinnati • Detroit • Johannesburg • London
Madrid • Melbourne • Mexico City • New York • Paris • Singapore • Tokyo • Toronto • Washington

To my sister, Kimberly Lynn Moore

Acknowledgments

Special thanks to Theron Shreve and Robert Kern for getting this project started and for their initial input, and to Meredith Brittain for her excellent editing. Thanks also to the other members of the Coriolis team that helped with this project—Kim, Tony, Cynthia, and Mary.

About The Author

Shelley O'Hara (Indianapolis, IN) has written more than 60 books, including the first edition of *Official Netscape Beginner's Guide to the Internet*, and is the coauthor of *Official Earthlink Beginner's Guide to the Internet*. She is the author of nine bestsellers in the Easy series. O'Hara, who has a BA from the University of South Carolina and an MA from the University of Maryland, also does training for the Division of Continuing Education Studies at Indiana University-Purdue University at Indianapolis.

Table Of Contents

Introduction

The Internet is changing a lot of things—how you work, how you do business, how you shop, how you get the latest news, how you interact with others. It's hard to estimate just how many millions of people are connected. Grandmothers, grandfathers, aunts, uncles, neighbors, kids, friends, enemies, businesses, co-workers, cousins, and nieces are all going online. You might think everyone—except you—is connected.

Now maybe you are thinking of taking the plunge. Perhaps you aren't sure why you should get connected. What is all the excitement about? Is it all hype? Why even get connected? You may not want to jump on the bandwagon until you are sure where the bandwagon is headed.

Or you might want to get connected, but you're not quite sure how to go about it. What do you have to do? How much cost is involved? Is it difficult?

Or maybe you already are connected, but now you are asking yourself, "What do I do next?"

Or perhaps your children are bugging you to get connected so that they can take advantage of all the Internet has to offer. What are the advantages for your children? What are the pitfalls?

If you can identify with any of the above scenarios, this book is for you. The book explains what the Internet is so that you can decide whether getting connected is right for you. You'll find the language easy to understand. New terms are clearly defined when they first appear, and the short Glossary at the end of the book is a handy reference. (You don't have to worry that you need a separate Internet-decoder dictionary to understand the text.)

Have you decided to get connected? Good. Part I of the book describes what you need to get connected. It explains exactly what you need to do and approximately how much it will cost you. Getting connected takes a little bit of effort, but you only have to get set up once. After that, you are ready to surf the Internet.

The rest of the book teaches you *how* to surf—that is, it tells you all the great things you can do on the Internet using Netscape Navigator. Netscape Navigator is a program that lets you browse the World Wide Web, send email messages to other Internet users, hook up with other users with similar interests, and download files. You'll learn how to use Navigator to do all these things. Each procedure is set out in easy-to-follow steps and includes plenty of illustrations so you can follow along.

Who Can Use This Book?

Anyone who is thinking about or wants to get connected to the Internet can use this book. The book is for people of all ages, all professions, and all backgrounds who have one thing in common: the desire to learn about the Internet using a book that is easy to understand.

You may be a business owner who wants to get connected to see whether your business can benefit from being on the Internet. Or you may be a homemaker who wants to use the Internet to expand your interests. You may work out of your home and want to use the Internet as a tool for research and networking with others. Perhaps you are a child or parent and want to experiment with all that's available. You may be retired and want to use the Internet to keep in contact with your friends and family and to connect with new friends. The possibilities are endless. One of the coolest things about the Internet is that it truly has something for everyone.

What You Need To Use This Book

To use this book, you need a computer—either a PC or a Macintosh. This book will work for either type of system, although the figures show Windows 95 screenshots. (Your screen will look slightly different if you have a Macintosh.) If a certain procedure is different on the two systems, instructions for both are included in the text.

You also need a modem, an Internet connection, and Netscape Navigator. How to get these items is covered in Chapter 2. This book uses Netscape Navigator version 4, the latest version.

How This Book Is Organized

This book is divided into four parts. Review the chapter-by-chapter break-down to get an idea of the content.

Part I: Getting Connected

Part I focuses on the key things you need to know to get connected.

Chapter 1, "Why Do I Want To Get Connected?", discusses what you can do once you are on the Internet. Some people hesitate to get connected because they have no idea what the Internet has to offer. This chapter gives you the information you need so you can decide whether you even want to get connected.

Chapter 2, "What Do I Need To Get Connected?", covers the hardware and software you need to actually get *on* the Internet. You also learn how to find an Internet Service Provider, a company that provides the connection to the Internet.

Chapter 3, "How Do I Get Connected?", discusses the basic procedure you follow to get connected to the Internet. You have to get your hardware set up, sign up with an Internet Service Provider, and install software. This chapter tells you what to expect.

Part II: Getting Around

Part II focuses on all the skills you need to use Netscape Navigator.

Chapter 4, "Learning Navigator Basics," tells you how to start Navigator, gives you a tour of the Navigator screen, explains how a typical Web page is set up, and shows you how to get help.

Chapter 5, "Navigating The Internet," shows you methods for moving around on the World Wide Web. Most Web pages include links to other pages. You first learn what a link is and then you learn how to navigate the Web by using links and bookmarks and by typing addresses.

Chapter 6, "Searching The Internet," explains how to find a particular company, topic, or organization on the Internet. The Internet isn't organized into neat little cubbyholes. The information is varied and scattered. This chapter will help you find the sites that will be of interest to you.

Chapter 7, "Exploring Web Pages," covers all the ways you can work with a Web page. You learn ways to view a page, print a page, copy and paste text from a page, find something on a page, and save a page. You also learn about different multimedia elements, such as sounds, movies, and interactive pages.

Chapter 8, "Using Plug-ins," covers using extra helper programs with Navigator. You learn how to find these programs and how to set them up.

Chapter 9, "Kids And The Internet," discusses kid-related sites as well as some precautions you should keep in mind if you have children that might use the Internet.

Chapter 10, "Downloading Files," tells you how to find and download (copy from the network computer to your computer) files. You may want to copy clip art, program files, reports, and other information. For all the help you need on downloading, turn to this chapter.

Chapter 11, "Customizing Navigator," highlights some of the changes you can make to how Navigator looks and works. You can change how the screen appears, select a new home page, organize your bookmarks, and create shortcuts.

Chapter 12, "Sending And Receiving Mail," covers how to send email messages to other Internet users. The chapter explains how to find addresses, create and send mail, and handle mail you receive.

Chapter 13, "Participating In Newsgroups," starts by explaining what a newsgroup is (an electronic bulletin board where you can post and review messages). Then you learn how to subscribe to newsgroups, read messages, and post your own messages.

Part III: Getting Down To Business

Part II gives you the chance to practice the skills you will use over and over again on the Internet. Once you master these skills, you are ready to explore any part of the Internet. Each chapter in Part III describes some specific things you can do as well as highlights some sites you might want to try.

Chapter 14, "Shopping," points out some of the places you can shop on the Internet.

Chapter 15, "Reading The Latest News," showcases some of the best places to get news on the Internet.

Chapter 16, "Looking It Up," explains the resources you can use to look up information on the Internet, such as someone's email address or a toll-free phone number. You can explore some of the government pages, too.

Chapter 17, "Getting The Latest Sports News," previews some of the best sporting pages. Entertainment is one of the main reasons for cruising the Internet, and sports is one of the best forms of entertainment.

Chapter 18, "Researching Financial Information," covers some of the places to get financial information and advice.

Chapter 19, "That's Entertainment," tells you where to find the latest on movies, music, books, and more.

Chapter 20, "Getting Computer Information And Help," lists some of the numerous computer resources on the Web. You can find product information, read the latest news, and get technical support from the sites in this chapter.

Chapter 21, "Finding A Job," explains how to access and use some of the Internet's career resources.

Chapter 22, "Having Fun," is something of a catchall and showcases some of the fun, wild, even wacky sites on the Web. You can look up your horoscope, play games, and more.

Part IV: Appendices And Glossary

The final section of the book includes two appendices and a glossary.

Appendix A, "Troubleshooting Guide," lists some common problems along with their solutions.

Appendix B, "More About Netscape Communicator," covers some other components of Netscape Communicator—Netcaster, Conference, and Composer. You may want to use these programs after you have mastered the basics of browsing, sending mail, and working with newsgroups.

The Glossary is a handy reference of key terms used in the book.

Let's Get Started

The Internet is exciting, informative, and entertaining. You will be surprised and delighted at what you find as you enter this new world. Once you get your feet wet, you may want to check out the other Netscape Press titles that cover Netscape products in greater depth.

Part I

Getting Connected

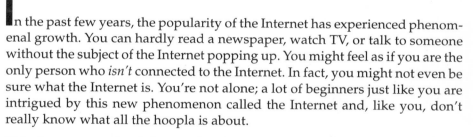

CHAPTER 1

Why Do I Want To Get Connected?

In the past few years, the popularity of the Internet has experienced phenomenal growth. You can hardly read a newspaper, watch TV, or talk to someone without the subject of the Internet popping up. You might feel as if you are the only person who *isn't* connected to the Internet. In fact, you might not even be sure what the Internet is. You're not alone; a lot of beginners just like you are intrigued by this new phenomenon called the Internet and, like you, don't really know what all the hoopla is about.

This chapter starts by defining what the Internet is and then explains why you might want to get connected. You'll learn the difference between the World Wide Web and the Internet. You'll master some of the Internet lingo such as *URL* and *FTP*. And you'll start to see what all the hoopla *is* about.

What Is The Internet?

The *Internet* is a group of thousands and thousands (probably hundreds of thousands) of different computer networks, all loosely connected through the phone lines. To understand how these networks are connected, think of the U.S. highway system. All the major cities are connected by highways, and you can get to just about any city in the United States (except those in Hawaii) using highways. To get to a city, you may have to go through other cities, both small and large. Also, you can take one of several routes to the same city.

Just The FAQs

What is a FAQ?

FAQ stands for Frequently Asked Question. Many areas of the Internet post FAQs. If you have a question, you can check out the FAQ instead of asking someone else or trying to figure it out yourself. Many chapters in this book include a list of FAQs that deal with the chapter topic.

What is the Internet?

The *Internet* is a group of hundreds of thousands of different computer networks, all loosely connected through the phone lines. When you have access to the Internet, you have access to all those networks and the information they contain. You can also communicate with all the other Internet users.

What is the World Wide Web?

The *World Wide Web* is the set of programs that run on the Internet and is a way of presenting information. On the Web, information is presented graphically, using both text and pictures. In some cases, the Web pages may also include sounds or movies that you can play back.

What is Netscape Navigator 4?

Netscape Navigator is a Web browser, a program that enables you to view and work with information on the World Wide Web. Version 4 is the most recent version.

What is Netscape Communicator?

Netscape Communicator is a suite of Internet tools, including Netscape Navigator for browsing the Web, Netscape Messenger for sending and receiving email, Netscape Collabra for working with newsgroups, and several other components.

What can I do once I am connected to the Internet?

Once connected, you can send and receive messages from other users, access information from other computer networks, post and review messages on a bulletin board, download files, and more.

The Internet works the same way. There are several hundred thousand networks (like cities) all connected through the phone lines (like highways). You can get to any network from your computer by traveling through the phone lines. The path you take to get there doesn't matter; the destination does.

And why is the destination important? Two reasons—people and information.

Connecting With Others

It's hard to estimate just how many people are connected to the Internet. A rough guess would be more than 40 million people in the United States alone, and that guess is probably too low. Every day more and more new people, like you, are getting connected to the Internet.

So as an Internet user, you have access to millions and millions of people and all their knowledge. You can send messages, exchange opinions, and share files with any one of the other millions of users. Instantaneously.

The Internet is just one more way—like phones, mail, and faxes—to communicate with others. And that communication is inexpensive, always available, and immediate.

Getting Information

In addition to being connected with other Internet users, you have access to vast stores of information on the various smaller networks that make up the Internet. (Keep in mind that the people who set up the individual networks will decide what you can see and what you can't.) That benefits you in several ways. First, you can access information you might otherwise be unable to obtain. Second, you can get the most up-to-date information—for example, the most current stock price. Third, that information is available at your convenience. You don't have to wait for the newspaper. You don't have to make a call and wait until someone (hopefully a person) answers the phone. You don't have to go anywhere other than to your computer. You can get connected at 2:00 A.M. in your pajamas if you want to.

The Internet is dramatically changing the way people communicate, the way people work, and the way people do business. Instead of writing letters to your aunt, you can send her an email message. Information is more readily available and more widely distributed, making it easier to review from anywhere and possible to work from home. Home offices and small businesses now have more resources to help them compete and stay up-to-date on recent developments.

What Makes Up The Internet?

When you hear people talk about the Internet, you may hear other terms, such as the *World Wide Web* (or *Web*) and *Usenet*. Is the World Wide Web the Internet? Or are they different? What pieces and parts make up the Internet?

The Internet doesn't contain different physical divisions. For example, the World Wide Web is not located in the West and Usenet is not located in the East. The presentation of information, however, does vary on different parts of the Internet. And the way information is presented has evolved as the Internet has become more popular. In this chapter, you'll learn about some of these different methods, starting with the most common.

WWW: The Internet With Pictures (And More)

The most popular way to present information on the Internet is graphically. You'll find graphics on the World Wide Web (or Web or WWW), which is part of the Internet (but not the only part).

The Web was introduced in 1993 and has grown exponentially since then. The explosion of the Internet is largely due to the World Wide Web's popularity and ease of use. The World Wide Web is to the Internet as Windows is to DOS.

You can view information by clicking with a mouse rather than needing to know cryptic commands. All content on the World Wide Web is displayed on *Web pages*, which can be one screen or longer. Instead of viewing just text, you can see pictures and text, making the presentation of information much richer. Some Web pages may even include sounds, videos, and animations. Figure 1.1 shows a sample Web page.

In addition to text and pictures, a Web page may also include *links* to other Web pages. Links enable you to quickly display related pages; the process of selecting links and viewing information is called *browsing*. You browse information by simply clicking on a picture or word. (You'll read more about browsing the Web in Part II of this book.)

To use the World Wide Web, you need a *Web browser* such as Netscape Navigator 4. (The first browser, Mosaic, was developed by Marc Andreessen, the co-founder of Netscape.) A Web browser is your window to the Internet and lets you not only view and work with Web pages, but also access other areas of the Internet.

Each page on the World Wide Web has an address, called the *URL* or *Uniform Resource Locator*. To move quickly to a page, you can type its address. For example, the address of the Web page shown in Figure 1.1 is **http://www.nba.com**.

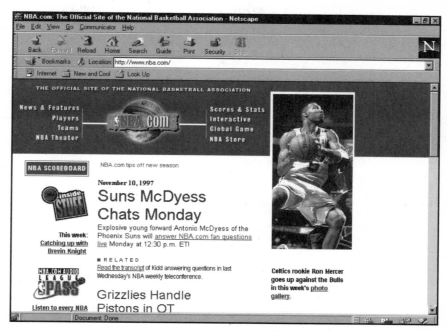

Figure 1.1   Information on the World Wide Web is presented in a graphical format that makes it inviting and easy to use.

Gopherspace: Text Only

In the early days, accessing information on the Internet was difficult because you had to memorize and type Unix commands. To make it easier to access information, *Gopher* was created. Gopher is a menu-driven utility for finding file-transfer sites as well as other textual information. In Gopherspace, you'll find text-only information, which is the best format for documents such as library resources or academic research.

Like Web pages, Gopher sites also have addresses, which start with "gopher". You can get to any of the Gopher sites by using Navigator. The address of the Gopher menu shown in Figure 1.2 is **gopher://gopher.panix.com:70/**.

File Transfer With FTP

FTP stands for *File Transfer Protocol*, which is a method of accessing another network's files. For example, you might download free software or the latest version of a software program from an FTP site. Or you might exchange files with your office from your home using FTP.

Keep in mind that you can't log on to just any computer and swipe just any files. The person who sets up the FTP site will determine what files are available.

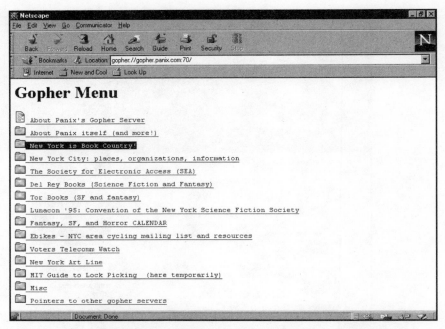

Figure 1.2   You can use a Gopher menu to navigate through textual information on the Internet.

Some networks allow only restricted access; you must have a password and an assigned name to log on to the network and view information. Other networks, called *anonymous FTP sites*, allow anyone to access their files.

FTP sites have addresses that start with *ftp*. You can go to any of these sites by typing the address in Navigator. You can find the list of files shown in Figure 1.3 at the address **ftp://ftp.netscape.com**.

If you are wondering whether someone can access the files on your computer while you are connected to the Internet, stop worrying. They can't unless you specifically allow access to your computer (and that's a fairly complicated job).

Mail

To send mail, you use your email program to address and create a message. Figure 1.4 shows Netscape Messenger's mail program. You can view the messages in your inbox, create a new message, and deal with the messages you have received. For more information about sending mail, see Chapter 12.

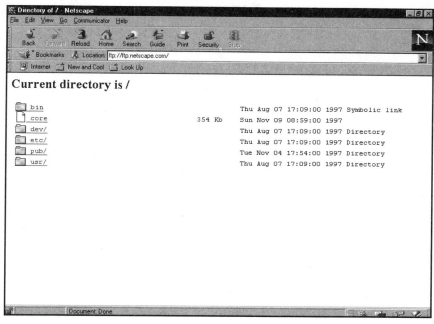

Figure 1.3   From an FTP site, you can download files to your computer.

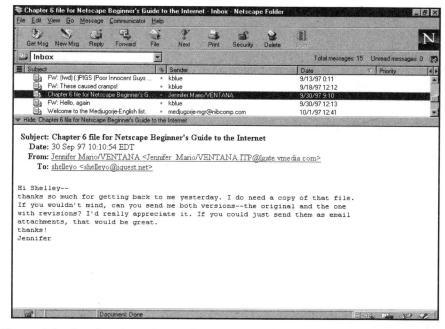

Figure 1.4   Send and receive mail using your email program (here,
             Netscape's Messenger).

Newsgroups And The Usenet

You might think a *newsgroup* would be a place to get the latest world news, but instead, it's an online discussion group—kind of like an electronic bulletin board. Readers of the newsgroup can read existing messages and post their own messages for others to read. They can reply to an existing message or post a new message. *Usenet* is the name of the collection of newsgroups.

Newsgroups are generally devoted to a special area of interest. For example, you might want to join a mystery-novel newsgroup, a cooking newsgroup, or a newsgroup composed of Elvis fans. There are newsgroups for just about everything. Once you subscribe to a newsgroup, you can read any of the messages posted to it. You can also post your own messages, either to start a conversation or in response to a current message. A newsgroup gives you the opportunity to connect with and share ideas with other people interested in the same topic you are.

Each newsgroup has a name made up of parts that are separated from one another by periods. The first part of the name defines the broadest category (for example, "alt" for alternative, "sci" for science, or "rec" for recreation), and subsequent parts of the name break that category into ever more specific subcategories. For more information, see Chapter 13, which covers accessing Internet newsgroups. Figure 1.5 shows some messages in a newsgroup.

Netscape Communicator includes a *news reader* (called Collabra) that lets you subscribe to newsgroups of interest to you. You can then easily review the messages and post your own ideas. You may also use a different news reader, perhaps one supplied to you by your Internet Service Provider (ISP) (see Chapter 2 for more about ISPs).

Mailing Lists

In addition to sharing ideas on a newsgroup, you can subscribe to *mailing lists* and take part in email discussions. To do so, you send an email message requesting a subscription to a mailing list that interests you. When someone in the group sends a message, it is emailed to everyone in the group. Unlike a newsgroup message, which is posted publicly for everyone to see, mailing-list messages are more private and are sent only to those on the subscription list. As with newsgroups, you can find mailing lists on virtually any topic. You can both subscribe to mailing lists and read any messages using your mail program. See Chapter 12 for more information on how to subscribe to a mailing list.

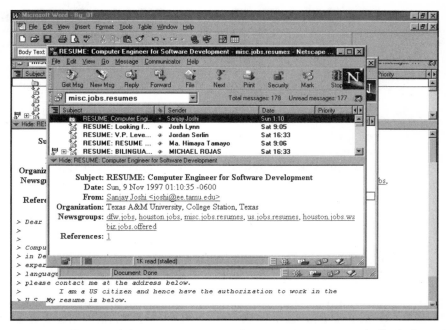

Figure 1.5 *You can join a newsgroup and post messages on a bulletin board to share your ideas with others.*

And More . . .

You can have content delivered to your computer from a Web site using a new type of content publishing called *push technology*. Netscape Communicator includes Netcaster, a program used to deliver content to you via the Internet. You can read more about this program in Appendix B.

You can use *Telnet* to connect with and work on a remote computer. Because you need special Telnet software and need to know how to use special commands, Telnet is not covered in this book.

You can also use *Internet Relay Chat* to chat with other online users. A chat is like a phone conversation, but instead of talking, you type your comments. Anyone in the same *chat room* you are in can respond. If you want to hold a conference call, you can use Netscape Conference (a component of Netscape Communicator).

As with Telnet, chatting and telephone conferencing are for more advanced users. You'll probably want to look into these features as you become more proficient at using the Internet.

Who Owns The Internet? And Other Questions

The Internet seems so pervasive that you may be worried someone powerful is in charge. Or you may be wondering who's making all the money. You may even be thinking how *you* can make some money. This section explains these aspects of the Internet.

Who Owns The Internet?

No one owns the Internet—or rather, *everyone* owns the Internet. No one person or company owns or controls the entire Internet. Instead, each person or company owns their own network and the information on that network. What is made available and how the information is distributed is up to that individual or company.

This lack of ownership or control is what makes the Internet so appealing to many people. You don't have to follow anyone else's rules, although there are some simple rules of etiquette (called *Netiquette*) that you are expected to follow. But it's not as if the Internet police will arrive at your door if you don't follow proper Netiquette. You may hear from other users, though, if you are rude or disruptive.

You can say whatever you want on the Internet; the content is not censored. (That is, no one reviews the content to be sure it conforms to some standard.) The Internet's uncensored nature is great because it allows you to find information on just about any topic and to voice your opinion without fear. Keep in mind, though, that everyone has the same rights as you do. You might come across information you find offensive or don't agree with. *C'est la vie*. And if you have children, remember that they will have access to all the same information. You can buy programs that help you limit and block access to certain areas of the Internet. (See Chapter 9 for more information on kids and the Internet.)

Although you will have to pay someone for the time you are connected to the Internet (see Chapter 2), one giant company is not raking in all the money. No one has a monopoly on Internet access. On the downside, the Internet can be difficult to use because there is no single set interface. A help line is not available for you to call if you have problems.

Finally, anyone can publish on the Internet—even you. The Internet is an open forum. Just because information is published on the Internet, however, doesn't mean it is *useful*. And the information isn't organized into neat little cubbyholes. Instead, it's scattered. Finding what you are looking for can sometimes be challenging. Before you despair, keep in mind that Navigator provides links to several search tools you can use to find information. And this book also highlights some key resources.

How Do Businesses Make Money On The Internet?

Practically every major business is getting set up on the World Wide Web. Does that mean they are making money? And if so, how are they making that money? It depends on the type of business.

Businesses that sell a product or service can reach a wide audience using the Internet. For successful businesses, all the costs for setting up and maintaining their Web sites are offset by the sales they make. But don't think it's an easy job making those sales. Sure, you have an audience of millions of users, but how many of them are interested in what you have to offer? And how do you reach them? It's considered unacceptable to send junk mail via the Internet, so it's difficult to reach your audience directly. You have to get them to come to you—to your Web page, that is.

Some businesses, like car dealers, don't sell directly over the Internet. Instead, they use the Web as an advertising and information medium—to attract customers to the places where they do sell.

Some sites are set up specifically for shopping—a kind of cybermall. Chapter 14 highlights some of these commerce sites.

Businesses that publish content, such as magazines, often offset the cost of their Web sites by selling advertising. Some of the search tools, described in Chapter 6, also do this. Like television stations, content providers may get revenue from advertisers rather than make their audience pay. Or they may charge a subscription fee for access to their services and information. For example, to get the full interactive version of the *Wall Street Journal*, you have to subscribe and pay a fee.

What Am I Charged For On The Internet?

To use the Internet, you are charged a fee by the company that provides your Internet access (described in Chapter 2). If you purchase something via the Internet, you have to pay for that, too. If you sign up for a special service that charges a fee, you will, of course, be billed. But don't think you can unwittingly enter a fee-charging area. When something costs money, you will most likely have to complete some type of form, which means you will always be aware when you have to pay for a service. The rest of the content—in fact, most of the content—is free.

What Can I Do With The Internet?

Now that you know the basics, you are probably beginning to see what you can do on the Internet. Here's a summary of the most common uses for the Internet:

- *Send and receive email*—You can send email to anyone who is connected to the Internet if you know his or her email address. You can send a message to your old college roommate. You can send a fan letter to your favorite author. You can also subscribe to mailing lists. Chapter 12 covers sending and receiving email.

- *Browse the World Wide Web*—You can look up something, get the latest news, find financial information, shop, look for a job, research a product, get entertainment information, and more. Part III of this book covers some specific ways you can use the Internet.

- *Download files*—You might get the latest version of a software product or exchange files with a co-worker or even someone in another office. Chapter 10 explains how to download files.

- *Share your ideas with other users who have similar interests*—You can join a newsgroup on topics ranging from Appalachian literature to skateboarding, computer programming to gardening. You can find more information on newsgroups in Chapter 13.

- *Have fun*—You can play games, look up your horoscope, find recipes, dissect a frog, and more. Chapter 22 covers some of the out-of-the-ordinary things you can do on the Internet.

The possibilities are endless. If there's something you want to do, you can probably find a place to do it on the Internet. This book will get you started on this exciting adventure.

Moving On

Now that you know what the Internet is and what you can do with it, you are probably eager to get started. Chapter 2 covers what you need to get connected to the Internet.

CHAPTER 2

What Do I Need To Get Connected?

To get connected to the Internet, you need three basic things: the hardware, the software, and the connection. What type of hardware do you need? What software do you need, and where can you find it? How do you make the connection? This chapter answers all these questions and more.

What Hardware Do I Need?

To access the Internet, you need a computer and a modem. Sounds simple enough. But not only do you need these items, you also need to be sure they are fast enough and powerful enough. As with most things in life, you can never have enough speed or power.

Displaying Web pages, especially those with a lot of graphics, can take some time. How fast you are able to view a page depends on both your computer and your modem. First, the image has to be sent from the Internet *server* (see the "Clients And Servers" sidebar) to your PC via your modem. This is probably the biggest bottleneck. The faster the modem, the faster the transfer. Second, your machine has to process and display the image on your screen. If you have a slow system, you might see delays here, too.

This section tells you the minimum recommended system and modem requirements. The key words here are *minimum* and *recommended*. You might get by using a less powerful system, but you aren't likely to find Internet cruising as much fun as you would with a mid- to high-end system.

Just The FAQs

What do I need to get connected to the Internet?

To get connected to the Internet, you need a computer, modem, phone line, and an *Internet Service Provider (ISP)*. You also need software for browsing the Web, handling email, transferring files, and participating in newsgroups.

What type of computer do I need?

At the minimum, you need a 486 with 8MB of RAM, a mouse, a sound card, and Windows, if you're using a PC. For a Mac, you'll be happiest with a Power Macintosh, Power Mac clone, or high-end 040 Mac (like a Quadra). External speakers are also handy.

What type of modem do I need?

At the minimum, you need a 28.8Kbps modem. You can use a 14.4Kbps modem if that's what you have, but you might not be happy with its performance on the Web.

Who provides the connection?

To get connected to the Internet, you need a service provider. You can use one of the popular online service providers such as America Online or Prodigy. These commercial online companies have their own content areas and also provide access (sometimes limited) to the Internet. Or you can select an ISP. An ISP does not include its own content areas and provides complete access to the Internet.

How much do I have to pay to get connected?

The charges you incur when you connect to the Internet can vary. With an ISP, you might pay $19.95 for unlimited online time, but you should shop around among ISPs for the best possible price.

Clients And Servers

When you read about the Internet, you may see the terms *client* and *server*. Basically, these two terms describe the type of relationship between you (and other Internet users) and the systems you access. The client is a computer that can access services on a network. The server is the system and its software that provide that service to the client.

What Type Of Computer Do I Need?

To get connected, you need an IBM-compatible, Macintosh, or Mac-compatible computer. This book is applicable for both types of systems, but the book's figures show a Windows system. If you have a Macintosh, just remember that your screen will look a little different.

At the minimum, you want a system with the following:

- *A 486 microprocessor or higher*—A 486 is acceptable, but you'll get the best results with a Pentium or Pentium II. Also, the higher the speed, the better. For a Mac, you want at least an 040 processor (as in the Quadra), but you would do better with a Power Mac machine.

- *16MB or more of memory*—You can get by with 12MB of memory, but you'll be happier with 16MB or more.

- *A sound card (if you're using a Windows machine) and speakers*—Some Web pages include sounds that you can play; also, games almost always take advantage of sound. These pieces aren't absolute requirements, but your Internet experience won't be as rich without them.

- *An accelerated graphics card (optional)*—If you want to be able to display pages as quickly as possible, an accelerated graphics card can enhance your machine's performance.

Internet Boxes And TV Connections

Some companies have begun marketing *Internet boxes*, simple computers that provide access to the Internet. Ranging in price from $300 to $700, these "appliances" are touted as an inexpensive way to get connected to the Internet. Are these a good idea? I wouldn't try one for a while. As with any new concept, it takes several versions to get the kinks worked out and to see whether the concept will take hold.

Also, you can purchase systems that turn your TV into a Web-browsing tool. For example, Gateway 2000 (a computer manufacturer) sells the Destination PC/TV. Functioning as both a PC and a TV, this type of combo system ranges in price from $2,500 to $4,500 or more, depending on what options you select.

If you are buying a new computer, make sure the machine you are considering meets these requirements. They are applicable to most computing tasks, not just Internet cruising. If you already have a computer, check your system to be sure it meets these requirements. If it doesn't, you may want to consider making some upgrades.

What Kind Of Modem Do I Need?

In addition to the computer, you need a *modem*, which stands for *modulator/demodulator*. This hardware component enables you to use phone lines to connect to the Internet. The current phone lines use an analog signal, but computers use a digital signal. Therefore, you need a modem to translate the signals. The modem takes data and translates it from digital to analog and sends the data over the phone line. The receiving modem then translates the same data back from analog to digital.

Getting Connected In The Future

Currently, the phone system is being updated so that you can send digital data over the new fiber optic phone system. When this work is complete, you will be able to connect directly to the phone line, without a modem. As an alternative, the cable companies will be able to use their network system to deliver information. To receive data from the cable system, you will need a special type of cable modem—the type that provides a speed of 10,000Kbps, which is 350 times faster than a 28.8 modem. Wow! Either method will significantly increase the speed at which data is transmitted, but both are still some time from completion. (Some cable companies provide service in limited areas, but this type of service is still not widely available.)

If you are buying a new computer, consider buying one that is bundled with a modem. If you have a computer but not a modem, adding a modem is an easy upgrade. You can buy an excellent device for $150 to 200. If you already have a modem, make sure it is fast enough. The rest of this section discusses some differences among modems.

Modem Speed

Modem speed is measured in bits per second (bps) or kilobits per second (Kbps). Either a 28.8Kbps or a 33.6Kbps modem is acceptable. A 28.8 modem can transmit 28.8 kilobits per second (28,800 bits per second). A 33.6 modem can transmit 33.6 kilobits per second (33,600 bits per second).

You may see advertisements for a faster modem—the 56Kbps modem. Ideally, this modem is faster, but there are a few catches. First, the 56Kbps modem can only *receive* information at that speed; you cannot *send* information at that rate. Second, your ISP must be able to support a 56Kbps modem. Some do, some don't. If your ISP does not, you won't be gaining any advantage in speed. Finally, even if the ISP does support 56Kbps modems, the phone lines may have problems with line quality, so you might not achieve the advertised speed.

If you are hooking up your business to the Internet, you may want to consider an alternative setup. You can get a digital phone line connection using *ISDN*. This type of connection is about twice as fast as a 56Kbps modem, but is significantly more expensive. The cost of this type of setup includes installation (around $100), monthly fee ($25 to $85 a month), and modem ($300 or so). Also, this type of setup may not be available where you live. (You have to live near a local ISDN network.) If your business depends on an Internet connection, though, the extra speed of an ISDN connection may be worthwhile.

Internal Vs. External

You can purchase a modem that is an electronic card you insert into a slot inside your computer (although this is much more common for PCs than for Macs). The phone cable plugs into an outlet on the card. Or you can purchase an external modem that sits on your desktop and is connected to your computer via a cable. The phone line then plugs into the modem.

Internal modems are usually less expensive than external modems, but they also use up an expansion slot, and you can't see what's happening if you have to call technical support. External modems use indicator lights to show the status of your connection, which can help technical support staff troubleshoot any problems.

Bus Type

A *bus* is the electronic pathway that connects different components of your PC. Different types of PCs have different types of buses. For PCs, ISA and PCI are the two most common types of connectors. For Macs, PCI or NuBus are the most common. You need the same type of connector on the modem as you have in your computer. Check your system documentation.

Fax And Other Features

Modems differ in the features they offer. For example, many modems can function as fax machines. Also, the software included with the modem may vary. If you have any questions about the features of your modem, ask your salesperson to explain them.

Do I Need Another Phone Line?

You can't do much with just a computer and a modem. Your connection to the outside world—to the Internet—is the phone line. You can use an existing line, but then you must coordinate when that line is a regular phone line and when it is an Internet connection. When you are using the phone line to connect to the Internet, you won't be able to receive or make voice calls—and special features like call waiting may interrupt your online session. A better solution is to have the phone company install a second line and to use this line for your computer. You can check with your local phone company for information about rates for this second line.

What Software Do I Need?

In addition to the hardware, you need software to get connected and to handle all your Internet activities. Your computer comes with an operating system. For PCs, you need Windows 3.1 or Windows 95. For a Macintosh, you need System 7.5 or higher. You also need software for each of the key things you do on the Internet. You need software for browsing the Web, for sending and receiving email, for reading messages in newsgroups, and for handling file transfers. Here are the specifics:

- To browse the World Wide Web, you need a Web browser. This book covers one of the most popular Web browsers, Netscape Navigator. See the next section, "Getting Navigator."

- If you want to send and receive email (covered in Chapter 12), you need a program to handle it. You might use a separate program such as Eudora, usually provided in your Internet kit or by your ISP. Netscape Communicator includes an excellent email facility, Messenger, which should give you all the features you'll need.

- To participate in newsgroups, you need a news reader. Netscape Communicator includes Collabra, a good news reader program.

- To handle file transfers, you need an FTP program. Navigator can handle most FTP transfers for you. If you need a separate program, like CuteFTP or Fetch, your ISP should provide it or enable you to download it. Also, larger online services like AOL provide an FTP interface.

Getting Navigator

The person who created the first Web browser (Mosaic, created by Marc Andreessen) also created Netscape Navigator. This is currently one of the most popular browsers available and is the browser this book is based on. (After all, this book is the *Official **Netscape** Beginner's Guide to the Internet*.) You'll find that most Web pages are designed for the features and capabilities of Navigator, largely because of its popularity. For beginners, Navigator is a great choice for a browser. Keep in mind, though, that there are other browsers—such as Microsoft's Internet Explorer—available.

Where Can I Get Navigator?

Your ISP may bundle a copy of Netscape Navigator with its service. (For information on finding and comparing ISPs, see the "What Are The Ways I Can Get Connected?" section later in this chapter.) If you don't receive a copy of Netscape Navigator from your ISP, you can download the software from Netscape's Web site. (A *Web site* is a collection of Web pages dedicated to the same topic or company.) Downloading software can be a problem because you first need a way to get connected. If you already have a Web browser, but want to try Navigator, go to **http://www.home.netscape.com**.

Once Netscape's home page (shown in Figure 2.1) is on your screen, you can use one of several links to get information and download the software. To update a previous version of Navigator, try SmartUpdate. To get information about purchasing Navigator, try Store. For product information, click Products. From the download pages, you can find complete instructions on what to expect and what to do. Simply follow the on-screen directions.

If you don't have a browser, you can call Netscape and order a copy of Navigator. You might also try a retail store.

How Much Does It Cost?

If you are a student, staff, or faculty member of an educational institution, charitable nonprofit organization, or public library, you can use Navigator for free. You can contact Netscape for information on this program.

Anyone can evaluate the product free for 90 days. After the set evaluation time, you must register the software and pay a fee. Expect to pay around $59 for registration or for a retail copy of Netscape Navigator.

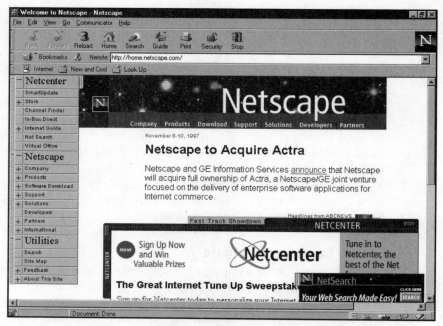

Figure 2.1 You can download the latest version of Netscape Navigator from the Netscape home page.

Which Version Do I Need?

The most current version of Navigator is version 4. This version enables you to browse Web pages, download files, and more. Navigator 4 is included with Netscape's Communicator.

> **TIP**
>
> *You can find out what version of Navigator you have by selecting About Netscape from the Help menu on a PC or from the Apple menu on a Mac.*

What's New In Version 4?

If you are have a previous version of Navigator, you may wonder what is new in version 4. Here's a list of key highlights:

- *Revamped interface*—The Netscape home page now includes revamped toolbars for quick access to your favorite sites. Use the Component bar, for instance, to access email, news, and so on.

- *Access to the Netscape Guide by Yahoo!*—If you want to find some key sites, you can view the Netscape Guide by Yahoo! and select from several categories including Shopping, News, Computers, and more.

- *View security information*—You can view complete security information about a page using the new Security button. Data encryption also protects data transmitted over the Internet.

- *Customization features*—You can customize and set up your own personal toolbar. In addition, bookmarks are easier to add and update. (See Chapter 11 for more information on customizing.)

- *Better plug-in handling*—*Plug-ins* are small programs that provide extra capabilities (such as playing sounds) to your browser. Navigator 4 downloads and installs plug-ins automatically. For more information on this topic, see Chapter 8.

- *Behind-the-scenes features*—As a user, you won't notice some additional changes to Navigator 4, but this version includes features that make it easier for Web developers to create cool pages, full of interactive content.

What's The Difference Between Navigator And Communicator?

Netscape Navigator is the browser, and some users may prefer to use this singular program. But you can also get and use Netscape Communicator, which is an entire suite of Internet products. The Standard version of Communicator includes the following programs:

- *Navigator 4*—Use this program to browse Web pages.

- *Netscape Messenger*—Use this program to send, receive, and handle email messages. (See Chapter 12 for more information on email.)

- *Netscape Collabra*—Use this program to participate in newsgroups. (You can read more about this topic in Chapter 13.)

- *Netscape Composer*—Use this program to create your own Web pages. (Appendix B includes a description of this program.)

- *Netscape Netcaster*—Use this program to deliver content to your PC from one of several "channels." (Read more about this new type of push technology in Appendix B.)

- *Netscape Conference*—Use this program to communicate in live phone conversations via the Internet.

TIP

You can also get the Professional Edition, which includes Netscape Calendar, AutoAdmin, and IBM Host On-Demand, tools for administering corporate sites.

Other Software Options

If you don't have Communicator, you can get separate programs for email, news reader, and FTP from your ISP (covered in the next section). A lot of the software is *shareware* (you pay a small fee to register the software) or *freeware*.

Some modems come bundled with Internet software. So if you need to purchase a modem, shop for one that includes a complete Internet access package.

Finally, you can buy commercial Internet kits that include the software you need. These kits also help you find an ISP, and sometimes they even include a modem. The kits start at $20.

What Are The Ways I Can Get Connected?

You've got the hardware and the software. Are you set? Not quite—you still need a way to get connected. The connection is usually provided by a third party called an *Internet Service Provider (ISP)*. This section explains some strategies for getting connected.

Trying An Online Service Provider

Before the Internet became so widespread, many computer users signed up for and used an online service to communicate with other users. America Online, CompuServe (before it was purchased by America Online), the Microsoft Network, and Prodigy are among the most popular of these independently owned and operated commercial services. Each company controls what information is provided by its service, and you pay a subscription fee to that company.

When the Internet became so popular, many online companies knew that to keep their customers they also needed to provide Internet access. So in addition to the email, forums, and content they provided, they expanded to allow their users to access the Internet through their online service.

Using an online service as a gateway to the Internet has some advantages. First, if you already subscribe to the online service, you can try out the Internet without a big investment in additional software. Second, sometimes the technical support staff of the online service can help you get connected. (Sometimes they provide the connection, but if you have any problems or questions, you are on your own.) Third, these companies provide great chat areas and content that you can only get as a member. For example, you can find forums on finance, shopping, travel, weather, and so on, which are not open to the entire Internet.

If you use the Internet a lot, though, an online service probably isn't the most economical choice. The "Comparing Online Vs. Independent ISPs" section describes the pros and cons of both an online service provider and an independent provider.

Using An ISP

If you don't want the restrictions or extra content of an online service provider, you can connect with an ISP. There are more than 5,000 ISPs, ranging from big nationwide providers to local services. The cost, type of service, and other features vary from ISP to ISP. (For information on how to compare ISPs, see the "Comparing ISPs" section later in this chapter.) You may find that the cost of this type of connection, plus the services provided, is more suited to your needs.

Comparing Online Vs. Independent ISPs

In the past, online services charged a set fee for a certain amount of time online. If you exceeded that time, you were charged hourly, which made connection time fairly expensive if you exceeded your set limit. Now most online providers offer the same flat fee as ISPs; however, you should check out the Internet connection fees to be sure. The plans offered change frequently.

Your Internet access may be limited, depending on the online provider. Not every online provider offers complete Internet access. You might not be able to access all newsgroups or all areas of the Internet. And you may be limited to using the browser, news reader, and email programs supplied by the online service rather than the ones you prefer.

Finally, most of the emphasis for online services is on their content—probably about 90 percent. They are not dedicated Internet companies. On the other hand, the ISPs are exclusively Internet companies, providing complete Internet access, but almost no specialized content.

Finding An ISP

If you think you want to go the ISP route for getting connected, you first need to find one and then do some comparison shopping to make sure you are getting the best deal. In the next year or so, you'll probably see ISPs advertised more heavily; try looking in the Yellow Pages. And be sure to pay attention to word of mouth, which continues to be one of the best ways to find a good ISP.

You can also try calling local computer stores and asking what ISPs they recommend. You can at least get the names and phone numbers of companies in your area. You might also try a local university. Or if you know people who are currently connected, ask them what company they use. If you purchase a commercial Internet kit, it will have a setup routine that will help you locate an ISP—that's another alternative.

If you are already connected (perhaps through an online service provider) and want to switch to an ISP, you can use a Web page to locate an ISP. Go to **http://www.thelist.internet.com** (see Figure 2.2). Using this Web page, you can find an ISP by name, by state, or by area.

Comparing ISPs

You don't want to sign up for just any ISP because ISPs can vary both in the services they provide and the cost. Use the information in this section to evaluate the different ISPs.

Is your connection to the Internet a local call? If not, is it an 800 number? Keep in mind that you are using the phone lines to make the connection and you have to pay for that service as well. Local calls or 800 calls are obviously the best since you don't want to pay long-distance charges on top of the ISP charge. If you live in a big city, you shouldn't have too much trouble finding an ISP that

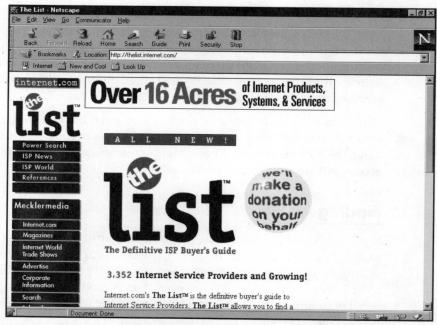

Figure 2.2   Use http://www.thelist.internet.com to find an ISP.

offers a local or 800 number. If you live in a rural area, finding an ISP that doesn't require a long-distance call is a priority. Be sure you aren't being charged extra to connect with a local number or 800 number. If you are, compare the toll-free access fee that you are charged.

What type of connection does the ISP provide? Most ISPs offer many types of connections, all with confusing names. You want to be sure the ISP supports your modem type, especially if you have a special modem like a 56Kbps or an ISDN modem.

If you are getting a large business connected, you might want to investigate a different type of connection. For most beginners, though, a PPP or SLIP connection is acceptable. *PPP* stands for *Point-to-Point Protocol*; *SLIP* stands for *Serial Line Internet Protocol*. Both are dial-up accounts; you are directly connected to the Internet. If you have to choose between the two (although you usually won't), PPP is the better way to go, for a lot of technical reasons that don't bear going into.

What is the setup fee? Some ISPs charge a one-time setup fee, but others don't. Check out this fee when you are comparison shopping. If there is a fee, it is generally about $25 to $35.

What is the subscription fee? The best type of rate—and the type you should ask for—is a flat rate. You receive a certain number of hours for a set fee. Here is where you really need to comparison shop. Some companies charge you a certain rate for a number of hours, then another rate above that amount. They may charge you for email messages and for storage. Keeping track of what the fees are can be a nightmare. That's why a flat rate is best. Ask lots of questions and be sure you understand exactly how you will be billed. The charge may also vary depending on the type of account you have, the modem, the number you use to connect, and other factors.

How many connections are provided? How many subscribers does the service have? Large providers may offer more connections, but they also have more subscribers. You don't want to encounter a busy signal every time you connect.

What software is provided? The ISP should provide you with all the software you need to get started, including a news reader, a browser, an email program, and an FTP program. You should also be able to use any browser you want, not just the one provided by the ISP. Some services come bundled with Netscape Navigator; some use Internet Explorer. You can compare the software provided and pick the one you want to use.

Does the company provide free technical support? How is technical support provided? Phone? Email? Not at all? As a new user, being able to get a "real" person to help you is an advantage. Look for a company that offers toll-free support and is available during more than just regular business hours.

Does the company provide other Internet services? Thinking ahead, you might want to expand your Internet skills and, for example, publish your own home page. Does the company also provide space on its server for users to publish home pages? Different ISPs offer different amounts of space and Web publishing services. Also, some ISPs provide FTP services while others don't.

Moving On

Part I of this book covers the three basic steps you need to complete before you get started. Chapter 1 covers how to decide that you want to get connected. This chapter explains how to get the equipment you need. Chapter 3 will discuss the final step: how to get connected.

CHAPTER 3

How Do I Get Connected?

Probably the hardest part about getting connected to the Internet is getting connected the first time. But you only have to go through the setup process once; after that, getting connected takes just a few mouse clicks.

This chapter covers the general process you follow to get connected the first time. Keep in mind that the specific instructions you follow are going to depend on your setup software. For example, if you purchase an Internet kit, it will provide complete instructions on getting connected. If you sign up with and get software from an Internet Service Provider (ISP), the ISP will detail all the setup steps you need to follow to use its software. This chapter just tells you what to expect.

Setting Up The Hardware

Already have all your hardware? Everything connected? Good. You can skip this section. You have already completed the first step of the setup process.

If your system did not include the hardware you need—basically, the modem—you need to install this component first. Your modem should have come with a list of specific installation instructions that you should read. This section covers the basic procedure for installing a modem.

Just The FAQs

How do I get connected?

To get connected, you need to do three things: install your modem (if necessary), set up your ISP account, and install the software for the Internet, including Netscape Navigator and the setup software provided by your ISP.

How do I install the software?

If you got your software from an ISP, it most likely provided specific installation instructions. If you got your software in an Internet kit, you probably received a book with details about installing the software; simply follow those instructions.

What happens when I install the software?

You usually install software by running a file called Install or Setup or something similar. This program sets up the appropriate folders for your files and then copies the files to your hard disk. It will probably also prompt you to enter certain information about your computer setup in order to fully configure the software (note that not all programs do this—you may be required to do some manual configuration after the installer runs).

What information do I need before starting the setup?

Your ISP provides you with all the specific technical information you need to get started, such as domain name server, domain name, username, password, email address, and so on. Don't worry too much about this information. Although you need to enter all of this information during the setup process, after that you only need to know your username and password.

Installing An Internal Modem

PC users have the option of using an internal or external modem. (While some Macs do have internal modems, such modems are pretty unusual, and they're difficult to find on the market. Hence, most Mac users prefer externals.) Internal modems are just flat green cards, sometimes called *adapter cards* or *expansion cards*. They contain jacks (usually two) that are accessible when the card is plugged into the computer.

To install an internal modem in your PC, you need to do the following:

1. Turn off and unplug the system, then remove the cover. Be sure you touch something metal to ground yourself before you start working on the innards of your computer, and always wear a grounding strap. (If you don't have one, you can probably get one for about $3 at your local computer store; it's worth the money.) Static electricity can damage your system components. Also, if you're using a PC, be sure you put the screws to the system case in a safe place. You'll need them later.

2. Locate an empty slot for your modem.

3. Take off the back cover for the expansion slot, then insert the card into the slot.

4. Make any adjustments needed to the switches on your modem. Depending on what COM port you are using for your modem—which depends on the other equipment you have installed—you may have to flip a few switches. Check your system documentation.

5. Put the system case back on, but don't secure the screws. You need to be sure the modem is installed properly first.

6. Connect the phone line to the jack on the card labeled "Line" or "Wall". (The other jack is for connecting a telephone, if you ever want to use that phone line for regular calls.)

7. Run the setup software for your modem, if necessary. Then test your modem by following the instructions included in your modem's documentation.

Installing An External Modem

Installing an external modem is even easier. You just have to plug in a few connections. Follow these steps:

1. Turn off and unplug the system.

2. You should have received a cable with your modem. Connect one end of the cable to a serial port on the back of your computer and the other end

to your modem. On a PC, the serial ports will probably be unlabeled, but you can tell which port is the correct one by matching the port to the cable. On a Mac, use the port with the telephone icon over it.

3. Plug your phone line into the jack that is labeled "Line" or "Wall" on the back of the modem. (The second jack—frequently the card contains two— connects a telephone, if you ever want to use that phone line for regular calls.)

4. Connect your modem's power cable to the modem, then to a plug. Switch the modem on.

5. If necessary, run the setup software for your modem. Then test your modem by following the instructions included in your modem's documentation.

TIP

For PC users, Windows 95 includes a Hardware Setup program you can use to install and tell Windows about any new hardware you add. This wizard leads you step by step through the process of setting up equipment such as a modem. You can access this program by clicking the Start button, selecting Control Panel, and then double-clicking the Add New Hardware icon.

Setting Up Your ISP Account

The next step in getting connected is to set up your ISP account. Chapter 2 covered how to find and compare ISPs so that you get the best deal. After you decide on one, you can phone the provider to get specific instructions on how to set up an account. You may need to give the ISP some information first, such as your name, address, phone number, billing information, and what type of system you have. The ISP will then mail you the necessary disks and instructions for getting started.

In the packet that you receive from the ISP, you will receive the technical information that you need to get set up. For example, you will most likely be assigned a domain name for the server, your username, the local access phone number, type of account (PPP, for example), and a password. You might also receive the address, account name, and password for your email.

You enter most of this information once and then forget about it. You use only your password and username each time you get connected.

If you decide to use an online service provider such as America Online, you won't need additional sign-on information, but you will need to figure out how to install the software and find the Internet features you are interested in. Look for an area called Internet or World Wide Web and then follow the instructions provided. (If you can't find the Internet access information, call the technical support number for your online provider.)

Installing The Software

As mentioned in Chapter 2, you need certain software to connect to the Internet. You will probably get this software from your ISP, along with installation instructions; simply follow those instructions.

Any type of software installation usually involves some of the same steps. You run the setup program (look for a file called Install or Setup). You select a drive and folder for your software, and then the installation program copies the programs from the CD-ROM or floppy disk to your computer.

The installation program may also need to know certain information about your computer setup. For example, if you have Windows 95, you can run the Internet Connection Wizard to set up your system. (To start this program, look for a program named Connection Wizard in your Programs folder.) This wizard leads you step by step through the process of setting up your connection (see Figure 3.1). You are prompted to enter information, such as the dial-up number, for each step. Follow the steps in each dialog box.

In Windows, the installation program also sets up the program icons you use to start the programs. For example, Figure 3.2 shows the various program items added when you install the ISP software.

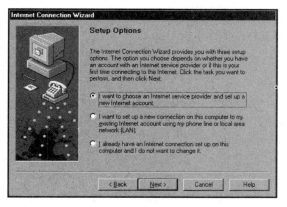

Figure 3.1   You can use the Internet Connection Wizard for your connection settings.

Figure 3.2   The Windows installation program sets up program icons for each program it installs.

Getting Connected

After you install the software, you can get connected for the first time by following specific instructions from your ISP. Keep in mind that the steps you follow depend on the type of system you have and your ISP. For example, if you have Windows 95, you may have a connection icon in the Dial-Up Networking folder. To get connected, double-click on the My Computer icon and then double-click on the Dial-Up Networking folder. You should see an icon for your ISP connection (see Figure 3.3); double-click on it to get connected.

On Macintoshes, connecting usually involves opening a control panel (usually ConfigPPP or something similar) and pressing the Connect button.

Once you are connected, you can run any of the software provided by your ISP. You should also download and install Netscape Navigator.

Figure 3.3   The installation programs set up an icon for getting connected to your ISP.

Installing Navigator

If you don't already have Navigator, you will need to download and then install it.

This is as simple as connecting to the Netscape home page. (The address is **http://www.home.netscape.com**.) My ISP, for instance, included a program icon for connecting and then downloading Navigator. Many ISPs include Navigator as their browser of choice when they send you software, and some will even provide you with a registered version. You can also purchase Navigator directly from Netscape or from a computer store. And if you have an Internet kit, you may have the Navigator program on disk.

Once you have the actual setup program, double-click its icon to start the installation. The installer leads you step by step through the process, prompting you for some responses— for example, to select a folder for the program files (see Figure 3.4). Simply follow the on-screen instructions. Once Navigator is installed, you are ready to go!

Moving On

The hard part is over. You are all connected. Now you simply need to start Navigator and start your Internet surfing. Chapter 4 covers the basics of starting and moving around in Navigator.

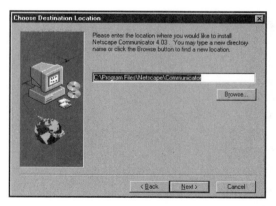

Figure 3.4   Follow the on-screen instructions for installing Navigator, a component of Netscape Communicator.

Part II

Getting Around

CHAPTER 4

Learning
Navigator Basics

Netscape Navigator is so easy to use that you can probably take one look at the opening Netscape home page and figure out what most of the items do. For example, you can try new sites (What's New or What's Cool) or check out the Netscape Guide by Yahoo!.

Still, if you aren't sure what all the tools on the screen do, read on. This chapter explains what you see on your screen and discusses the basics for moving around the Netscape home page. Even if you think you can figure out all the items, you should read this chapter for tips you might otherwise miss.

Starting Navigator

The way you start Navigator depends on the type of system you have. For Windows 95 and Macintosh systems, you simply double-click on the Netscape Navigator or Netscape Communicator icon. Next, you see a dialog box for logging on—that is, making the connection with your Internet Service Provider (ISP) (see Figure 4.1). What you see depends on your software.

To log on, you usually type your username and password. If you need help with your logon procedure, check the instructions provided by your ISP. Once you are connected, you see the Netscape home page, which you'll read about in the next section, "Understanding The Navigator Window."

Just The FAQs

How do I start Navigator?

To start Navigator, double-click on the Netscape Navigator icon or Netscape Communicator icon. You are prompted to then log on to your Internet connection.

What is a page?

All information on the World Wide Web is actually a document or series of documents, and each document is called a *page*. A page may be one screen of information or longer and can contain text, graphics, sound, animations, videos, and most important, links to other pages. The page is formatted using a special language called *Hypertext Markup Language (HTML)*.

What is a home page?

Your *home page* is the first page you see when you start Navigator. In most cases, the default is Netscape's home page, which includes lots of helpful information about Netscape. However, your ISP may display another page, or you can display the home page of your choice.

How do I get around?

You can move from place to place on the Internet by either typing in addresses called *Uniform Resource Locators (URLs)* or clicking on underlined words called *links*. Links are also sometimes called *hypertext* or *hyperlinks*. Pictures can be links, too.

What is a frame?

Netscape Navigator version 2 added *frames* to the page concept. Frames divide the page into *panes*. Each pane has its own content, determined by the author of the Web page.

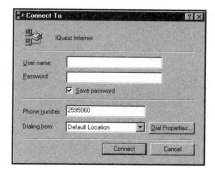

Figure 4.1   Before you can use Navigator to connect to the Internet, you have to log on to your ISP.

The first time you start Navigator, you are prompted to create a user profile. You can create and switch among different profiles, a handy feature if more than one person uses your PC to connect to the Internet. Follow the on-screen directions to enter the appropriate information. Use the Next button to go to the next step.

You will also see the setup page the first time you log on to Navigator. From here, you can register your copy, sign up for SmartUpdate, go to the Netcenter, and more. Use the links to get more information.

Understanding The Navigator Window

On the World Wide Web, all information is displayed as a *page*. The page may be one screenful of information or more and may contain text, graphics, and links to other pages. (You will find out more about Web pages later in this chapter.) The first page you see for any site is its *home page*. And the first page you see when you log on to the Internet is *your* home page—most likely, the Netscape home page (see Figure 4.2). If you don't see it, you can go there by typing "http://www.home.netscape.com" in the Location text box and pressing Enter.

Note that the figures in this book show the Windows version of Navigator. The Macintosh version is nearly identical. Instead of the Help menu, Mac users have an Apple menu. Also, the Netscape icon is in a different location.

The Navigator window contains several features to help you navigate around the Internet. The top parts of the screen (the title bar, menu bar, and toolbars) are always displayed, no matter what page you are viewing, as is the status bar at the bottom of the screen. You can use these on-screen elements to navigate among different Web pages; they don't appear just on the Netscape home page.

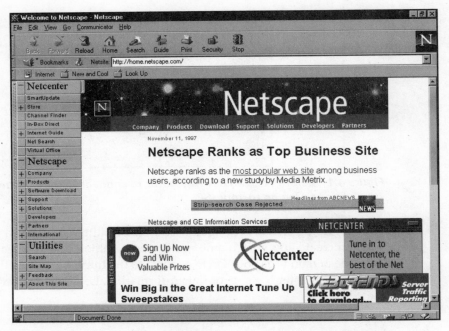

Figure 4.2 *The Netscape home page is your starting point on your Internet journey.*

In the main area of the page, you see the content of the current page. What you see here varies, depending on the page you are viewing.

TIP

Don't be alarmed if your screens don't match those shown in this book, because the content of most Web pages is updated frequently. What you see depends on when you view a particular page. For example, the information on the Netscape home page will be different when you display it.

Getting Information From The Title Bar And Status Bar

Both the top and the bottom parts of the Navigator window provide information. The title bar says "Welcome to Netscape", followed by the title of the current document. In addition to displaying messages about the current action, the status bar includes the following:

- *The progress bar*—This indicates the progress of the current operation; for example, when a document is being displayed, you see a visual indicator of how much has been transferred and how much is left to transfer. You can also tell when Navigator is busy downloading a page by looking at the Netscape logo in the upper right area of the screen. If you see shooting stars, Navigator is still busy.

■ *The security indicator*—This looks like a key or padlock and indicates whether the document is secure (key on blue background or closed padlock) or not secure (broken key on gray background or open padlock). For viewing a page, the document does not have to be secure, so don't worry if you mostly see broken keys or open padlocks. When you are sending sensitive information, such as ordering an item using a credit card, the document should be secure. (You can read more about security features in Chapter 7.)

■ *The Component bar (if you have Netscape Communicator)*—This row of icons enables you to move to different Communicator components, such as Messenger for reading mail, Collabra for reading newsgroup messages, and Composer for creating Web pages. You may see this in the status bar or as a floating toolbar.

TIP

To find out what the icons in the Component bar do, place the mouse pointer over an icon and watch the icon name pop up.

Using The Menu Bar To Select Commands

The menu bar appears under the title bar. You can use menu commands to set options that control how Navigator works (called *preferences*), to create mail, to go to a particular page, and more. To select a command, follow these steps:

1. Click on the menu name. You see a drop-down list of commands.

2. Click on the command name. Some commands are executed right away. Others display a submenu; you select the command you want from the submenu by clicking on the command. Sometimes, a dialog box prompts you for additional information. Enter your selections, then click on the OK button to confirm the command.

Depending on what you are doing, the commands in the menu may change. For example, when you are creating mail, you may see different commands than when you are browsing among pages.

The fastest way to select a command is not by using the menu system, but by using one of the toolbar shortcuts, covered next. The most commonly used commands have a toolbar button. If you have to use a menu command because no toolbar button will perform the desired task, this book tells you which command to use.

Using The Navigation Toolbar

To make it as easy as possible to access commands, the Navigator window includes several toolbar buttons. You can use these buttons as you navigate the Internet. Table 4.1 identifies and describes each button.

Table 4.1   Navigator toolbar buttons.

Button	Name	Click To
Back	Back	Display the previous page. Chapter 5 explains more about moving among pages.
Forward	Forward	Display the next page. Again, you'll learn more in Chapter 5.
Reload	Reload	Redisplay the current page. You may want to do this if you made any preference changes, if you think the information may have been updated by the network, or if you encountered a problem loading the page.
Home	Home	Display the Netscape home page. You can change which page is displayed by setting a different preference. Making this change is covered in Chapter 11.
Search	Search	Display the available search tools for finding sites on the Internet. See Chapter 6 for more information on searching.
Guide	Guide	Display the Netscape Guide by Yahoo!.
Print	Print	Print the content area of the current page.
Security	Security	Display the security settings of the current page. Chapter 7 discusses the security features in more detail.
Stop	Stop	Stop the transfer of page information.

TIP

You can shrink any toolbar by clicking the tab to the far left of the toolbar. This turns the toolbar into a tiny unlabeled button. (If you hold your cursor over this tiny button, the name of the toolbar will be displayed.) Click on the tab again to redisplay the toolbar buttons. To hide a toolbar entirely, open the View menu and select Hide Navigation Toolbar, Hide Location Toolbar, or Hide Personal Toolbar.

Using The Personal Toolbar To Check Out Sites

The Web contains *so* much information; new pages are added all the time. To help you find information that might be of interest, Netscape includes some directories or lists of sites. You can view these lists using the buttons in the Personal toolbar:

■ Use the Internet button to select some sites within a particular category. This button displays the Netscape Guide by Yahoo! (see Figure 4.3). You can select from several categories, including Business, Computers, Entertainment, Finance, Local, News, Shopping, Sports, and Travel.

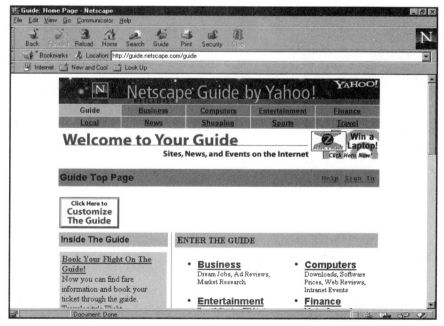

Figure 4.3   You can look through sites within a selected category using the Internet button. (Text and artwork copyright 1998 by Netscape and YAHOO!, Inc. All rights reserved. YAHOO! and the YAHOO! logo are trademarks of YAHOO!, Inc.)

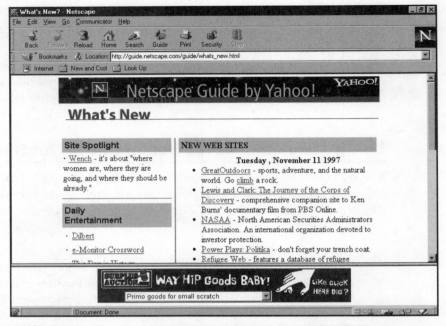

Figure 4.4   Check out new sites using the What's New directory. (Text and artwork copyright 1998 by Netscape and YAHOO!, Inc. All rights reserved. YAHOO! and the YAHOO! logo are trademarks of YAHOO!, Inc.)

- Click on the New and Cool button and then select the What's New command to see a list of new Internet sites. Figure 4.4 shows a recent What's New list. You can scroll through the list of sites and go to any of them by clicking on the underlined/colored link.

- Click on the New and Cool button and select What's Cool to see a list of sites deemed cool by the Netscape staff. Figure 4.5 shows a recent What's Cool list.

- Want to find a particular person or business on the Net? Click on the Look Up button, then select the People command to find a person (see Figure 4.6). Both Chapters 12 and 16 explain how to find someone on the Internet. You can also select Yellow Pages to look up a business.

TIP

You can customize the Personal toolbar and add buttons for your favorite sites. For information on making this change, see Chapter 11.

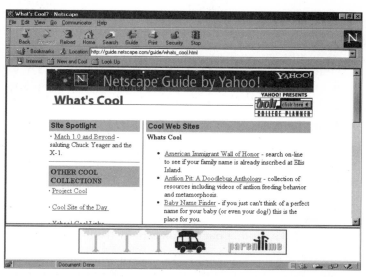

Figure 4.5   You can visit some cool sites from this directory list. (Text and artwork copyright 1998 by Netscape and YAHOO!, Inc. All rights reserved. YAHOO! and the YAHOO! logo are trademarks of YAHOO!, Inc.)

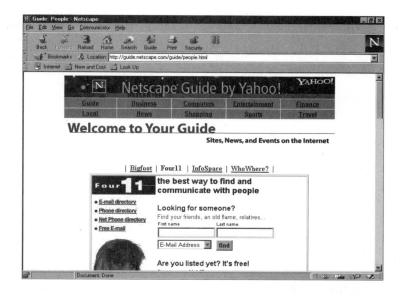

Figure 4.6   You can look up people using the Look Up button. (Text and artwork copyright 1998 by Netscape and YAHOO!, Inc. All rights reserved. YAHOO! and the YAHOO! logo are trademarks of YAHOO!, Inc.)

Understanding Pages

Before you can begin to "surf" the Net, you need to understand how the World Wide Web works—how the information appears and how you move from one area to another. This section defines the concept of a Web page.

How Is A Page Set Up?

Basically, all information on the Web is a series of documents formatted using a special language called *Hypertext Markup Language* or *HTML*. All documents are stored at a Web site, and each document is displayed as a page (although the text may be longer than one page or one screen). The page may include graphics, text, sounds, animations, and videos. In addition, most documents include links to other pages. You can use the links to jump to other related pages.

In most documents, text links appear underlined or in a different color, or both. You can jump to these links by clicking on the underlined text. For example, you could click on the underlined text in Figure 4.7 to jump to any of the related pages. In addition to text links, some pages include *hot spots* or graphic links. Just as you can with text links, you can jump to any of the sites in the *image map* in Figure 4.8.

When you click on a link, Navigator displays the corresponding Web page. From this Web page, you can go back to the page you were on or go to yet another one of the links from the current page. Jump from page to page, and soon you will be a regular surfer girl (or boy).

Most Web pages are actually a set of related documents. Sometimes the links point to documents at the same site, so if you click on one of these links, you see the related page, but you haven't left the Web site. Other links point to documents at a different site. When you select this type of link, Navigator goes to the site and downloads the page. You won't be able to tell from the page content whether you are at a different site, but you can look at the address in the Location box to note any site changes.

When a document will not fit in one window, use the scroll bars along the edges of the window. To scroll, click the scroll arrow in the direction you want to scroll, or drag the scroll box to move a relative distance.

What Is A Page Address?

Each Web page has a unique address called a *Uniform Resource Locator (URL)*. This address tells Navigator where to find the page, which page to display, and how to display it. For instance, the URL for a part of The Coriolis Group's home page is **http://www.coriolis.com/Site/MSIE/Customer.htm**.

Figure 4.7   A Web page usually includes links to other pages; text links are underlined.

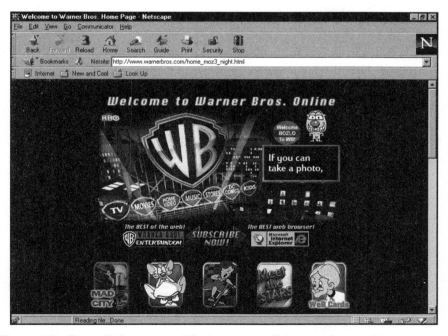

Figure 4.8   Some links are graphical; you can click on an icon or image to jump to another page.

A typical address consists of two or three parts: the protocol, the server, and the path name. The *protocol* tells Navigator how to display the page; for example, "http" stands for Hypertext Transfer Protocol, which is commonly used to display hypertext documents. FTP is another protocol; it stands for File Transfer Protocol. (You will learn more about transferring files in Chapter 10.)

The *server* or *domain name* (**www.coriolis.com** in the example) tells Navigator on what system the page is stored. Each Internet server has a unique address, and you can tell something about the server name by its extension. Here are some common extensions:

- *.com*—Commercial
- *.edu*—Educational
- *.gov*—Government
- *.net*—Network
- *.org*—Noncommercial or nonprofit

The *path name* (**/Site/MSIE/Customer.htm** in the example) tells Navigator the folder where the page is stored on the server. Sometimes the address includes the document name as well.

What Is A Frame?

To help navigate in the site, some Web pages are divided into *frames*. Often, frames divide the content area into one main content area and several panes of information. Figure 4.9 shows a page with frames. Notice that each frame displays separate content, and each frame can have its own set of scroll bars.

What appears in each pane depends on the author of the Web page. The panes might provide a table of contents and tell you where you are; they might provide links to other pages; or they might display additional pages within those panes. When you click on a link in a pane, you may see a change in the contents of the pane, another pane, or another area of the page. Navigating among panes is covered in the Chapter 5.

Getting Help

Something got you stumped? Can't find your *Official Netscape Beginner's Guide to the Internet, Second Edition*? If you want a quick reminder of how to perform a task, you can use the Help menu. You can use the NetHelp system or select any of the other Help commands, as described in this section.

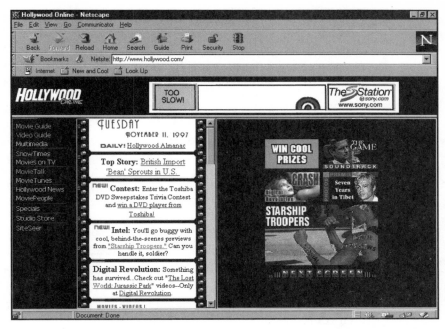

Figure 4.9   A Web page can be divided by frames into panes of information.

Using NetHelp

You can use the online help manual to look up topics in the table of contents or index. You can even search for a particular topic. Follow these steps:

1. Open the Help menu and select the Help Contents command. You see the NetHelp window. The left pane displays the different options you can use for this help guide. The right pane displays the current page, which is the table of contents by default (see Figure 4.10).

2. Click on the topic you want to look up. The information for that topic is displayed in the main help window (see Figure 4.11).

3. Click on the Index button to look up a topic in the index. You can either scroll through to find the topic you want, or move quickly to a particular topic by typing it in the text box (see Figure 4.12).

4. To search for a particular topic, click on the Find button. Then type the word or phrase you're looking for in the Find What text box. Click on the Find Next button.

The help window includes buttons that you can use to navigate through the online help document. You can do any of the following:

Figure 4.10   You can look up help information in the online help guide.

■ Click on any of the buttons along the top to get help about that particular component. For example, click the Messenger icon to see help about using this component.

■ Click on the Back button to go back to the previous page. Click the Forward button to go forward (after going back a page).

Figure 4.11   Select the topic you want information about by browsing the contents.

Figure 4.12   Look up a topic in the index.

- Click on the Print button to print the help information.
- Click on the Exit button or the Close (X) button for the help window to exit help.

Using Other Help Features

You can also use other help commands to get information. For instance, you can do any of the following:

- Display information about Netscape, plug-ins (add-on software programs that expand the capabilities of Navigator), or font displayers.

- See a list of release notes about the current Navigator version. (This command is not available on the Mac.)

- View product and support information.

- Get information on updating your software.

Simply select the command you want and then use the on-screen documents to find and read the information.

Exiting Navigator

When you are done cruising the Internet, you should log off so that you aren't using up the online time you are allowed by your ISP. To exit Navigator, you can click the Close button in the title bar. On a PC, this is an X in the top right corner of the window. On the Mac, it is an empty box in the top left corner. You can also open the File menu and select the Exit (Quit for the Mac) command.

You should also disconnect from your ISP using its instructions. You might need to click on a Disconnect button in an ISP dialog box or use a Sign Out command.

Moving On

Now that you have a basic understanding of how the Navigator screen is set up, you are ready to be set free in the wide, wild world of the Web. Chapter 5 explains how to navigate the Internet.

Navigating
The Internet

Suppose you are looking up something in a book. Do you always find what you need on the first page you turn to? Of course not—you sometimes have to turn to another page or even another book. The same is true when looking for information on the Internet. If you're lucky, the first page you start with will have what you are looking for. Sometimes you may have to display another page at that site; sometimes you may have to try another site. You might have to make one, two, three, or more jumps until you find what you are looking for. Fortunately, all this jumping around is easy—just click your mouse button. And as you jump around you might find something of *more* interest.

This chapter covers how to move around on the Internet. You will learn how to jump from link to link, go directly to an address, and save sites that you want to visit again.

Jumping From Link To Link

Suppose that you want to create a Web page about yourself. Could you fit your life story on one screen? You could probably cover the basics of your life in one page, but what if you want to go into a little bit of detail about your Irish heritage? What if you want to include information about your professional accomplishments?

Just The FAQs

How do you use links to jump to another page?

When you want to go to another Web page, you click on the *link* to it. Links may appear in a different color, underlined, or both. In addition to text links, some graphics are *hot spots*—links to other pages. When you click on a link, Navigator locates that server and document, then displays it on your screen.

How do you back up?

You can return to previously viewed pages. To go back a page, click the Back button in the Navigation toolbar. You can also use the Go menu and select any of the previously visited sites from the drop-down list box.

How do you go directly to an address?

If you know the address of a Web page, the fastest way to get there is to type the address in the Location box and press Enter.

What if I find a page that I like and want to return to it? Do I always have to enter the address?

If you find a page that you will visit often, you can save the page address as a *bookmark*. You can then easily and quickly go to it without having to re-enter the address.

Why won't a page display?

If you try to go to a link and get an error message, it might mean one of several things. First, if you typed the address, check it, because you may have typed it incorrectly. Second, the server might be down. Try going to that link another time. Third, the page may have been moved or even deleted from the server. You may see a note that explains where you can now find it.

What if you are an avid reader and want to include a list of your favorite books? Or perhaps you are a cook and want to include some of your best recipes. Now imagine you own a company and want to publish information on the Web. Can you do it on one page?

As you can see, fitting everything on one page isn't easy. That's why most Web sites are a series of related documents or pages. You can include one main page, with links to other pages that include additional information. By constructing your pages this way, you give your viewer the option of picking the information of interest to him or her. For example, perhaps a visitor to your home page couldn't care less about your Irish heritage, but does like to read mystery novels and wants to see whether you list any. This viewer could try your book-list page. Setting up links this way is beneficial to both the author and the viewer.

How can you tell what links a page includes? How do you jump from link to link? This section covers the basics on moving from page to page and back and forward among pages.

Moving From Page To Page

When you take a look at a Web page, notice that some text is underlined and appears in a different color (see Figure 5.1). These are links that you can click

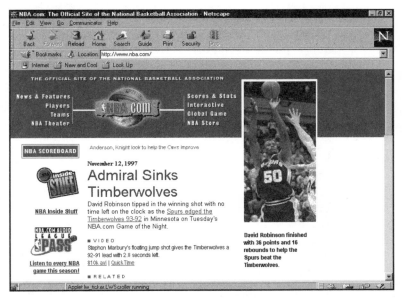

Figure 5.1   Click on any underlined or colored text to jump to that link.

on to jump to the accompanying page. Some pages include buttons that you can click on to go to another page. You will also notice pages that include images that serve as links or hot spots; click on the graphics to go to another page.

You can tell when your mouse pointer is over a link by its appearance: It looks like a hand with a pointing finger. Also, look at the status bar to see the address of the linked Web page.

When you click on a link, Navigator displays the page for that link. The page could be any one of the following:

- One of the related pages (that is, a separate document on the current server)

- Another section within the original page (an easy way to move to a different location within a document)

- A page on another network (meaning that Navigator has connected to that network to display the page)

TIP

If you're using a PC, press Ctrl+Home to go quickly to the top of a page. Press Ctrl+End to go to the end of the page.

Take your imaginary home page as an example again. If all you included on your Web pages were links to your own related documents, your page would be something of a dead end. A reader who gets there has nowhere else to go. Most well-designed Web pages include links to other Web pages. You might, for instance, include a link to a cooking site on the page with your recipes. Or you might include a link to pages on Irish history on your Irish-heritage page. Including links beyond your own little world opens up other avenues of exploration and makes surfing the Internet so exciting. You can never tell where you might end up.

TIP

You can tell where you've been—which links you've tried—by looking at their color. When you've visited a link, the color of the text changes. The default color is purple. (Links you haven't followed are blue by default.) That doesn't mean the link is unavailable. You can still click on it to visit the page again. The color change just helps you remember what you've visited and what you haven't. You can change the color of followed links and specify when they should revert back to their original color. See Chapter 11 for details.

Going Back And Forward

In your journey around the Web, you may find something you think might be interesting, but when you go to the page, you find it isn't what you thought it would be. Or you might want to go back to a page you've visited before. Navigator makes it easy to go back and forth between pages.

The Back And Forward Buttons

To go back to the last page you visited, click on the Back button in the Navigation toolbar. Or you can open the Go menu and select the Back command. If you aren't sure where the Back button will take you, put the mouse pointer over the button. The title of the page pops up. You can also display a drop-down list of sites you have visited by clicking and holding down the mouse button on the Back button. From that list, click on the site you want. Both of these features are new with Navigator 4.

Once you have moved back, you can also move forward. To do so, click the Forward button or open the Go menu and select the Forward command. You can likewise display a drop-down list of sites by clicking and holding down the mouse button on the Forward button and then selecting from any of the listed sites.

TIP

Forward or Back command grayed out? If the Forward and Back buttons are gray, it means you have not visited any other pages during this session. To move back, you have to have visited at least one page. To move forward, you must have gone back at least one page.

The Location List

If you are using Navigator on a PC (rather than a Mac), you can also use the Location drop-down list box to go to any of the last several locations you have visited in this session. One warning: This list includes only those sites you have visited by *typing* the address (covered in the "Entering The Address" section later in this chapter); it does not include those sites you have visited by clicking on links.

To go to a previous site, follow these steps:

1. Click on the down arrow to the right of the Location list. You see a list of the last sites you have visited (see Figure 5.2).

2. Click on the site you want to go back to. Navigator displays that page.

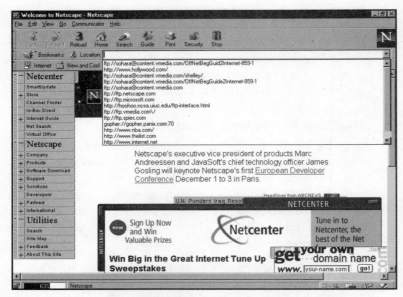

Figure 5.2 *Use the Location list to go back to some of the sites you've visited recently.*

The Go Menu

You can also return to a previously viewed page using the Go menu. When you open it, you see a list of the sites you have visited in the current session (see Figure 5.3), including the sites you have jumped to via a link. Click on the site you want to visit.

The History Command

Finally, you can also use the History command to view the list of sites you have visited. This is convenient, because sometimes you know you went to a certain site, but you can't remember the name. Rather than try to find the site via links or searching, display a history list, and from it, select any of the sites you have visited. Follow these steps:

1. Open the Communicator menu and select the History command. The list of the sites you have visited appears (see Figure 5.4). You can find out the name of the page, the site address, dates visited, and more from the list.

2. Double-click on the site you want to go back to.

TIP

Checking the history list is also a good way to monitor what sites have been visited. For example, you can check to see the sites your children are looking at.

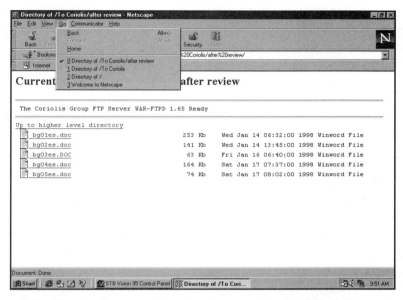

Figure 5.3   Use the Go menu to return to a previously visited site.

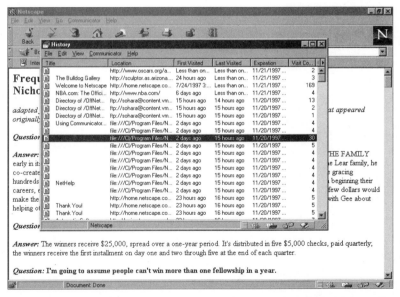

Figure 5.4   You can see what sites you have visited from the history list.

Getting Around In Gopherspace

You might remember the brief discussion of Gopherspace back in Chapter 1. Because information on Gopher servers is text-only and organized in hierarchical menus, these sites look a bit different than sites on the World Wide Web. Most information was presented in this format before the advent of the Web, and this format is still valuable, especially for research purposes where graphics may not be an enhancement.

To go to a Gopher server, enter the address, which begins with "gopher". For instance, the address of a Gopher site for the House of Representatives is **gopher://gopher.house.gov**.

As you can see from Figure 5.5, a Gopher server is mostly text and is mostly links. The documents (indicated with a document icon) are arranged into folders (indicated with a folder icon). You can move (or *burrow* or *tunnel*) through the various folders to find the information you want.

Moving among the folders and opening documents is similar to working with an FTP site. For more information on navigating FTP sites, turn to Chapter 10.

Going Home

If you start to feel like Hansel and Gretel leaving breadcrumbs in the forest, have no fear. You can quickly return to your starting spot, usually the Netscape

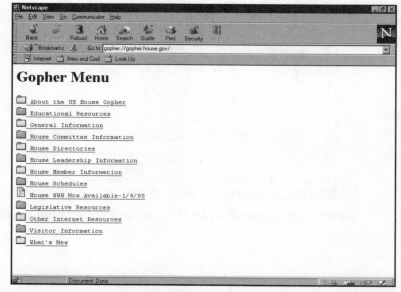

Figure 5.5   Gopher menus arrange documents into a hierarchical structure.

home page. To do so, click the Home button or open the Go menu and select the Home command.

In Chapter 11, you will find out how you can select a home page other than the Netscape home page.

Stopping A Link

Sometimes you will click on a link and wait and wait and wait and wait. You may wonder if something is wrong. One way to check whether Navigator is still busy is to look at the Netscape logo in the upper right corner of the window. If the logo is animated (the stars are shooting through the sky), Navigator is still busy trying to locate the server or download the document. You can also check the progress bar, which gives you an idea of the transfer's progress, or check the status bar, which displays messages telling you what is happening.

If you get tired of waiting or if you decide you don't want to go to that site after all, you can stop the link by clicking on the Stop button or opening the View menu and selecting the Stop Page Loading command. Navigator stops the transfer and redisplays the home page.

Try the site again later, perhaps during a time of day that isn't so busy. Some peak times are the early evening hours and Friday nights.

Moving Within A Frame

Some Web pages are constructed with *frames*; the information on such pages is divided into *panes*, with each pane containing a unique page of information. The entire set of frames is called a *top-level page* or *frameset* and has one unique address (even though each frame acts a lot like a separate page).

As you explore the Web, you'll find some pages that use frames and some that don't. Because navigating in a frame is somewhat different than navigating in a page, this section covers some techniques for working with frames.

Don't see any frames? Not all Web pages are set up in frames. If you display a page and don't see frames, don't worry. Some Web pages will fill the entire screen; it doesn't mean something is wrong.

Selecting A Frame

Some commands—like printing—affect only the selected frame. To select a frame, click within it.

Clicking On Links Within A Frame

Some frames contain links. What happens when you click on any of those links depends on how the author has set up the page. A new page will either be displayed within that frame, in another frame, or in *all* the frames. Finally, clicking on a link might take you to an entirely new site with no frames whatsoever. It's really not as confusing as it sounds. Once you experiment a bit, you'll get the hang of it.

Resizing Frames

The size and arrangement of the frames are set by the author, who also controls whether *you* can resize the frame. You can change some frames. For example, if you want to make one frame bigger, put your mouse pointer on the frame border. If your pointer turns into a bar with two arrows, you can resize the frame by simply dragging its border.

If the contents won't fit in the frame, use the scroll bars along the frame edges to scroll through the frame.

Going Directly To A Location

When you first start exploring the Web, you may not know exactly where you want to go. You might, for instance, want to take a "Sunday drive" and just browse around from site to site, using links. This method is great for getting an idea of what you can find on the Web. But this method can be undesirably time-consuming when you have a specific goal in mind.

You'll often want to go directly to a site, without having to make several jumps from link to link. In this case, you can use the Location text box to go directly to an address. To travel this way, you need to know the address.

Finding The Address

As you watch TV or read magazines, you may have noticed a new element in a lot of ads: the Web address. For example, you may see the address for Intel on its TV commercials. Or you might see a reference to the Web page for MTV during its shows and commercials. When reading a newsmagazine, you may notice Web addresses on advertisements for cars, computers, phone systems, bottled water, florists, and more—practically everyone has a Web page.

The address or URL, as covered in Chapter 4, looks like this: **http://www.perrier.com**.

You can also find addresses by searching for them, as described in Chapter 6, or by trying some of the sites highlighted in Part III of this book. You can find the Web addresses in both the chapters and the illustrations.

As another alternative, you can purchase a number of excellent books that list Internet attractions by category.

Computer magazines often highlight Web sites in articles and lists. Use these to try out new sites.

Finally, sometimes you can guess the address. For instance, you can type "www.nba.com" to go to the NBA's page. If the address is wrong, you'll just see an error message. You can then try a different name if you wish.

Entering The Address

Once you know the address, you can go quickly to a site. Simply select the current address in the Location text box and type the new address. As you start typing, the name of this box changes to Go To. Be sure to type the address exactly as it appears (some addresses are case-sensitive). Also, be sure you get the slashes and periods in all the right places. After you type the address, press Enter. Navigator displays the page.

TIP

Get an error message? You may not have typed the address correctly. Check your source and be sure you enter the address exactly as it appears.

As an alternative to the Location text box, you can use a menu command. Follow these steps:

1. Open the File menu and select the Open Page command. You'll see the Open Page dialog box (see Figure 5.6).

2. Type the address and click the Open button.

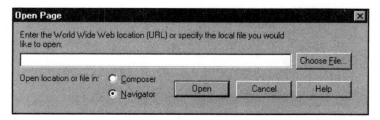

Figure 5.6 Use the Open Page dialog box to go directly to an address.

Shortcuts For Entering The Address

Navigator 4 includes a new feature that makes typing an address quicker. If you have typed the address before, you can simply type the first few letters. Navigator guesses the site and completes the address for you (see Figure 5.7). If this is the site you want, you can simply press Enter to have Navigator go to that site. If it's not the site, you can just keep typing.

You can also leave off parts of the address. For an address that starts "http://", you don't have to type "http://". If the address includes "http://www.", you can also leave off the "http://www.". And if the suffix is ".com", you don't have to type that, either.

Finally, if you don't know an address, you can try faking it. Usually the name is some version of the company name. For example, the address for HBO is **http://www.hbo.com**. It doesn't hurt to try a made-up address. If it's wrong, you just get an error message.

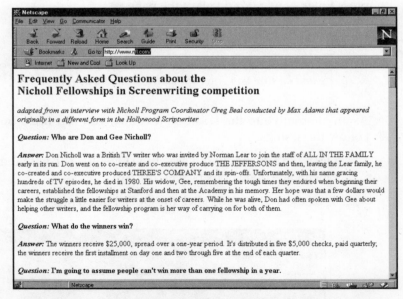

Figure 5.7   Navigator will automatically complete addresses you have typed recently.

Using Bookmarks

When you go traveling on vacation, you may find a place that you like so much you want to return. You might find a hotel that you love and want to stay there every time you are in the area. Or you might find one or two restaurants worthy of a return visit. The same is true of Internet traveling. As you journey from site to site, you may find places you want to visit again. You could keep a written record of the addresses and consult that list when typing in an address later, but as you know, addresses can be complicated to type. An alternative is to have Navigator save the address for you as a bookmark. Your bookmarks will be available any time you use Navigator.

Trying Some Of Navigator's Bookmarks

Navigator may set up bookmark folders with some sites; for example, you may be able to display sites relating to Business & Finance, Computers & Technology, Shopping, Sports, Travel & Leisure, and more. You can select from any of the folders and sites in the Bookmarks menu.

Creating A Bookmark For A Page

You can also create bookmarks for any pages you like. If you don't specify otherwise, Navigator adds the bookmark to the end of the list. To create a bookmark for a page, follow these steps:

1. Display the page you want to save as a bookmark.

2. Click the Bookmarks button and select the Add Bookmark command.

The address is stored as a bookmark and added to the end of your Bookmark menu. The next time you want to go to that page, you can do so quickly.

If you want to place the bookmark in a separate folder, you can do so when you create it. (You can also rearrange your bookmarks, as covered in Chapter 11.) Here's how:

1. Display the page you want to save as a bookmark.

2. Click and hold down the mouse button on the icon that appears next to the Location text box.

3. While still holding down the mouse button, point to the Bookmarks button and select the File Bookmark command. You will see a list of the folders in your Bookmark menu (see Figure 5.8).

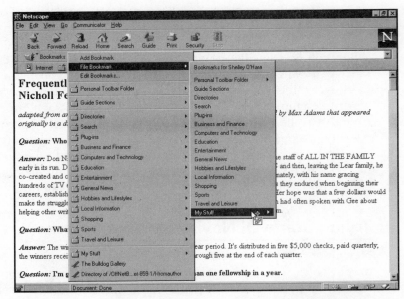

Figure 5.8 *You can file a bookmark in any of the folders set up in your bookmark list.*

4. Point to the folder where you want to place the bookmark and release the mouse button. The bookmark is added to that folder.

Going To A Bookmark

You can quickly return to a saved bookmark (or go to a bookmark Navigator has already set) by following these steps:

1. Click the Bookmarks button. A list of the current bookmarks appears (see Figure 5.9).

2. If necessary, point to the folder that contains the bookmark to see a list of the bookmarks in that folder (see Figure 5.10).

3. When you see the bookmark you want, click on it. Navigator displays that page.

TIP

You can create new folders and organize your bookmarks into groups rather than in one long list. The bookmarks in Figures 5.9 and 5.10, for example, include folders. Chapter 11 explains how to make this change.

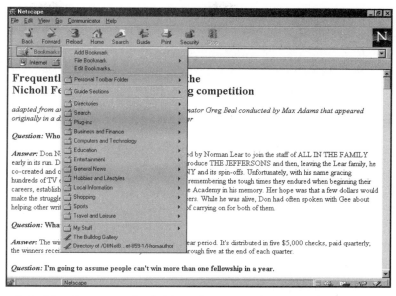

Figure 5.9   You first open the folder where you placed the bookmark.

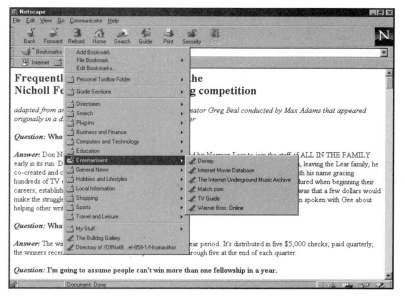

Figure 5.10   Select the bookmark you want.

Moving On

Browsing around somewhat aimlessly is a great way to explore the Web and see what's out there, but you may tire of this method soon if you want to find something specific. How do you find a particular company on the Web? Can you find pages dealing with a particular topic? Yes, you can. Chapter 6 explains how to use search tools to search the Internet.

CHAPTER 6

Searching The Internet

When you first start exploring the Internet, you might get a kick out of venturing from link to link, kind of wandering around in cyberspace. After a while, you might decide to use a more effective approach for finding something. For example, suppose that you are a tennis fan and want to see what Internet sites you can find about tennis. Or suppose you are looking for new job and want to do some research on the companies in your field.

Luckily, the Internet has several tools for searching, and Navigator makes many of them accessible from the Netscape home page. You can select from one of several different tools for searching the Internet, as covered in this chapter.

Internet Search Basics

The basics for searching the Internet are similar no matter what tool you use. You select the tool, enter what you want to find, and then review the search results. But which tools are available? And how do you find a search tool? This section covers the basic search procedures. The rest of the chapter gives you specific advice on using some of the most popular search tools.

Displaying The Search Tools

As mentioned, Netscape includes a Net Search area on its home page, and each time you access this page a different search tool is selected by default.

Just The FAQs

How do I search the Internet?

To find something on the Internet, you need to use a *search engine*. Navigator conveniently has a Net Search area on its home page. Plus, you can use the Search button to display a page with links to the most popular search engines.

No matter which search tool you use, the same basic procedure for searching is the same. Select the tool you want, enter the text to find, and then click on the Search button. You see the results of the search on a page.

What are the search results?

The search results are a page of links to sites that match what you entered. Usually the results include a short description of the matching sites so that you can decide whether the site is of interest. You can also view additional matches or related sites from the search results page, search again, and display additional help on how to search.

Which search tool is the best?

Each search tool has its pros and cons. You should try them all and then pick the one you like the best. Also, if you try one tool and don't find the match you want, try another one. The results from the search are likely to be different.

What if I don't know what I'm looking for?

If you aren't sure what you want to find, you can try another method: browsing. Most search tools also include category directories, which are a good way to see the types of sites you can find on the Internet.

How much does searching cost?

You don't have to pay a fee to use most search engines. You may have to skip over a few advertisements on the pages; the search companies usually offset their costs by selling advertising space.

You can also display the drop-down list and select from any of the available search tools.

In addition, you can find links to some of the premier search tools on one Net Search page so that you can easily access them. To display the available tools on a page, click on the Search button or open the Edit menu and select the Search Internet command. In either case, you see the Net Search page (see Figure 6.1).

As you can see from Figure 6.1, many different companies provide search tools (sometimes called *search engines* or *search indexes*). Netscape makes the most popular tools available as links along the left side of the page; click on the appropriate one to access Lycos, Yahoo!, Excite, or Infoseek. In addition, you can select from several other services, including AOL NetFind, HotBot, LookSmart, SEARCH.COM, and WebCrawler. Finally, scroll down the page to select from several other search engines (see Figure 6.2).

All of these search tools are provided for you to use free of charge. The company that creates and maintains a search engine often sells advertising or other products, which offsets the cost of providing the search tool.

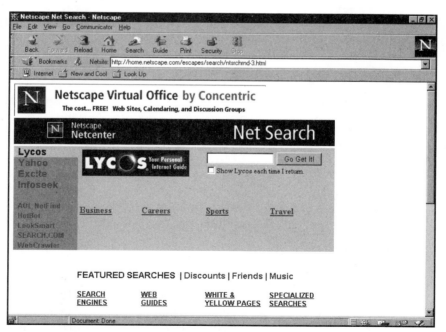

Figure 6.1   Use the Net Search page to select a search tool.

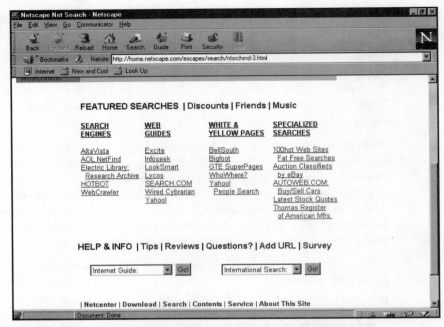

Figure 6.2   You can select from a number of search engines on the Netscape Search page.

Selecting A Search Tool

If all the tools do a search, then what's the difference? Search tools differ in the following ways:

■ *How they search the page*—For example, some search engines search the home pages of sites and index the contents. Others review the site and then make a list of keywords or create a summary. The keyword list is then used as the index. Because each search engine searches a little bit differently, you can get different results from each one. Some sites are not really a search engine, but more of a directory (like Yahoo!).

■ *How the results are ranked*—Most search tools rank the search results, displaying the most probable matches first. The criteria that determine the most probable or most relevant vary from tool to tool. Some rank based on how well the site text matches what you typed. Some rank based on how many times your search phrase appears. Most pages include an explanation of how the sites are ranked on the search results page.

■ *What search options are available*—In addition to a simple search, most search tools provide some more advanced options for performing a search. You may be able to instruct the search engine to disregard occurrences of "table tennis" in a search for "tennis". You might be able to search just a part of the Internet—for instance, just newsgroups or just Web pages.

■ *Whether the sites are reviewed*—Some companies, in addition to providing search capabilities, also have a staff that reviews and rates sites. You can use the reviews to get an idea of the quality of a particular site.

TIP

If you use a particular search tool often, create a bookmark for it so that you can quickly display its home page. To create a bookmark, display the page, click on the Bookmarks button, and select the Add Bookmark command. Next time you want to use the tool, just select the site from the Bookmarks menu.

Comparing Search Engines

How do you pick a search tool, then? No one search tool is the best. Each has strengths and weaknesses, which are largely determined by what you are searching for and your own personal preferences. It's a good idea to try out each tool and see which one gives you the results you like best. If you don't find something using one tool, try another. The results will probably be different.

You can also usually find reviews of search tools in various computer magazines. The editors put each tool through a search test and rate its usability. Here are some highlights from a September 1997 "2nd Annual Search Engine Shoot-out" in *PC Computing*:

■ Excite indexes over 60 million pages. You can access this search tool from a link on the left side of the Net Search page.

■ Infoseek has a searchable index of 24 million pages. Infoseek is one of the search tools available on the left side of the Net Search page.

■ HotBot indexes the full text of 54 million Web and Usenet documents. You can select HotBot on the left side of the Net Search page.

■ AltaVista indexes over 31 million Web pages and 4 million articles from 14,000 Usenet newsgroups. You can access AltaVista from the bottom of the Net Search page (under Search Engines).

Entering The Search

To perform a search, follow these basic steps:

1. Click on the search tool you want to use. Figure 6.1 shows the search box for Lycos.

2. In the text box, enter the text that best describes what you want to find. You can enter a word or a phrase. Keep in mind that the more unique the entry, the narrower the search. For instance, if you enter "computers", you are going to get thousands of hits. If you enter "computer programming", you narrow the search. And if you enter "object-oriented programming", you further narrow the search. The "Setting Search Options" section later in this chapter gives some advice on using complex search criteria.

3. Click the Search button. (The name of this button varies depending on the tool.)

The search tool completes the search and then displays the results. Figure 6.3 shows the results of a Lycos search.

Reviewing The Results

The search results page usually includes the following:

- The text you searched for ("careers", in the example shown in Figure 6.3), as well as a summary of the results.

- A list of links to matching sites. You can go to any of the sites listed by clicking on the link.

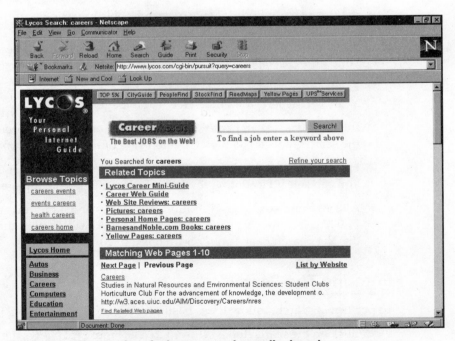

Figure 6.3   The results of a Lycos search are displayed.

TIP

Some search sites have reviews of various sites. Usually a reviewed site is indicated with an icon. You can read the review to get an idea of the site's strengths and weaknesses.

■ A link or button you can use to display additional matches, if you get more than one page of search results.

TIP

Some of the listed sites include a link called "Find Related Web pages" or "More Like This". You can click on this link to see related pages.

■ Links to pages that offer advice on how to search, how to use complex search strings, how to list your own Web page on that service, and other information.

■ A link or button you can use for starting over, if you want to try a different search.

■ Advertisements and links to other services. Notice that the advertisements are sometimes customized. In Figure 6.3, for instance, you see an ad for Career Mosaic.

Browsing The Search Directories Or Channels

In addition to their search capabilities, some search tools also include categories or channels that you can browse through. For example, Lycos offers several categories of links, including Entertainment, Business, Kids, Travel, Shopping, Money, and more. Yahoo! is more of a directory; it catalogs sites into groups like Arts, Business, Computers, Education, Employment, Entertainment, Games, Government, Health, Internet, Investing, Kids, Media, Movies, Music, Recreation, Reference, Regional, Science, Society, Software, Sports, Travel, and Weather. You can browse the sites in any of these categories. You can also look up businesses, people, or city maps.

Infoseek has several channels, such as Automotive, Business, Careers, Real Estate, and so on.

Excite has several channels of content, divided into sections like News, Sports, Travel, and so on.

Browsing is a good method when you don't know what you are looking for, but want to get an idea of the types of sites that are available.

Visiting The Home Page Of The Search Tool

The Net Search page provides links to several popular search tools that make starting a search from this page easy and quick. You can also go directly to the home page for the search engine. From this page, you can find help links for using the search tool and setting other options. Table 6.1 shows the addresses of the most popular search tools.

Browsing With Yahoo!

The Yahoo! search service describes itself as "a searchable, browsable, hierarchical index of the Internet." This search service categorizes Internet sites. You can search through its index listings to find sites, companies, and topics of interest, or you can browse through the various categories.

To use Yahoo!, follow these steps:

1. On the Netscape Net Search page, click on the Yahoo! link. You see the search form for Yahoo! at the top of the page (see Figure 6.4).

2. Type the text you want to find using either lowercase or uppercase. For example, you might type "careers".

3. Click the Search button. Yahoo! displays the first set of matching categories (see Figure 6.5). You can scroll down to see the individual sites.

4. Jump to any of the categories in bold by clicking on the one you want. Figure 6.6 shows some categories for Business and Economy: Employment: Careers. You can also display the next set of matches by clicking on the Next Matches link. Scroll down the page to find this link.

5. Continue to click on subcategories until you see sites listed. Yahoo! displays the sites within the category as well as a short description of each one. In Figure 6.7, you see a list of sites for the Radio subcategory.

Table 6.1   Popular tools for searching the Internet.

Search Tool	Address
Lycos	http://www.lycos.com
Yahoo!	http://www.yahoo.com
Excite	http://www.excite.com
Infoseek	http://www.infoseek.com
HotBot	http://www.hotbot.com
AltaVista	http://www.altavista.digital.com

Figure 6.4   Use Yahoo! to search the Internet. (Text and artwork copyright 1998 by YAHOO!, Inc. All rights reserved. YAHOO! and the YAHOO! logo are trademarks of YAHOO!, Inc.)

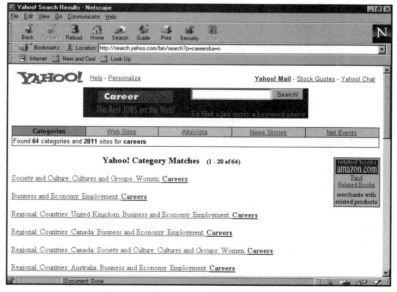

Figure 6.5   When you search, Yahoo! displays matching categories. (Text and artwork copyright 1998 by YAHOO!, Inc. All rights reserved. YAHOO! and the YAHOO! logo are trademarks of YAHOO!, Inc.)

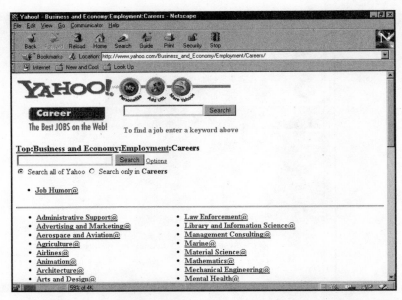

Figure 6.6 *You can select from subcategories within the main category. (Text and artwork copyright 1998 by YAHOO!, Inc. All rights reserved. YAHOO! and the YAHOO! logo are trademarks of YAHOO!, Inc.)*

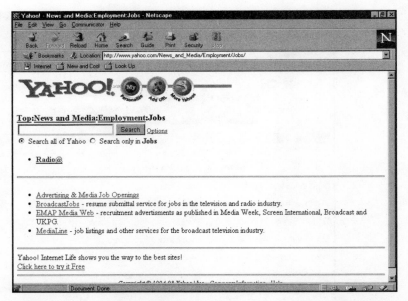

Figure 6.7 *After you select the subcategory, you see a list of selected sites. (Text and artwork copyright 1998 by YAHOO!, Inc. All rights reserved. YAHOO! and the YAHOO! logo are trademarks of YAHOO!, Inc.)*

In addition to a simple search, you can browse through categories, set search options, review current news headlines, and check out some Yahoo! picks, as described in the following sections.

Browsing Yahoo!'s Categories

In addition to searching Yahoo! for a particular company, organization, or topic, you can browse through the different categories or search within a category. For example, you might select the Sports category from the start page and view the Sports sites of Yahoo! (see Figure 6.8).

Setting Search Options

If your search turns up too many matches and you don't want to have to wade through 50 or more entries to find the one you want, you can limit your search.

If you want to set search options, click on the Options link (next to the Next Search button on the search results page). Then select the options you want and try the search again. From this search-entry form, shown in Figure 6.9, you can enter the keyword(s) to find and select what to search (Yahoo!, Usenet, or email addresses). You can select a search method and search area as well as

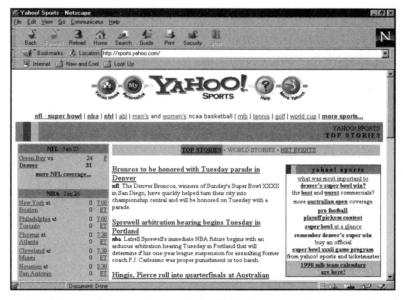

Figure 6.8   *You can browse through the Yahoo! categories to see what is available. (Text and artwork copyright 1998 by YAHOO!, Inc. All rights reserved. YAHOO! and the YAHOO! logo are trademarks of YAHOO!, Inc.)*

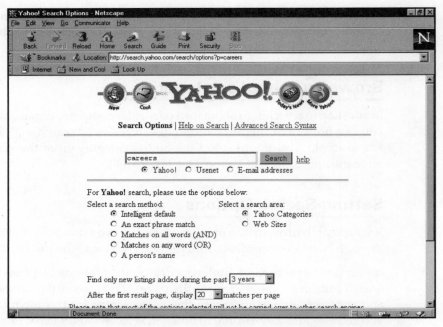

Figure 6.9 Select search options on this search form. (Text and artwork copyright 1998 by YAHOO!, Inc. All rights reserved. YAHOO! and the YAHOO! logo are trademarks of YAHOO!, Inc.)

limit the search to listings added during a specified time period. You can also select how many matches are displayed per page. Make your selections and then click on the Search button.

Reviewing Current News And Stock Information

In addition to indexing sites, Yahoo! has links to current news events. From the Yahoo! home page, click on the Today's News button to display headlines or summaries for news in any of the following categories: Top Stories, Business, Technology, World, Sports, Entertainment, Politics, Health, Weather, Human Interests, and Community. Select the category you want and then select the current news stories you want to read.

Use the Stock Quotes link to enter or look up a stock symbol and then get the latest quote for that stock. Review classified ads using the Classifieds link.

Using Infoseek

As with Yahoo!, you can use Infoseek to search for a particular topic, organization, or company. Results are scored from 0 to 100 based on the words or phrases you use in the search, and the sites with the 10 highest scores appear by default. Infoseek also includes links to many news and reference resources.

To use Infoseek to search the Internet, follow these steps:

1. Click on the Infoseek link on the Net Search page. You see the form for using Infoseek (see Figure 6.10).

2. Type the word or phrase that best describes what you want to find. The Infoseek help pages offer these tips on getting the best search results:

   ■ Use the proper capitalization, especially if you are searching for a proper name. If you don't use caps, Infoseek treats the entry like any other word. For example, to find sites relating to the White House, type "White House". If you type "white house", you will get a list of sites relating to any white houses.

   ■ To search for several names, separate the entries with a comma.

   ■ Put quotation marks around words that must appear next to each other. For example, to search for the French Open, enter "French Open". If you don't use the quotation marks, you'll get results that include either French or Open.

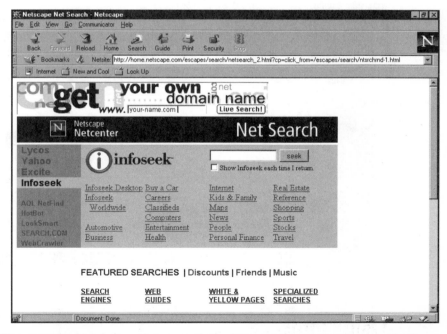

Figure 6.10 **Use Infoseek to search the Internet, browse categories in the Infoseek directory, get stock information, and more.**

■ Enter a plus sign before words that must appear in the document. Use a minus sign before words that should not appear in the document. For example, to find documents on tennis, but not table tennis, enter "tennis -table". Be sure to type the space before the hyphen.

One of the characteristics of Infoseek that contributes to its popularity is that when you enter a question, Infoseek interprets it and displays relevant sites.

3. Click on the Seek button. Infoseek performs the search and displays the first 10 matches (see Figure 6.11). The results page lists the name of the site, the address, the score, the size, and a short description. You can use this information to help find the site(s) of interest.

If you find too many sites, limit the list to those of interest by searching the list of found sites. Type the word or phrase you want to find and then click on the Search Only Within These Pages option button.

If you don't find the results you want, go ahead and display the next set of matches or try a new search. You can also use the links to related topics that appear along the left edge of the screen.

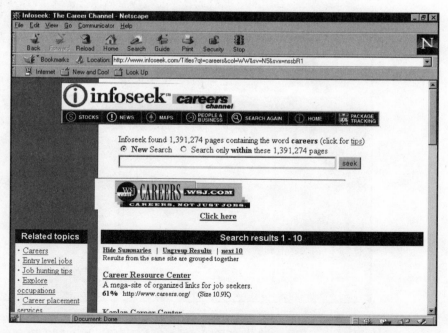

Figure 6.11   The results of an Infoseek search are ranked from the highest to lowest probable match.

Browsing Infoseek's Categories

Infoseek also includes several relevant categories such as Business, Automotive, Computer, Entertainment, Healthy, Internet, Kids & Family, Travel, Shopping, Real Estate, and more. Click on the category you want to review and then try any of the highlighted sites.

Getting The Latest Stock And News Information

Links from Infoseek allow you to get the latest stock prices or the latest news. For stock information, click the Stocks icon on the opening Infoseek page. From the Stocks page, you can enter or look up the stock symbol of a company and then get the latest quote. You can also check portfolios and intraday charts (see Figure 6.12).

Looking Up Something

Among the coolest categories of Infoseek links is Desk Reference. Use this page to look up words in the dictionary or thesaurus; you can also look up quotations in Bartlett's Quotations (see Figure 6.13).

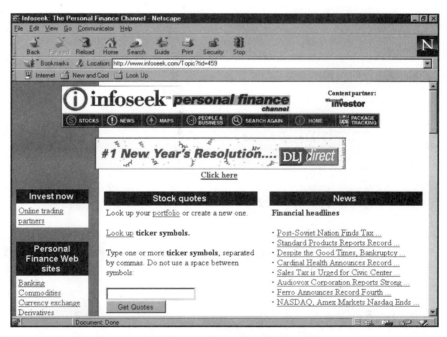

Figure 6.12   Look up stock information using Infoseek.

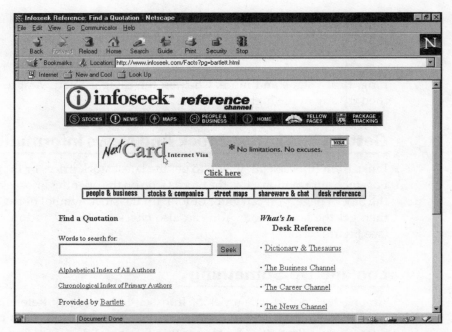

Figure 6.13   Infoseek includes links to many other resources, which you can use to look up facts.

If you need to look up an address, click on Street Maps. The self-explanatory People & Business and Shareware & Chat buttons are useful, too. And finally, you can also use Yellow Pages to look up businesses. (Some of the other search engines also include a link to Yellow Pages.)

Searching With Lycos

Lycos, an alternative to Infoseek and Yahoo!, searches its indexed lists of sites and displays links to the first 10 matches. To use Lycos, follow these steps:

1. Click on the Lycos link on the Net Search page. You see the Lycos search form (see Figure 6.14).

2. Enter the text that best describes what you want to find. By default, Lycos will find pages that include any of the words you enter in the search form.

3. Click on the Go Get It! button. Lycos displays a list of results (see Figure 6.15). You can go to any of the sites by clicking on the appropriate link. To display additional links in the list, click on the links for the other pages at the bottom of the page.

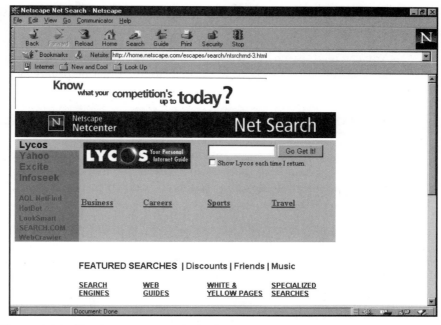

Figure 6.14   Use Lycos to search the Internet.

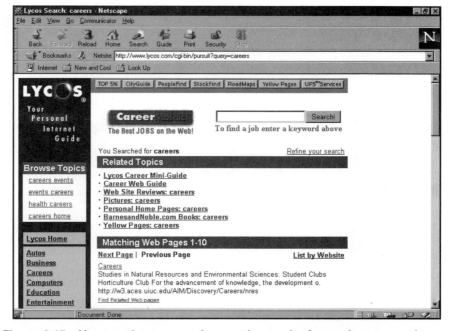

Figure 6.15   You see the top matches on the results from a Lycos search.

Getting More Results

The search results page also includes a section called "More Ways to Search". You can also search again just in the results you found. Use the Related Topics and Browse Topics sections of the page to find other helpful related information.

Looking For A Site With Excite

Excite's search software scans pages and then comes up with a keyword and summary. Excite uses these as the criteria for the search when looking for a particular Internet site. The results are ranked in percentages. Follow these steps to use Excite:

1. Click on the Excite link on the Net Search page. You see the form for searching using Excite (see Figure 6.16).

2. Enter the word or words that best describe what you want to find. If you enter more than one word, Excite looks for pages that include one or both of the words, giving a higher weight to documents with both terms.

3. Click on the Search button. Excite displays the results (see Figure 6.17). You see the name of the site, a percentile ranking, the address, and a

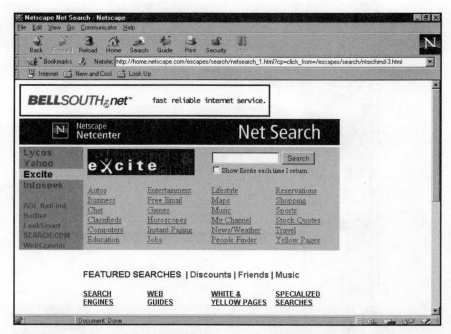

Figure 6.16 *Use Excite to search for a keyword or browse through the listed categories.*

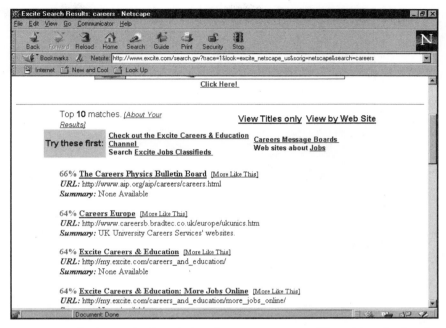

Figure 6.17   Excite ranks listed sites by a percentage of how closely the site matches your search phrase.

description. To go to any of the listed sites, click on the link. To view additional sites, click on the Next Results button. To display pages similar to one that is listed, click on the More Like This link that accompanies it.

Refining Your Search

To refine your search, you can add other related words to the search. Excite recognizes and groups keywords together. For instance, the search for "bulldog" found these related words: bulldog, citadel, razorbacks, sporting news, and others. You can limit the search by checking any of the words and then clicking on the Search button. (You can find these options at the bottom of the page.)

Browsing Excite's Channels

Excite also has several channels, such as Arts, Business, Chat, Classifieds, Computers, Education, Entertainment, Games, Hardware, Health, Horoscopes, Instant Paging, Lifestyle, Maps, Movies, Music, My Channel, News, PeopleFinder, Relationships, Reservations, Shareware, Shopping, Sports, Stock Quotes, Travel, Yellow Pages, and Weather. Click on any of these links from the initial Excite page to display that channel (for instance, Figure 6.18 shows

Figure 6.18   Browse any of Excite's channels.

the Entertainment channel). You can go to any of these highlighted sites by clicking on the link.

Trying Other Tools

The tools we've described–Yahoo!, Infoseek, Lycos, and Excite—are some of the most popular ones, but they aren't the only tools available. Try some of the other tools listed and linked on the Net Search page—for example, HotBot, a popular search engine. As you can see from the HotBot home page shown in Figure 6.19, you have lots of search options. You can select a date range, choose a continent, limit the media type, and more.

Another popular search engine is AltaVista, shown in Figure 6.20.

Keep in mind that even this list of search tools isn't complete. As the Internet continues to grow, more and more tools and utilities for working with the Internet are created. You may find new search tools to try.

TIP

You can select which search engine you want displayed by default. To do so, click on the Show Each Time I Return checkbox for the search tool you want.

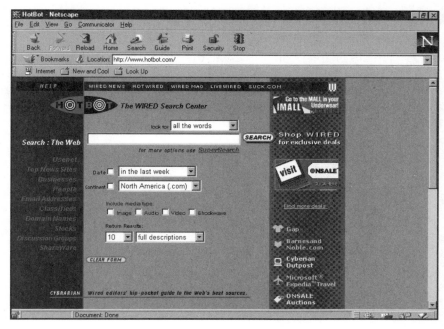

Figure 6.19   HotBot includes many options for searching.

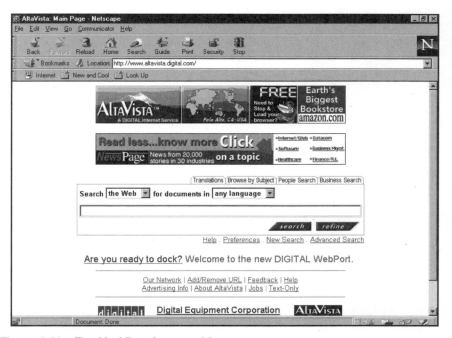

Figure 6.20   Try AltaVista for searching, too.

Moving On

In this chapter you learned all the basic techniques for searching the Internet. What can you do once you find the site you seek? Chapter 7 tells you how to do more with Web pages—namely, how to copy, print, and search the pages you visit.

Chapter 7

Exploring Web Pages

You may wonder what else you can do besides simply review the information on a Web page. Is that all there is? No. You can also change the view, print, copy, and search the page.

If the page includes reference information that you want to review, you can print that information. Or perhaps the page includes a graphic logo (that is distributed freely) that you want to include in your document or on your Web page. You can copy the image. If the page is fairly long and includes a lot of text, you may want to search the page to find a particular word or phrase. Curious what HTML looks like? You can view the document source. You can also view the security settings for the page.

Some Web pages include sounds and movies that you can play back. Or you may find a form that asks you for information—to enter a contest, for instance. This chapter covers all the skills and techniques you need to know to do more with Web pages than simply view them.

Viewing Web Pages

When you click on a link, Navigator transfers the linked page from the network server it resides on and displays it on your screen. Depending on how the page is set up, you may see text, graphics, an *image map* (a graphic with links), links to other pages, and links to play sounds, videos, or animations.

Just The FAQs

Besides viewing a Web page, what else can I do with it?

Besides viewing a Web page, you can save or print it, search for text on it, and copy text and images from it. You can also play back sounds and movies and complete online forms.

Can I freely copy text and graphics?

The text and graphics on a Web page may be copyrighted, meaning that you cannot use them in your work without permission. If you are not sure whether you can use the text or image, check with the site.

How do I print a copy of the page?

Open the File menu and select the Print command. When the Print dialog box appears, click on OK to print the page.

How do I check out the security of a page?

New with Navigator 4, you can display the security settings of a particular page to check out settings such as encryption, verification, and so on.

How do I play back a sound or movie?

To play back a sound, click on the sound link. Navigator downloads the file and then plays it. To play back a movie, click on the movie link. The movie file is downloaded and then the file is played using the plug-in application.

How do I complete a form?

Forms contain elements similar to those in a dialog box: text boxes, drop-down lists, option buttons, checkboxes, and so on. You select these options just as you do in a dialog box.

The default view shows the formatted text and images. If you want, you can select to view the page in another format. This section discusses different options for viewing pages.

Viewing Images

The huge rise in the popularity of the Internet is in a large part due to the emergence of the World Wide Web, and one of the things that makes the Web so popular is the ability to view both text and images on a page. As you cruise the Web, you'll find that most pages include images. A Web page can include two types of images: an *inline* image that is part of the Web page itself and an *external* image that is a separate file. To view an external image, you need to download the file and then view it using a separate application.

Because images are more complex than text, transferring and displaying images can slow you down. You can choose to turn off the images and then load them on demand, as described in the next section. You can also select to view an image in a separate window.

Turning Images Off And On

If a page contains an inline image, that image is displayed by default when you see the page. If the inline images are complex, transferring the page may take some time. You may decide that you don't want the images displayed. If so, turn off the option that displays images automatically by following these steps:

1. Open the Edit menu and select the Preferences command.
2. Click on the Advanced category to display these options, shown in Figure 7.1.
3. Deselect the Automatically Load Images command.

Now when you view a page with inline images, you see a small icon, usually with some type of descriptive text. Notice that the Navigation toolbar includes an Images button. Click on this button to display the images on the page.

TIP

Turning off Automatically Load Images does not affect the current page or any previous pages you have viewed. It affects only new pages that you view after you deselect it.

Some Web pages have two versions: a text version and a graphics version. If you want the fastest connection, you can choose the text version. You can always switch to the graphics version if you want to see the pictures. Look for these options on the page.

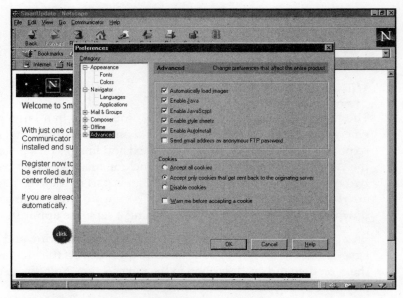

Figure 7.1   You can turn off the display of images.

Viewing External Images

Some Web pages include external images that are displayed in their own window. You can view this type of image by clicking on its link. Navigator lets you view the most common types of graphic file formats, including GIF and JPEG. If the image is in another format, you may need a *helper application* for displaying the image. (If Navigator cannot automatically display the image, you will be prompted to select the application to use to view the image.)

Some inline images are actually small thumbnail versions of the actual image. To see the external image, click on the thumbnail. For example, you can view the external image of any of the thumbnails in Figure 7.2. (By the way, that's my bulldog, Jelly Roll, in the last row, fourth from the left.)

Reloading A Page

To speed up your Internet cruising, Navigator saves a copy of pages you have viewed in a *cache*, a special area of memory. If you go back to one of these pages in the same session, Navigator can retrieve the page more quickly from the cache than it can from doing a network transfer again. That means that when you go back to a page, you may be seeing the cached version.

Most documents are not updated that frequently, so the cached version is most likely the same as the network one. On the other hand, if you are viewing stock quotes or some other timely information, the page information may be

Figure 7.2   Click on the thumbnail image. . .

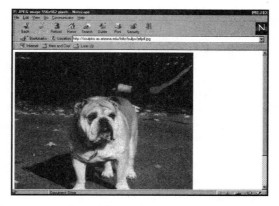

. . . to view the entire external image.

updated often. If you want to *reload* the page—i.e., get it again from the network server—click on the Reload button or open the View menu and select the Reload command. You may also want to do this if a glitch in the connection caused the page to display improperly.

TIP

You can increase or decrease the font size of the text. To do so, open the View menu and select Increase Font or Decrease Font.

Searching Web Pages

Some Web pages are just a screen or two of information, so scanning through them to find something you want is easy. Other Web pages may be much longer.

When you are looking for something in a long document, scanning through it screen by screen is too time consuming. Also, you may easily miss what you are looking for. Instead, you can use a different method: Search for text on a page.

TIP

The Find In Page command searches for text only on the current page. It does not search the Internet for that text. For help on searching the Internet, see Chapter 6.

To search for text on a page, follow these steps:

1. Open the Edit menu and select the Find In Page command. Navigator displays the Find dialog box (see Figure 7.3). (Note that this dialog box looks different in Mac versions of Navigator.)

2. In the Find What text box, enter the word or phrase you want to find.

3. If you want Navigator to match the text exactly as you have typed it, check the Match Case (PC) or Case Sensitive (Mac) checkbox. (If you don't care about matching the case, leave this option unchecked.)

4. Select the direction to search: Up or Down. On a Mac, select Wrap Search to search from the current location to the bottom of the page, then from the top back to the current location. You can also select Find Backward to search in the opposite direction.

5. Click on the Find Next (PC) or Find (Mac) button. Navigator moves to the first occurrence of the text and highlights it (see Figure 7.4). With PC versions, the dialog box remains open. Move to the next occurrence by clicking on the Find Next button. To close the dialog box, click on the Close button or the Cancel button. On the Mac, the dialog box closes once the first occurrence is found. Select Edit/Find Again to find the next occurrence.

6. If you search the entire document and find all the occurrences, or if the text is not found, you see an alert box that says "Search String Not Found" (PC) or you hear a beep (Mac). If you see an alert box, click on OK. (It's a good idea to double-check your typing. If you entered the word correctly, try searching for a different word or phrase.)

Figure 7.3   You can search a page for a word or phrase.

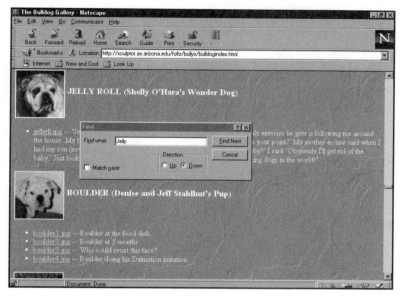

Figure 7.4   When Navigator finds the word or phrase, it is highlighted, and the dialog box remains open.

Printing Web Pages

You've probably heard it a thousand times: The computer industry was supposed to, but didn't, create the paperless office. In fact, people probably use more paper now than ever; having a hard copy version of information just seems desirable in many cases. You might want to read the information at your leisure away from your computer, or perhaps you want to use the printouts as a reference. Whatever the reason, you can use Navigator to preview a page, set up the page layout, and then print a page, as covered in this section.

Setting Up The Page

By default, Navigator uses certain margins and creates a header and footer for all printouts. You can check and change these defaults for PC versions. To change them, follow these steps:

1. Open the File menu and select the Page Setup command. You see the Page Setup dialog box (see Figure 7.5).

2. Deselect or select any of the following: Beveled Lines, Black Text, Black Lines, Last Page First.

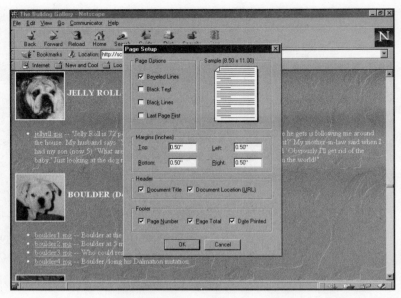

Figure 7.5   Use the options in the Page Setup dialog box to control how printouts appear.

3. Enter new margins for the top, bottom, left, or right margins.

4. By default, the printout includes the document title (the name that appears in the title bar) and document location (URL) in the header. To turn off these elements, deselect the appropriate checkboxes.

5. By default, Navigator prints the page number, page total, and date printed in the footer. You can turn off any of these elements by deselecting the appropriate checkbox.

6. When you are finished making changes, click on the OK button.

Previewing The Page

If you want to get an idea of how the printed page will appear—how much text will fit on one page, which items will print—you can preview the page (Windows versions only). If you made changes to the page setup, you may want to preview them first.

To preview a page, first display it. Then open the File menu and select the Print Preview command. Figure 7.6 shows a preview of a Web page.

You can use any of the toolbar buttons to change how the preview appears. Table 7.1 lists each toolbar button and what it does.

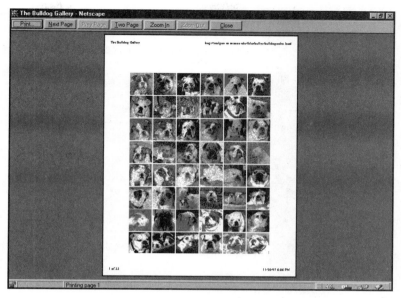

Figure 7.6   Use Print Preview to see how a page will look when printed.

Printing The Page

To print the page, follow these steps:

1. Open the File menu and select the Print command or click on the Print button. You see the Print dialog box (Figure 7.7).

2. Make any changes you want to the print options, such as the number of copies or the printer used.

3. Click on the OK button. Navigator prints the page.

Table 7.1   Buttons on the Print Preview toolbar.

Click On	To
Print	Print the page.
Next Page	Display the next page in a document with more than two pages.
Prev Page	Display the previous page. This option is available only when you use the Next Page button to go to the next page.
Two Page	Display two pages at a time. This option is available only when the document is more than two pages long.
Zoom In	See a close-up view of the preview.
Zoom Out	Go back to the regular view after zooming in.
Close	Close the preview.

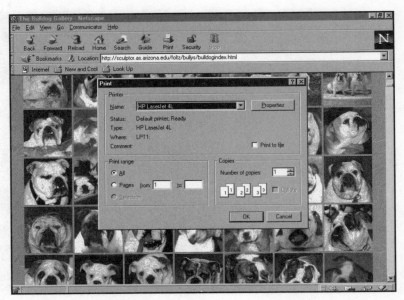

Figure 7.7   Select the printer to use and the number of copies to print from the Print dialog box.

TIP

If the page is composed of frames, you can print a selected frame. To do so, click within the frame you want to print. Then open the File menu. Instead of the Print command, use the Print Frame command to print the frame.

Saving Text, Graphics, And Links

If you want to use the information or images in a Web page, you can easily save them to disk or copy and paste them to a different document. Keep in mind that the text and images are probably copyrighted. You cannot use anything you find without permission. In fact, you should probably assume that you *can't* use it. If in doubt, contact the site to inquire about getting permission. (Sites usually include an email link you can use to contact them.)

Saving A Page

Suppose you come across a page with information that you want to use. You can save the page for later use, either as a source (HTML) file (useful if you are trying to learn this formatting language) or as a text file (useful if you want to use the text). The inline images are *not* saved with the file; you can save external images, as covered later in this section. Follow these steps to save a page or frame:

1. Display the page or frame you want to save.

2. Open the File menu and select the Save As command. You see the Save As dialog box (Figure 7.8).

3. Select the drive on which you want to save the file using the Save In drop-down list. Select the folder in the folder list.

TIP

On a PC, you can create a new folder for the file by clicking on the Create New Folder button and typing a folder name. You can also move up through the folder structure using the Up One Level button in the dialog box.

4. To change the format in which the file is saved, display the Save As Type drop-down list (PC) or Format List (Mac) and select the file format you want.

5. Enter the file name in the File Name text box.

6. Click on the Save button. Navigator saves the page.

Figure 7.8   You can save a page or frame to your hard disk.

You can also save a linked page without going to the link. To do so, put your pointer over the link and then click the right-mouse button (Windows and Unix users) or hold down the mouse button (Mac users). From the pop-up menu that appears, select Save Link As. On the PC, you see the Save As dialog box where you can select a folder and drive for the page.

Opening A Saved Page

You can view a page that you have saved at any time using Navigator. Keep in mind that you are viewing the saved version, not the one on the network. You won't see any of the inline graphics, and you won't be able to jump to any of the links. To view a saved page, follow these steps:

TIP

If you open the page in Word 97 or another browser and are connected to the Internet, you can use the links.

1. Open the File menu and select the Open Page command. You see the Open Page dialog box (shown in Figure 7.9).

2. Type the path to the file in the text box.

   Or

Figure 7.9 *Type the page name or use the Choose File button to display a list of saved pages.*

Click on the Choose File button to select the file from a list. In the Open dialog box, select the drive where the file is saved. Select the folder from the folder list; you can move up through the folder structure and change the types of files that are listed. When you see the file you want, double-click on it.

3. Click on the Open button in the Open Page dialog box. Navigator displays that page.

TIP

You can also choose to open the file in Composer, a Web authoring program included with Netscape Communicator. Click on the Composer option button and then click on the Open button. For a description of what you can do with Composer, see Appendix B.

Saving An Image

Some images are provided for anyone's use. For example, you may find clip art that is distributed freely. Or you may want to use a company's logo as a link to their site from your own page. (Be sure to get permission for copying and using any images, if necessary.)

To save an image, follow these steps:

1. Right-click on the image and then select the Save Image As command. (Mac users hold down the mouse button to display the pop-up menu and select Save This Image As.) You see the Save As dialog box (Figure 7.10).

2. Enter a file name in the File Name text box.

3. Select a drive from the Save In list and a folder in the folder list. For the PC, you can use the Up One Level button to move through the folder structure.

4. If you want, change the file type by displaying the Save As Type drop-down list and selecting another format. (This step applies to PC versions only.)

5. Click on the Save button.

Copying And Pasting Text And Links

In addition to saving a page or image, you can copy and paste text and images. For most pages, only Copy is available. You cannot cut from pages or paste to pages. Follow these steps to copy and paste text:

Figure 7.10   Use the Save As dialog box to save a graphic image.

1. Select the text you want to copy. To select all the text on the page, open the Edit menu and choose the Select All command. The text should appear highlighted.

2. Open the Edit menu and select the Copy command.

3. Move to the location—usually another document—where you want to paste the text. For example, you can create a new Microsoft Word document and then paste the text into this document.

4. Open the Edit menu and select the Paste command. The text is pasted into the new document.

TIP

You can also use keyboard shortcuts: Ctrl+C for copy and Ctrl+V for paste.

If you have ever entered an address, you know that typing the address correctly isn't always easy. The address can be as complex as something like **http://www.sculptor.as.arizona.edu/foltz/bullys/bulldogindex.html**.

You have to be sure to type each part of the address correctly, getting the periods and slashes in just the right places.

TIP

If you want, you can copy an address and then paste it in another document or even in the Go To text box.

Sending Web Pages

If you find a page you really like and want to let others know about the page, you can send it to them. You can actually send a page in a mail message (if the recipient's mail program supports HTML messages). The recipient of the mail message only has to click on the link to go to that page.

To send a page, follow these steps:

1. Display the page you want to send.

2. Open the File menu and select the Send Page command. You see a Composition window with the subject line completed. The text of the message also includes a link to the current page (see Figure 7.11).

3. Enter the address of the person to whom you want to send the message. For help on creating mail messages, see Chapter 12.

4. Click on the Send button.

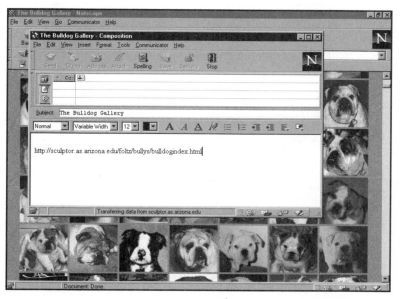

Figure 7.11 You can send an email message with a hyperlink to a site.

Viewing Page And Security Information

When you are browsing the Web, you may want to get additional information about the page, especially about the security of the page. You can view page information, including the overall structure of the document, and you can also check out the security of the page.

Viewing Page Information

To view page information, open the View menu and select the Page Info command. You see a separate window listing the structure, location, source, and other information about the page (see Figure 7.12). When you are done viewing this information, click on the Close (X) button for the window.

Checking The Security Of A Page

To view security information, click on the Security button in the Navigation toolbar, click on the lock icon in the lower left corner of the Netscape window, or open the Communicator menu and select Security Info. You see the Security Info page (see Figure 7.13). You can see whether the page is encrypted or view the verification settings. For instance, check out where the site comes from to

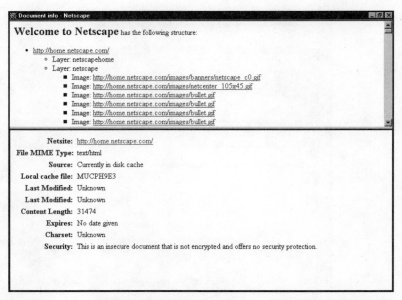

Figure 7.12   You can view page information such as the overall structure of the page.

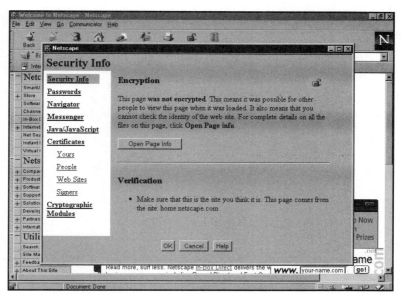

Figure 7.13   Check out the security information for the page.

be sure of its source. For more information on the security settings, such as certificates, click on the Help button and review online help. You can, for instance, get a certificate to identify yourself to another person or organization.

Viewing The Page Source

If you want to see how the document is formatted, you can view the document source. This view of the document shows you the *tags*, or HTML codes, that control page features such as bold and italics and also contain the links to other pages. Even if you aren't interested in Web page publishing, you may just want to take a look at the document source to satisfy your curiosity.

To view the document source, display the page you want to view. Then open the View menu and select the Page Source command. You see the text formatted using HTML (Figure 7.14). You can scroll through the document to see the various tags—for instance, **<B>** turns on boldface and **</B>** turns off boldface. A reference to another document takes the following form: **<A HREF = "http://address /document name"> link text </A>**. You can get an idea of how HTML works just by looking at the source.

When you finish viewing the document, close the document window by clicking on the Close button.

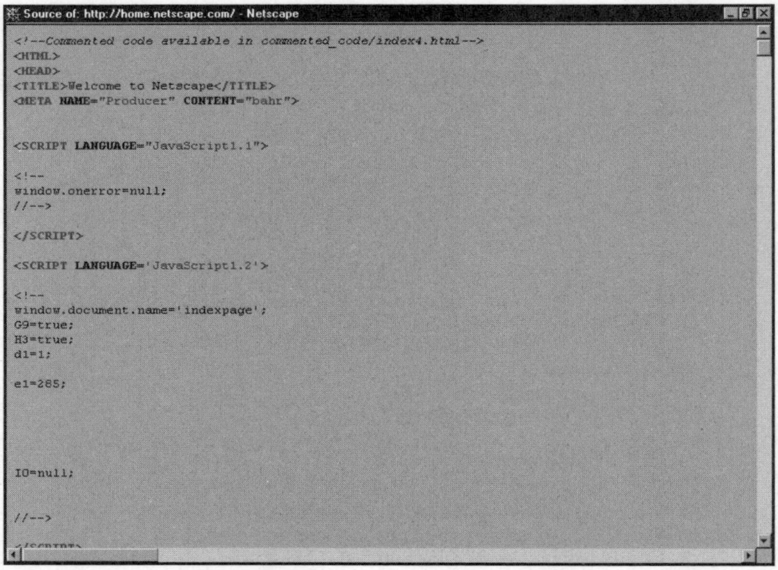

Figure 7.14   You can view the source document of a Web page.

Playing Sounds And Movies

Part of the thrill of the World Wide Web is that it is a *multimedia* environment, meaning that in addition to text and pictures, you may also find sounds, videos, and movies. For example, you can listen to the theme song from the *X-Files* or hear Phil Jackson's thoughts after winning the NBA championship for the 1996-97 season. You can even play a short video clip from a movie. This section explains how to play back sounds and movies.

Playing Sounds

Ready to hear the latest song from your favorite rock band? Want to hear news clips? World Wide Web pages can include links to sound files, which you can download and then play back. Sounds are stored in different file formats; to play back a sound, you also need a program that can handle that file format. Navigator 4 can play back most of the common file formats.

TIP

You can also use other applications to play back sounds. For example, you can use Media Player (included with Windows 95) to play WAV files. As another option, you can download some sound applications for free. A good audio and video player *that enables you to play back a sound as the sound file is downloaded (which saves time) is RealPlayer. You can get a copy of this software program at **http:// www.realaudio.com**. Simply go to the site and then follow the on-screen instructions for downloading and installing it.*

As you explore the Web, you may come across pages, such as the one in Figure 7.15, with sound files. To play the sound file back, click on the sound icon. First, however, Navigator has to download the sound. Because sound files are quite big, you shouldn't expect immediate gratification. Instead, you have to wait until the entire sound file is downloaded. Then Navigator plays the sound and displays a sound-control window.

Use the buttons in the sound playback window (see Figure 7.16) to replay the sound, pause or stop the playback, and adjust the volume.

Playing Back Movies

Some Web pages include movies as well as sounds; these may be video clips, animations, or multimedia movies. Like sounds, movies come in a variety of file formats. Navigator 4 can play back some of the most popular formats, including QuickTime.

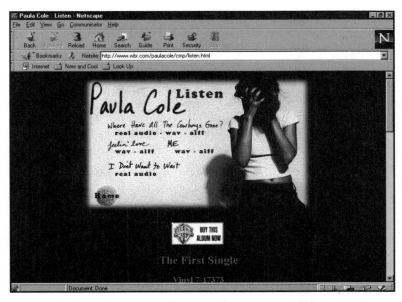

Figure 7.15   You can find sound files, such as samples from new albums.

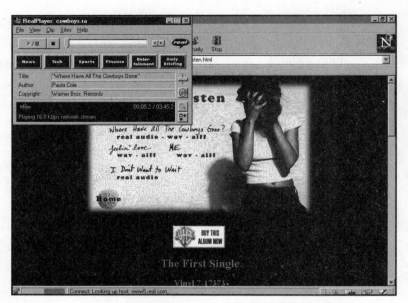

Figure 7.16   Click on the Play button to play the sound again.

Another popular movie program is Shockwave. You can use this program to play back multimedia files and Macromedia Director movies. (Macromedia Director is a popular program for creating multimedia movies.) To download a free copy of Shockwave, go to **http://www.macromedia.com**. *The page gives you instructions on how to select your operating system, download, and install this program.*

When you come across a page with a movie, you can download the movie by clicking on the movie icon; then you can play back the movie with another click of the mouse. Keep in mind that downloading a movie can take a lot of time. You can always see how much time is left and how much progress has been made in the status bar.

Once the movie is downloaded, you see the first image (shown in Figure 7.17). To play the movie, click on this image. The video clip is replayed on your screen.

Completing Forms

As you explore the Internet, you may find that some pages have forms you can complete. For example, you may want to register for a contest or sign up for a mailing list. The forms are usually sent back to the network server and

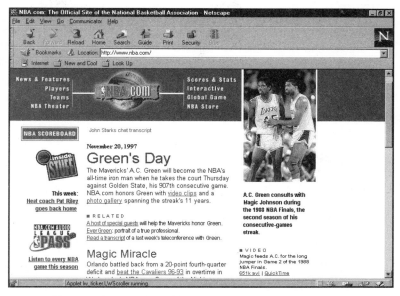

Figure 7.17   To play the movie, click on the image.

then processed by software called *Common Gateway Interface (CGI)*, the standard for sending and receiving data. Figure 7.18 shows a sample form.

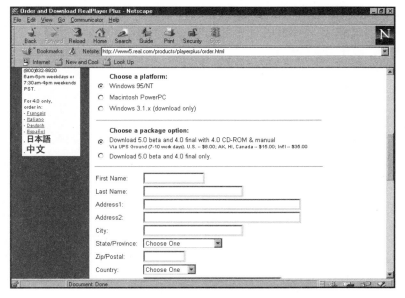

Figure 7.18   Some pages include forms you can use to submit information.

Forms are pretty straightforward; they work just like a dialog box. You may see text boxes, checkboxes, option buttons, and selection lists; you complete these items just as you do in a dialog box. Usually the form gives you instructions and includes a button for submitting it. After you complete the entries, click on the Send or Submit button. In some cases, you will get information back after submitting the form. Sometimes you receive an acknowledgment that the data was received, but at other times you get no confirmation.

Moving On

In this chapter, you learned how to work with Web pages, which is probably what you will see and use during most of your Internet experience. In addition to text and pictures, you may come across sounds, animations, and video clips—you also learned how to work with these Web page elements.

Chapter 8 covers adding extra programs called *plug-ins* to Navigator. These programs are especially helpful for handling multimedia aspects of Web pages.

CHAPTER 8

Using Plug-ins

The Web is a multimedia environment, as you learned in Chapter 7. You can find text, graphics, sounds, animations, videos, applications, and more on the Web pages you browse. You are lucky because Netscape Navigator includes components that let you listen to most sounds, view most videos, and run most Java applications. In addition to these built-in features, you can add other components—plug-ins—for handling these special elements. In this chapter, you'll learn how to find out which plug-ins you already have and how to add others.

What Is A Plug-in?

As mentioned, a *plug-in* is a special add-on program that expands the capabilities of Navigator. For instance, you can use the RealPlayer plug-in to play sounds or videos or the Shockwave plug-in to play movies.

Here's how a plug-in works. Navigator associates certain file types with an application. When Navigator encounters a data type it does not automatically recognize, it looks for the plug-in associated with that data type and then runs that plug-in. These programs work with Navigator as if they were part of Navigator itself.

Just The FAQs

What is a plug-in?

A *plug-in* is a special add-on program that expands the capabilities of Navigator. The program runs seamlessly—as if it were a part of Navigator—and enables you to view movies, hear live radio broadcasts, and experience other multimedia features of Navigator.

What plug-ins do I have?

Navigator automatically installs some popular plug-ins. You can see a list of them by opening the Help menu and selecting About Plug-ins.

How do plug-ins work?

Each file type is associated with a particular program. When Navigator finds a file its program components do not recognize, it looks for the file types associated with the installed plug-ins. If Navigator finds a match, it runs the plug-in for that file type.

Where can I find plug-ins?

A good place to find plug-ins is the link on the About Plug-ins page. You can select from several categories of plug-ins, including Audio, Video, 3D, and others.

How do I install a plug-in?

You click on the link to download the plug-in. Then you usually decompress the files and run the setup program. The Web page should give you exact download and installation directions.

Reviewing What Plug-ins You Have

Because some plug-ins are installed automatically, you may not know what plug-ins you have. To review a list of installed plug-ins, open the Help menu and select the About Plug-ins command. When you scroll through the list, you see a description of each of the plug-ins on your system (see Figure 8.1), as well as the associated file type.

Finding Plug-ins

When you want to add to Navigator's capabilities, you can find and download other plug-ins. There are several hundred available for listening to sounds, displaying presentations, viewing images, playing videos, and more. Check Navigator's About Plug-ins page for a good set of links, or you can try some of the sites listed in this chapter.

Checking Out Navigator's About Plug-ins Page

Navigator conveniently provides a link to popular plug-ins on the About Plug-ins page. Display this page by selecting Help, About Plug-ins. Then click on the link for more information. On the Inline Plug-ins page, you see the number of currently available plug-ins; categories include: 3D and Animation,

Figure 8.1   You can view the installed plug-ins using the About Plug-ins command on the Help menu.

Audio/Video, Business and Utilities, Image Viewers, Presentations, What's New, Plug-in Extras, and Support by Platform (see Figure 8.2). Click on any of the categories to display the available plug-ins. You can also scroll farther down the page to view other plug-in resources and a list of "cool" plug-ins. Figure 8.3 shows the available Audio/Video plug-ins; click on any of the links to get information and download the program.

Trying Some Other Plug-in Sites

You can also find plug-ins as you browse the Web. Usually if a sound, movie, or image on a Web page requires a certain plug-in, the page says so and provides a link where you can get more information on downloading that plug-in. You can also go directly to a company's home page to get information about a plug-in. You might also find plug-ins from magazine articles about the Internet. See Table 8.1 for a list of some popular plug-ins, as well as the addresses of their home pages. Most of these are available as links on the Netscape About Plug-ins page.

Installing Plug-ins

Some plug-ins are installed when you install Navigator. You can obtain additional plug-ins using SmartUpdate and you can also download plug-ins from

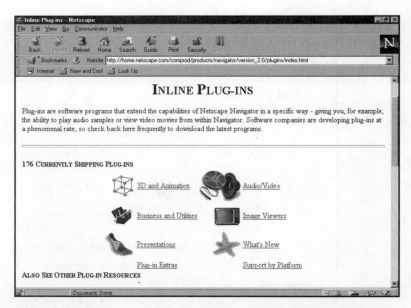

Figure 8.2 Select from any of these categories to display currently available plug-ins.

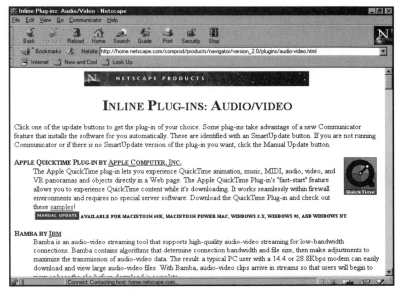

Figure 8.3   Click on any of these links to download the plug-in.

other Web pages, as covered in the "Downloading From A Web Page" section later in this chapter.

Table 8.1   Popular plug-ins and their Web addresses.

Plug-in	Description	Web Address
Adobe Acrobat	Adobe has a particular file format that is supported across different platforms (Unix, Macintosh, Windows). Use this program to handle this type of file.	**http://www.adobe.com**
Apple QuickTime	Use this popular program to play QuickTime movies.	**http://www.quicktime.apple.com**
Inso Quick View Plus	Use this program to view different types of files.	**http://www.inso.com**
Macromedia Shockwave	Use this popular program to play multimedia files.	**http://www.macromedia.com/shockwave**
RealPlayer	Use this program to listen to sound files and live radio broadcoasts as well as to play back videos.	**http://www.real.com/products/player**

Using SmartUpdate

Navigator includes a new feature called *SmartUpdate* that checks the components you have installed on your system and then recommends any additional programs, including plug-ins, you may want to add.

To use SmartUpdate, follow these steps:

1. Click on SmartUpdate in the Netcenter panel. You see the Welcome screen.

2. Click on the icon to continue.

3. If necessary, register your profile, which includes your name, street address, and email adress. You also sign up for a digital certificate from Verisoft used to verify your identity (this is a one-time-only procedure). Follow the on-screen instructions. After you have registered and your identity has been confirmed, SmartUpdate will display a list of components for upgrading.

4. Click on any of the links to download additional components.

Downloading From A Web Page

You can also find and install other plug-ins using links on Web sites. For instance, you can visit Macromedia's home page and use the links to get information and download Shockwave. Figure 8.4 shows the download page.

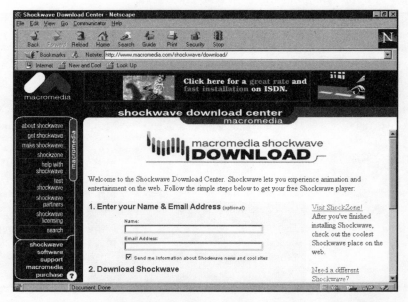

Figure 8.4   One popular plug-in is Shockwave, which you can find at the Macromedia Web site.

Once you find a plug-in you want to try, follow these steps to download and install it:

1. Go to the home page for the company that provides the plug-in. For example, the address for Macromedia Shockwave is **http://www.macromedia.com/shockwave**.

2. Click on the link to download the program. For Shockwave, click on the Get Shockwave button.

3. Follow the on-screen download instructions. What you do will vary from plug-in to plug-in. For Shockwave, for instance, you enter your name and email address. Shockwave determines which software is needed for your system.

4. Decompress the file (usually a plug-in is compressed into a single file) by double-clicking on it and following the on-screen instructions. The file should be in the folder you selected when you downloaded it. (It's helpful to create a new, temporary folder in which to place the file, as well as to write down the file name so you don't forget it.)

5. Install the program. (Decompressing the files does not install the program.) To do so, look for an Install or Setup file. Again, the on-screen instructions will tell you exactly what to do. Shockwave has a self-installation program that both decompresses and installs the program. Other plug-ins will vary.

Once the plug-in is installed, you can use it. For instance, you can use Shockwave to play back Macromedia movies and animation applications.

What Is Java?

Java is a full-featured programming language that is used to write small programs called *applets*. Applets are embedded on Web pages and enable two-way interaction on the Web, which is what makes them so exciting for users. You don't have to have a special program to run a Java applet because the program code resides at that site and travels over the Internet. You can run applets within Navigator. The language is exciting for programmers because a Java program can run on any type of platform—Windows, Mac, or Unix. And the user doesn't have to do anything special to run the applet because it is built into the page by the Web developer.

Java programs can perform a variety of functions. For instance, you can find a Java program for doing crossword puzzles, displaying a clock, calculating your biorhythm, viewing images, displaying stock tickers, and more.

Navigator also includes Dynamic HTML, an add-on to Hypertext Markup Language (HTML). Online help says that Dynamic HTML helps authors create Web pages that are "richer, faster, and more interactive." JavaScript is a programming language used for creating Java applets; this language is built into Communicator.

For more information about Java, visit the home page of Sun Microsystems at **http://www.java.sun.com**.

And if you want to try out some Java resources, you can find a great directory at Gamelan: The Java Directory at **http://www.developer.com/directories/pages/dir.java.html**. You can choose to view new and cool applets. You can also scroll down the page and opt to view applets by category. Figure 8.5 shows a recent list of "cool" Java applets.

Moving On

In this chapter, you learned about plug-ins—extra programs that add to the features of Navigator. You also learned how to find and install these add-on components.

Chapter 9 explains the issues you should address if children use your PC to access the Internet. You can find out about some good kid-related sites as well some security precautions you can take.

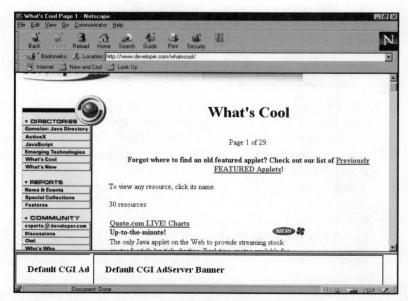

Figure 8.5   Find Java applets from this directory.

CHAPTER 9

Kids And The
Internet

You may have purchased a PC specifically so that your children would have access to this wonderful resource. You might want them to have all the advantages of being connected to such a vast collection of information. But what issues should you think about when letting your children access the Internet? How can you ensure their safety? This chapter discusses not only what children can do on the Internet, but also some things a parent should do.

Safety Issues For Kids And The Internet

Your primary concern as a parent is your children's safety. You may also want to ensure that your children do not access sites with objectionable content. How can you control access? This is a growing concern in the media, bringing up issues such as free speech, censorship, rating systems, and monitoring. Right now the two best things you can do are set parental guidelines and consider using some type of blocking and/or monitoring program. This section discusses both of these ideas.

Setting Some Rules

The best way to ensure your children's safety on the Internet is to set some guidelines. Let them know what is acceptable and what is not. Here are some

Just The FAQs

Is it safe for children to access the Internet?

Yes—if you set certain guidelines and monitor their usage.

What is the best precaution?

The best precaution is parental control. You should discuss with your children what is acceptable and what is not. You should also set guidelines for certain situations.

How can I control access?

You can purchase programs that block certain content. These programs may also enable you to monitor which sites your children have visited. Examples include Net Nanny, Cyber Patrol, CYBERSitter, and Surfwatch.

What can kids do on the Internet?

Like adults, children can find a wealth of information on the Internet. They can research topics, pursue hobbies, find help with homework, and more. They also can connect with other children with the same interests via chats, forums, and email messages.

Where can I find good kid sites?

Several of the search tools include a Kids category. You can browse these links. You can also find articles about highly rated sites in computer and other magazines and in newspaper articles.

suggestions; you can also incorporate any other guidelines or restrictions you feel necessary:

- Tell your children never to give out personal information such as their address, phone number, school name, or anything else. If they are prompted to enter this information to register for something—like a contest or prize—have them check with you first.

- Tell your children never to give out any personal information about your family, such as parents' names, work information, and so on.

- Strongly insist that children never set up a meeting with someone that they meet online unless the parents have agreed.

- If your children find something upsetting—an ugly message, an offensive site—tell them to come to you.

- Explain that both "good" sites and "bad" sites exist and tell them to stay away from sites with anything you specify as objectionable.

- Set limits on how much time children can stay online and what types of activities they can do. For instance, can they participate in chats? Is it okay to send email messages?

- Consider browsing with your children. Let them do the clicking, but you can work together. Look up the famous "Thinker" by Rodin. Check out information about sharks. Find help for a science project. Browsing is something you can do together.

Blocking Sites

In addition to setting your own rules, you may want to purchase a separate monitoring/blocking program. These programs vary in what features they offer, but most enable you to block sites that contain certain objectionable words. The program may also include features for monitoring and checking what sites your children have visited. The price varies: For some you pay just for the software; for others, you pay for the software and also a subscription fee to keep your list of objectionable sites updated. The programs also vary in the degree of customizing you can do. Popular programs include Cyber Patrol, Surfwatch, Net Nanny, and CYBERsitter. These programs are briefly described in this section.

Cyber Patrol

This program lets you block access to specific Internet sites by using its list of objectionable or blocked sites (the CyberNOT list) or by setting your own preferences. As a parent, you can select what categories are turned off (sexually explicit material, violent material, material related to drugs and alcohol, and so on) and what type of blocking is in effect (no blocking, selective blocking, or full blocking). In addition, you can restrict the time of day and amount of time your children spend on the Internet. And you can also find sites specifically for children with the CyberYES list.

You can download the program and try it out (see Figure 9.1). If you decide to continue using it, you can expect to pay around $30 to $35 to register the program, plus a subscription fee for updates. For more information on this program, visit the Cyber Patrol Web site at **http://www.microsys.com/cyber**.

Surfwatch

A team of reviewers sets a list of Web, Gopher, and FTP sites that are not for children. This list is available through a subscription and is updated frequently. You can expect to pay less than $50 for the software and $5.95 for updates. For information on Surfwatch, go to **http://www.surfwatch.com**.

Net Nanny

This program lets you screen Web sites, newsgroups, and text messages by creating your own list of objectionable words. While this gives you a good deal of control—and you can use the Starter Dictionary to start your list—it does require some time and effort. A plus is that you can also block access to certain files on your PC—to safeguard important information that you don't

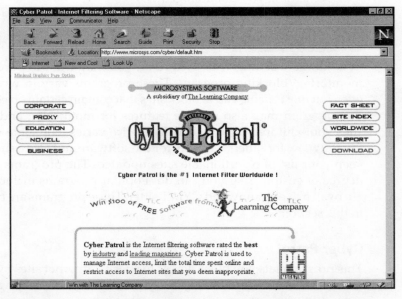

Figure 9.1   Visit the Cyber Patrol site for information on this product.

want accidentally or otherwise messed with. You can also print and review a log of all your children's activities. Expect to pay $20 or so for a downloaded version or $40 for a retail version (sold through a store or through Net Nanny). For more information on Net Nanny, visit **http://www.netnanny.com**.

CYBERsitter

CYBERsitter updates its blocked sites list frequently (sometimes daily), and you can download the list as often as you want. Although the program does not allow you to select from different categories of information, it does use a "smart" filter so that words that might be offensive in one context but not in another are blocked when necessary. You can also have CYBERsitter track and list every site visited. The program costs around $40. For more information, go to **http://www.solidoak.com**.

What Can Kids Do?

Now that you are at least a little assured your child won't be viewing adult or offensive content, you can relax and take advantage of all the benefits the Internet has to offer. Like adults, children can do a wealth of things on the Internet. Here's just a quick list to give you some ideas:

- *Research projects*—The Internet provides millions of resources right in your own home; it probably makes the old bound set of encyclopedias extinct. Your children can research practically any topic. You can even find sites specifically for helping with homework.

- *Keep up with a hobby*—My seven-year-old *loves* basketball. We spend a lot of time at the NBA page looking up scores, stories, stats, and more. He can find just about anything about his favorite teams and players. You can find all kinds of sports sites, a Beanie Babies site, a Barbie site, and more. If your children have particular interests or hobbies, you can probably find a site relating to them.

- *Meet other children*—Your children can find pen pals and send or receive email messages. This is a great way to connect with someone from another city, state, country, or culture.

- *Play games*—You can find trivia games, contests, and other fun activities—such as playing with LEGOs (see Figure 9.2)—at the many kid-related sites on the Internet.

- *Read kid-specific news, magazines, and other publications*—You can find books and book reviews for children.

- *Get advice*—Not only can children find advice, but parents can also find a wealth of parenting information.

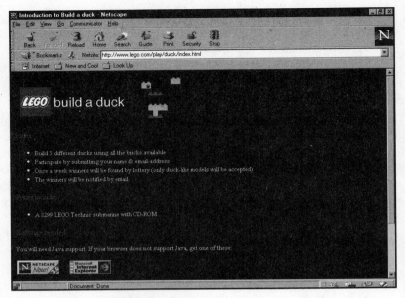

Figure 9.2   Build your own LEGO creation.

*As a parent, you can also find information that reviews sites, books, and software for children. For instance, try SuperKids, an education software review at **http:// www.superkids.com**.*

Finding Kid Sites

You can try a few different strategies for finding kid sites. First, you can use the search tools. Second, you can try some of the sites listed in this chapter. This section covers both methods.

Searching For A Site

You can use any of the search tools covered in Chapter 6 to search for a particular site or topic. For instance, if you want information about Nancy Drew books, you could search for a site on this topic. Second, you can review some of the search engines' site directories. Infoseek includes a directory of kid-related sites, and Yahoo! has Yahooligans!, "the Web guide for kids."

To try a search engine, follow these steps:

1. Click on the Search button in the toolbar.

2. Select the search tool you want to use. You should see the different categories available for browsing. For instance, in Figure 9.3, you can see the Kids & Family category for Infoseek.

3. Click on the Kids & Family category. You see the list of kid-related sites. Figure 9.4 shows these sites for Infoseek, and Figure 9.5 shows the list for Yahoo!. As you can see, you can select from a variety of sites relating to activities, travel, education, news, and more. (You may have to go to the search engine's home page to view the categories. See Chapter 6 for more information on using search tools.)

4. Click on any of the links to go to that site.

Trying Some Other Sites

In addition to these sites, you can visit other fun sites, as listed in Table 9.1.

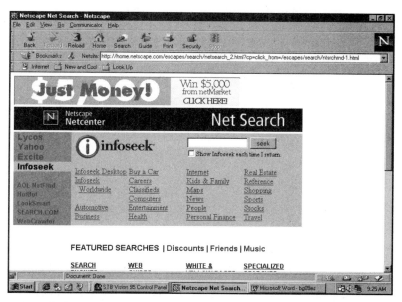

Figure 9.3   Select the Kids & Family category on Infoseek for interesting sites for kids.

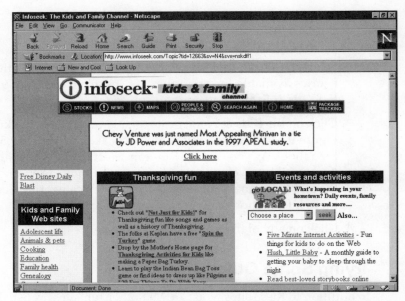

Figure 9.4 Infoseek's kid page features both timely fun (here, Thanksgiving) and other events and activities.

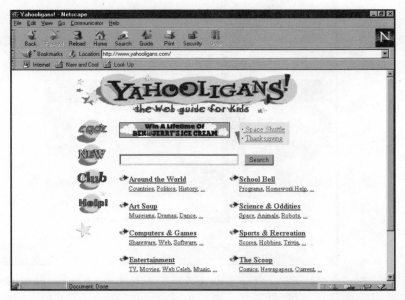

Figure 9.5 Yahooligans! is a guide specifically for children. (Text and artwork copyright 1998 by YAHOO!, Inc. All rights reserved. YAHOO! and the YAHOO! logo are trademarks of YAHOO!, Inc.)

Table 9.1   Other fun sites for kids.

Site	Web Address
Barbie	http://www.barbie.com
Beanie Babies	http://www.beaniebabies.com
Crayola	http://www.crayola.com
Disney	http://www.disney.com
LEGO	http://www.lego.com
Monopoly	http://www.monopoly.com
Nickelodeon	http://www.nick.com
Seussville	http://www.randomhouse.com (see Figure 9.6)
Sports Illustrated for Kids	http://www.pathfinder.com/SIFK
Time for Kids	http://www.pathfinder.com/TFK
Toys "R" Us	http://www.toysrus.com
Warner Brothers	http://www.warnerbros.com

Figure 9.6   Visit Seussville for loads of fun for kids.

Moving On

In this chapter, you learned about some specific issues regarding kids and the Internet. You learned how to control access, as well as what you can expect to find for children.

Chapter 10 discusses another task you can accomplish on the Internet: copying files from a network to your PC. You might want to download the latest version of a software program or try out a new game. Read on for the ins and outs of downloading files.

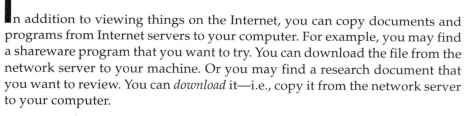

CHAPTER 10

Downloading Files

In addition to viewing things on the Internet, you can copy documents and programs from Internet servers to your computer. For example, you may find a shareware program that you want to try. You can download the file from the network server to your machine. Or you may find a research document that you want to review. You can *download* it—i.e., copy it from the network server to your computer.

This chapter explains all you need to know about downloading files, including different ways files are made available for downloading. You will also learn how to find and download files.

Knowing Where To Get Files

What's available? Where can you find the files? A wide variety of documents is available, including programs (freeware, shareware, and commercial upgrades to products that you purchase), text documents, clip art, technical reports, books, and more. *Freeware* is software that is provided for free. Anyone can use it. *Shareware* is software that is provided for evaluation. If you like and use the software, you have to pay a small fee to register your copy. In addition to these programs, you may also find some text, programs, and images that are in the public domain. Such materials are not copyrighted, so they are free for anyone to use. Some political texts are an example of information in the

133

Just The FAQs

What does it mean to download files?

When you *download* a file, you copy it from Internet servers to your computer. For instance, you may want to download a shareware program that you want to try. Or perhaps you are interested in the latest version of Navigator. You can download programs, documents, pictures, sounds, and other file types.

Where can I find files to download?

You can find links to download files on many Web pages. For example, if you go to the Web page for Macromedia Shockwave, a multimedia player, you can download this software program using the links. You can also find files to download at FTP sites.

What are FTP sites?

FTP stands for *File Transfer Protocol*. FTP sites are set up for file transfer and the files are organized into folders. An address to an FTP site looks like this: **ftp://ftp.uu.net**.

What is an anonymous FTP site?

Some sites require a login name and password in order to access the files on their network. Other networks are open to anyone; they are called *anonymous* FTP sites.

How do I download files from an FTP site?

To download a file from an FTP site, you first find the desired file by navigating through the folder structure. Then simply click on the file. When the Save As dialog box appears, select a folder in which to save the file.

public domain. Still other texts—technical reports, books, magazines—are provided for your review, but they are copyrighted, so you cannot use them without permission.

You can expect to find files on the Internet in two ways. Sometimes files for downloading are included as links on a Web page. For example, Figure 10.1 shows the links to download shareware at **http://www.jumbo.com**, a collection of shareware.

You can also find files on *File Transfer Protocol (FTP)* sites, which are set up for downloading files. The files are stored on the network in folders; you simply navigate through the folders to select the file you want. Figure 10.2 shows an FTP site.

Downloading Via A Link

Some Web pages, in particular those set up to promote a particular computer program, include links for downloading software. The links make it easy to download the software because you don't have to know anything about navigating around an FTP site. You simply need to know how to move from link to link and how to follow instructions. The links take care of moving you to the FTP site (if necessary) and selecting the files.

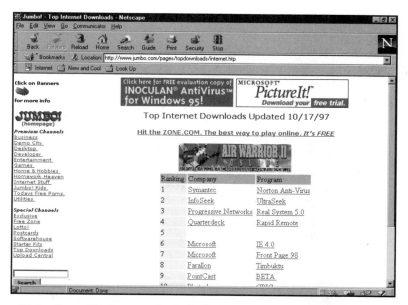

Figure 10.1   Some Web pages include links to files you can download.

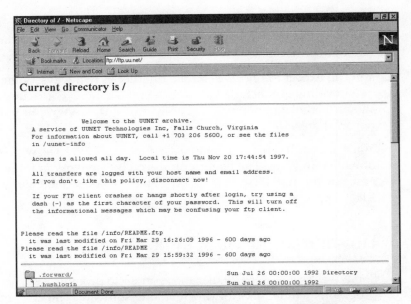

Figure 10.2   Files at an FTP site are arranged into folders.

The process for downloading via a link depends on the Web page, but most pages include specific instructions. Simply click on the link and then follow the on-screen instructions. For example, Figure 10.3 shows the instructions for downloading Macromedia's Shockwave plug-in.

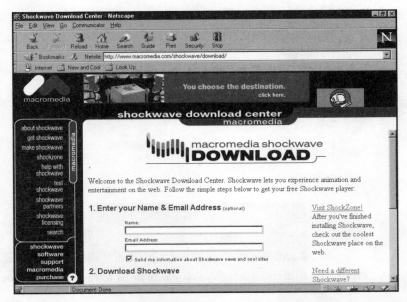

Figure 10.3   If a file is available for downloading via a link, you simply follow the on-screen instructions.

When you find links for downloading, keep these tips in mind:

■ Sometimes you use a form to make selections for the download. For example, you may be prompted to select the version, your operating system, the language you want, and your location. When you complete the form, the site displays the appropriate links for downloading the software.

■ Usually the Web page includes the particular steps you need to follow for downloading. It's a good idea to print these instructions so that you can refer to them during the download. Use the File | Print command to print the Web page that displays the instructions.

■ For a particularly popular download—such as Netscape Navigator—the files may be stored on several different servers. You can select the one closest to you to make sure you get the fastest download. Also, if one is busy, you can try another one.

■ After you select what you want to download, you see a Save As dialog box. Use it to select a folder in which to place the file. You can also enter a new file name, although it's usually best to keep the same name, especially for program files.

■ If you are downloading a program, you usually have to follow some additional steps to install and set it up. Most of the time, the program file (or files) is *compressed*, so you have to decompress it. (Compressing files is a way of shrinking them so they don't take up as much space or time to download. You cannot use compressed files; you must decompress them.) Sometimes you simply double-click on the compressed file to decompress it. Other files may require a program, such as WINZIP or PKUNZIP, to decompress them. If you require special decompression software, the Web page should tell you. WINZIP, for example, is a popular decompression program; you can find this utility at many of the shareware/freeware sites. You may also have to run a setup program to properly configure the downloaded program. Again, the Web page should provide complete instructions.

Downloading From An FTP Site

Some Internet sites consist of nothing but files available for downloading. You simply go to the sites and select the file(s) to download. This section discusses this type of file download.

Finding Sites

You can find FTP sites listed in books, indexes, magazine and newspaper articles, and other directories. You can also find lists of FTP sites on the Internet. For instance, try the Monster FTP Sites List at **http://www.hoohoo.ncsa. uiuc.edu/ftp/**.

From this site you can review any part of the massive FTP list (see Figure 10.4). You can also download the list and review it as a text or HTML (Web page) file.

Going To An FTP Site

To go to an FTP site, enter the address in the Go To text box in Navigator. An FTP address always starts with "ftp" and looks similar to a Web page address. For example, the following is the FTP site where you can find documents on a wide variety of subjects—from the JFK conspiracy to fairy tales: **ftp:// ftp.uu.net**.

When you go to the FTP server, usually the first thing you see is an opening screen that gives you instructions for logging in. For some sites, you have to enter a login name and password. If you have been given access to the site, use the name and password assigned to you. (If you want access, contact the administrator for that site to see how you can get access.) For anonymous sites (available to anyone), you can log in as a guest—usually as "guest" or "anonymous"—

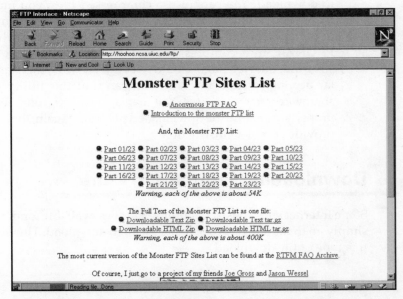

Figure 10.4   Find just about any FTP site from this monster list.

and use your email address as your password. Sometimes you don't need a login name.

Reviewing The FTP Screen

You won't find a lot of instructions on navigating around the FTP server—unlike when you download via a link. Still, you can tell a lot about the available documents from the file list, and moving around is pretty easy. For example, the first column includes an icon indicating the file type. Folder icons indicate folders; document icons indicate text files (see Figure 10.5). The next column displays the item name. Then, in the next columns you usually see the size (for files only), creation date, and file type.

Moving Among The Folders

Most FTP sites include hundreds and hundreds of files. To make it easy to find the file you want, most files are placed in folders. To select a document, you first have to move through the folder structure until you find the one you want.

To open a folder, click on it. You see the contents of that folder, as well as a link to move up a folder (see Figure 10.6). Continue clicking on folders until you find the document you want.

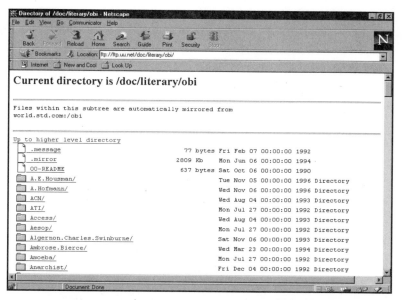

Figure 10.5   *The file list on an FTP site includes all the folders and documents in the current folder.*

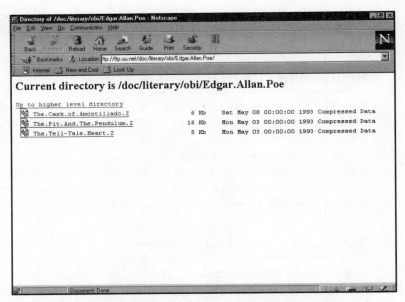

Figure 10.6   When you click on a folder, you see its contents.

To move back through the folder structure, click on the Up To Higher Level Directory link or click on the Back button in the Navigation toolbar. If you don't want to browse aimlessly, you can try looking for an index of the available files. Some sites contain a folder or file named something like About, Readme, or Index. If you find a folder, look for index files that list the available folders as well as a document list.

Downloading The File

Once you find the file you want, you can download it to your computer by simply clicking on it. If Navigator recognizes the file type, you see the file in the Navigator window or within the associated application window. If Navigator doesn't recognize the file type, it prompts you to select an application for viewing the file. This section describes how to view and then save the file.

Selecting How To Handle The File

For some file types, you are prompted to select the application to use to view the file (see Figure 10.7). You can click on the More Info button for more information about adding an application to Navigator. Click on the Pick App button to select a program for viewing the file. To skip viewing and simply save the file to your hard drive, click on the Save File button.

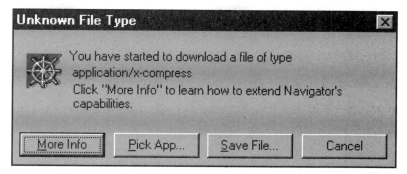

Figure 10.7 Select whether to view the file before downloading it (Pick App) or save the file without viewing it first (Save File).

Selecting The Application To Use

If Navigator can display the file, it will do so automatically. Also, some files are not really suitable for viewing. For instance, you can't view a ZIP file. If you want to use another application (an external viewer) to view the file and you have that application, know how it works, and know its file name, you can have Navigator deal with the file using this external viewer. To do so, follow these steps:

1. Click on the Pick App button.

2. In the Configure External Viewer dialog box (see Figure 10.8), type the path name to the file. Or use the Browse button in the dialog box to browse through your folders and find the file.

3. Click on the OK button. Navigator uses this application to deal with the file.

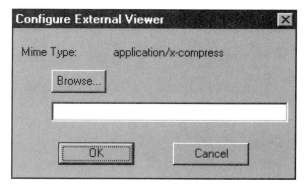

Figure 10.8 Enter the name of the application to use to view the file.

Saving The File

When you want to save the file, you display the Save As dialog box. For some file types—usually programs—you see this dialog box automatically. For files Navigator can't display, click on the Save File button to display the Save As dialog box. For files Navigator first displays on screen, open the File menu and select the Save As command.

From the Save As dialog box (see Figure 10.9), follow these steps to save the file (Windows users):

1. Display the Save In drop-down list (click on the Down arrow) and select the drive where you want to save the file.

2. In the file and folder list, select the folder in which to store the document. In Windows 95, you can use the Up One Level button to move up through the folder structure. Click on the Create New Folder button to create a new folder for the document.

3. In the File Name text box, enter a name for the document.

4. Click on the Save button. The file is copied from the FTP server to your PC.

On a Macintosh, follow these steps:

1. Use the drop-down folder list and the file list box to select the drive and folder where you want to place your file. You can make a new folder with the Create Folder button.

2. If you want to save the file under a different name than the one provided, enter it into the File Name box at the lower left.

3. Click on the OK button to download the file from the FTP server to your Mac.

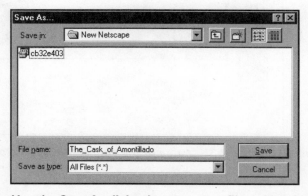

Figure 10.9   Use the Save As dialog box to save a file you've downloaded.

Using SmartUpdate To Update Navigator

New with Navigator 4 is SmartUpdate, a feature you can use to automatically update your version of Navigator. To update Navigator, you download the new files from Netscape's Web site.

To get information or use this feature, click on SmartUpdate under Netcenter. As you can see from the opening page in Figure 10.10, "SmartUpdate remembers which components you've installed and suggests new components to make your system work better for you." To use this feature, you must register first; after that, you can go to SmartUpdate, which checks your system and suggests any new components to install. You can use the links on the SmartUpdate page to download any suggested components.

Adding Your Own Files To An FTP Site

Do you have your own files that you want to share with the world? If so, how can you copy them from your computer to an FTP server (*upload* them)? It depends. First, not all FTP sites will accept submissions. And for some, you

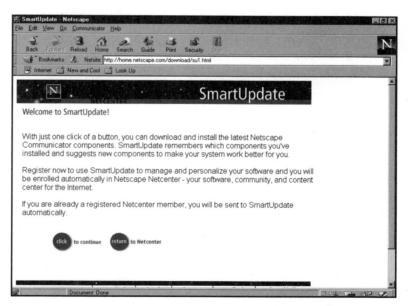

Figure 10.10   Use Navigator's SmartUpdate to update your version of Navigator and any other components.

must have permission to upload files. Second, the process for submitting files varies from server to server. You need to get specific instructions from the FTP server.

At most FTP sites, you should be able to find a document that describes the type of submissions that are accepted as well as the procedure for uploading. A good place to look is in the About folder, a Readme file, or something similar.

Here are the basic steps for uploading a file:

1. Go to the FTP site to which you want to upload the file.

2. Select the folder in which you want to place the file.

3. Open the File menu and select the Upload File command. You see the File Upload dialog box (Figure 10.11).

4. Change to the drive and folder in which the file you want to upload is stored.

5. Select the file to upload.

6. Click on the Open button. The file is copied from your hard disk to the FTP site.

Figure 10.11   In addition to downloading files, you can upload files (copy them from your computer to the FTP site).

Moving On

As you explore the Internet, you will come across many different types of useful information, including programs, documents, research, clip art, and other files that you can review and use. This chapter explained how to access and download such files, as well as the process for uploading files to FTP sites.

Chapter 11 covers customizing Navigator. If you don't like the default options in Navigator—options that control how it works and looks—you can set them to your own preferences. You can change how the screen appears, create a hierarchical bookmark menu, create shortcuts to favorite Internet spots, and more. Turn to the next chapter for help on making these types of changes.

Customizing Navigator

When you first install Netscape Navigator, it looks and works a certain way, and that way works just fine for most users. As you become more proficient with the program, you may want to make some changes. For instance, you may want to change how the Navigator screen appears by turning off the on-screen elements you don't use. Or you may want to organize your bookmarks into folders rather than one long list.

As a Navigator user, you have a great deal of control over how the program operates. This chapter covers the most common things you can do to customize Navigator.

Customizing The Toolbars

By default, Navigator displays certain items on screen, including the toolbars. You may want to turn them off so that you can see more of the Web page. You can also change their appearance.

Hiding The Toolbars

To turn off a toolbar, open the View menu and select Hide Navigation Toolbar, Hide Location Toolbar, or Hide Personal Toolbar to hide the corresponding toolbar. Figure 11.1 shows the Navigator screen with all three of these toolbars

Just The FAQs

What kinds of changes can I make to customize Navigator? And why would I want to make any changes?

Some changes are frivolous—such as changing the colors of links. Other changes make Navigator better suited to your needs. For example, if you have your own home page, you can use it as your starting point instead of Netscape's home page. You can create a shortcut to an Internet site on your Windows desktop. Or if you have a lot of bookmarks, you can organize them into folders.

What home page is displayed by default? Why use a different home page?

If you don't make a change, the home page you see when you log on to the Internet is most likely Netscape's home page or the home page set by your Internet Service Provider (ISP). But you may prefer to use another page. For instance, you may want to start at a stock market page if you are into managing your finances. Or you may want to set up your own home page and start there.

What colors can I change?

You can change the color of unvisited links, visited links, text, and background. For links, you can also turn off underlining.

How can I create a shortcut?

If you are running Windows 95, you can create a *shortcut* to an Internet site. The shortcut icon appears on your desktop; you can double-click on it to start Navigator, log on, and go to the corresponding site. You can also move the shortcut icon to another spot, such as onto your Start menu in Windows 95.

How can I make my bookmarks easier to find?

Rather than have one long list of bookmarks, you can organize your bookmarks into folders, putting similar types of bookmarks together. You can also add buttons for sites to your Personal toolbar.

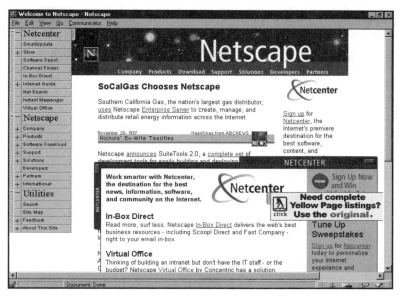

Figure 11.1   You can turn off the toolbars so that you have more room for the Web page.

turned off. To turn a toolbar back on, open the View menu and select the appropriate command.

TIP

> *You can display a* ToolTip *(a pop-up of the button's name) for each of the buttons. To see the ToolTip, put the mouse pointer on the edge of the button. Also, when the pointer is over a button, a short description appears in the status bar.*

Changing How The Buttons Appear

Many folks find the icons in the toolbar easy to use and remember; others would rather see the names of the options. In addition to controlling whether the toolbars are displayed, you can select how you want toolbar buttons to appear: as pictures, text, or pictures and text. To make a change, follow these steps:

1. Open the Edit menu and select the Preferences command. You see the Preferences dialog box.

2. Click on the Appearance item. You see the options for toolbar buttons (see Figure 11.2).

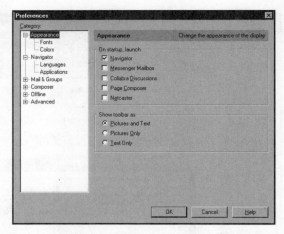

Figure 11.2   Use the Appearance options in the Preferences dialog box to make changes to the toolbar format.

3. Select how you want the toolbar to appear: as Pictures And Text, Pictures Only, or Text Only.

4. Click on the OK button. Figure 11.3 shows the toolbar displayed as text.

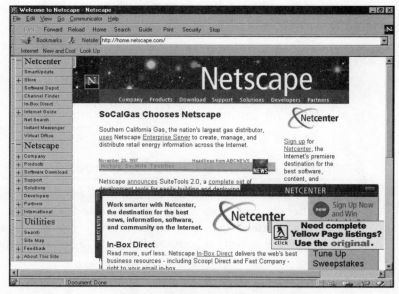

Figure 11.3   You can change the toolbar so that just text appears on the buttons.

Adding Buttons To Your Personal Toolbar

The Personal toolbar contains some default buttons with links to popular sites (Internet, New and Cool, and Lookup). In addition to these buttons, you can add buttons to other favorite sites.

To add a button, go to the page. Then drag the icon next to the Location text box (called the *Netsite icon*) to the toolbar. Navigator adds a button for that site.

To go to the site at any time, simply click on the toolbar button. For more information on rearranging and removing buttons, see the "Organizing Your Bookmarks" section later in this chapter.

Changing How Web Pages Appear

In addition to changing how the Navigator tools appear, you have a good deal of control over how Web pages and, in particular, links are displayed. You can turn off underlining for links as well as change their color. You can also select a color and font for the text on a page. Why make a change? You probably won't find any useful reason for doing it; most of the time you're just adding your own personal style to the Web pages.

TIP

It's a good idea to stick to the default settings when you are still a beginner or when other new users are still learning Navigator. For instance, because most new users understand that underlining indicates a link, turning off underlining may confuse them. Also, creators of Web pages usually design their pages carefully, so changing colors or other aspects might skew the results of their emphasis and design.

Changing The Link Style And Color

By default, all links are underlined. Visited links appear in a different color for 30 days and then revert back to the original color. If you want, you can turn off underlining and select a different color. You can also select a different color for unvisited links and for the text and background of a page. Follow these steps to make a change:

1. Open the Edit menu and select the Preferences command. You see the Preferences dialog box.

2. Under Appearance, select Colors to display the options shown in Figure 11.4.

3. To turn off the underlining, deselect the Underline Links checkbox.

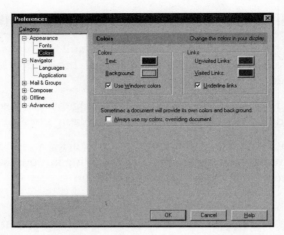

Figure 11.4   Select colors for links, text, and background from this dialog box.

4. To use a different color, click on the color next to the item you want to change. For instance, if you click on the color next to Visited Links, you'll see the Color dialog box (shown in Figure 11.5).

5. Click on the color you want to use and then click on OK. To define a custom color, click on the Define Custom Colors button and then click in the color area to select a color. Click on OK to close the Color dialog box.

   Mac users should click on the Custom checkbox and then on the Color box next to the word "Custom". A standard Apple color picker appears, allowing you to choose from a full array of colors. Use the sliders to adjust the color until you find one you like. Then click on the OK button to close the picker.

6. If you want to always use your colors and background image and override the colors used in a document, check the Always Use My Colors,

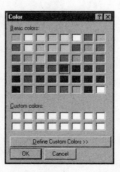

Figure 11.5   Select the color you want to use from the Color dialog box.

Overriding Document checkbox (Windows) or the Always Use My Colors, Overriding Page checkbox (Mac).

7. When you are finished making changes, click on the OK button.

Changing The Fonts

Web pages use only two styles of fonts: proportional and fixed. In a *proportional* style font, the characters vary in width. For instance, "j" takes up less space than "m". In a *fixed* style font, each character takes up an equal amount of space. Most fonts on a Web page are in a proportional font. For Windows, the default font is Times New Roman; for the Mac, it's Times. Some pages—for instance, those with fields you can edit—may appear in a fixed font. For Windows, the default for fixed fonts is Courier New; for the Mac, it's Geneva. The author of the Web page determines the font style for each page element, but you can select the specific font displayed for each style.

TIP

Don't know what a particular dialog box option does? Windows users who want some help on options can click on the Help button and use the online help to read about available options. To close the Help window, click on its Close button.

To change the fonts used for pages, follow these steps:

1. Open the Edit menu and select the Preferences command. You see the Preferences dialog box.

2. Under Appearance, select Fonts. You see the Fonts options (see Figure 11.6).

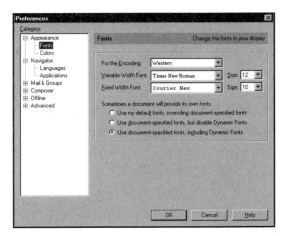

Figure 11.6   Select a font to use for fixed text and variable-width text.

3. To change the font, display the drop-down list next to the font (Fixed Width Font or Variable Width Font). Then select the font you want to use.

4. To change the font size, click on the drop-down Size list next to the font and then click on the font size you want to use.

5. Click on the OK button to close the Preferences dialog box.

Turning Off Images

Another change you can make for Web pages is to select whether images are displayed or not. Because displaying images takes time, you may want to turn them off. You can always choose to display them later. Follow these steps:

1. Open the Edit menu and select the Preferences command. You see the Preferences dialog box.

2. Select the Advanced option. Figure 11.7 shows the available options you can change.

3. Deselect the Automatically Load Images checkbox and then click on OK.

After you follow these steps, any pages that you open will not display the images. If you do come to a page on which you want to view the images, you can choose to load them by clicking on the Images button (which Navigator automatically adds to the Navigation toolbar). For more information on working with images, see Chapter 7.

Selecting A Different Home Page

Each time you start Navigator, you most likely see the Netscape home page, which is a good place to get started. (You may see a different page, selected by your ISP.) The Netscape page includes links to many Netscape products and information. You don't have to use this page, though; if you prefer, you can use a blank page or some favorite Web page. Or if you have become quite the Webmaster, you may have created your own Web page and want to use this as your starting point. You can use any Web address as the home page.

To select a home page, follow these steps:

1. Open the Edit menu and select the Preferences command. You see the Preferences dialog box.

2. Click on the Navigator item to display the options (see Figure 11.8).

3. Do any of the following in the Navigator Starts With section:

   ■ To use a blank page, select the Blank Page button.

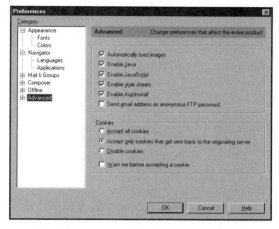

Figure 11.7   You can turn off the display of images from this list of choices.

- To use a different page, select Home Page and then enter the address or URL in the Location text box.
- To use the current page, select Home Page and then click on the Use Current Page button. You can also use the Browse button to select a page.
- To go to the last page you visited, select Last Page Visited.

4. Click on the OK button.

The next time you start Navigator or whenever you click on the Home button in the Navigation toolbar, the page you have selected as your home page will

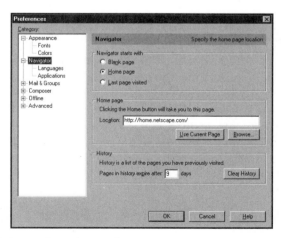

Figure 11.8   Set your home page here.

be displayed. Note that if you start Navigator with a blank page, it will start with a blank page, but when you click on the Home button, Navigator will display whatever address appears in the Home Page Location text box (Netscape home page, by default).

> **TIP**
>
> *To specify how long sites remain in your* history *(a list of pages you have previously visited), enter the number of days on the Appearance tab. To clear the history, click on the Clear History button.*

Setting Your Startup Options

When you open Navigator, only the browser is started. You must use a command to start mail or the news reader. If you want to automatically have your mail program started (and check your mail), or if you use the news reader a lot and want it started, you can set up Navigator to start either or both programs. Follow these steps:

1. Open the Edit menu and select the Preferences command. You see the Preferences dialog box.

2. Click on the Appearance tab to display the options.

3. In the On Startup Launch area, check the programs you want started.

4. Click on the OK button.

Organizing Your Bookmarks

When you add a bookmark to Navigator, it is added to the end of one long list, and the default name (the name of the bookmarked page) is used. If you have just a few bookmarks, you can easily find and select the one you want because the list is still short. If you have many bookmarks, though, the list is more difficult to navigate. Instead, you may want to organize the bookmarks into folders. Also, you can change the name of a bookmark. This section covers not only how to make these changes, but also how to delete a bookmarked item, add a separator line, sort bookmarks, and make changes to your Personal toolbar.

Viewing Your Bookmarks Folder

You can view the contents of your Bookmarks folder by clicking on the Bookmarks button. To make a change to the setup of this folder, follow these steps:

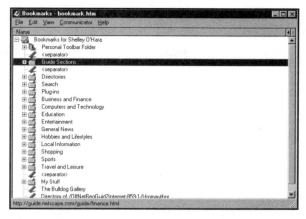

Figure 11.9   The Bookmarks dialog box displays the folders and bookmark items you have created.

1. Click on the Bookmarks button.

2. Select Edit Bookmarks. You see the Bookmarks window (see Figure 11.9). If you have created folders, you see these listed. You may also see folders set up by Navigator.

3. If necessary, expand the folder list to display the items by clicking on the plus sign (+) or the arrow. The list expands and the plus sign changes to a minus sign (-) (see Figure 11.10), or the arrow changes from right-pointing to downward.

4. To hide the bookmark items, click on the minus sign or arrow.

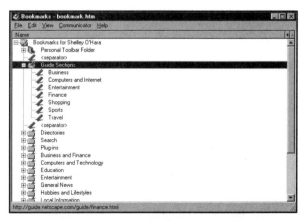

Figure 11.10   You can expand and collapse the list of folders.

TIP

You can go to any of the bookmarks in the list by double-clicking on the item or by clicking once on it and then using the File | Go to Bookmark command.

Creating Folders

To make your bookmark list more manageable, you may want to divide the bookmarks into different categories by creating folders. Use a folder to group similar sites together. To add a new folder, follow these steps:

1. Click on the Bookmarks button and select Edit Bookmarks. You see the Bookmarks window.

2. Open the File menu and select the New Folder command. You see the Bookmark Properties dialog box, shown in Figure 11.11. (Mac users will see the New Folder dialog box.)

3. Type a name for the folder. Use a short name that will remind you of the folder's contents.

4. If you want, type a description of the folder's contents in the Description text box.

TIP

You can create an alias *(a copy) of a bookmark so you can store the same bookmark in more than one folder. If you update the original bookmark, all aliases are updated as well. To make an alias, right-click on the bookmark you want and then select the Make Alias command. The alias appears in italics in the same folder as the original. You can then move the alias to another folder.*

5. Click on the OK button. Navigator adds the folder to the list.

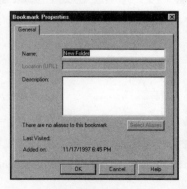

Figure 11.11   Enter a name for the folder and (if desired) a description.

6. When you are finished making changes, click on the Close box to close the Bookmarks window.

Moving Bookmarks

If you have already added bookmarks and want to reorganize them, you can move them from one folder to another. Follow these steps:

1. Click on the bookmark you want to move so that it is highlighted.

2. Hold down the mouse button and drag the item to the desired folder.

3. Release the mouse button. When you do so, the item is moved to the selected folder.

   Keep in mind that you don't have to move all the bookmarks to a folder. You can keep some on the main menu list as bookmark items.

4. When you are finished making changes, click on the Close box to close the Bookmarks window.

TIP

To add a bookmark to an existing folder, display that page. Then click on the Bookmarks button and select File Bookmarks. Select the folder in which to place the bookmark.

Deleting Bookmarks

To keep your bookmark list up-to-date and uncluttered, you can delete bookmarks that you no longer use. You may have gone hog-wild and added a bookmark to just about every site you visited. Now you realize you don't need all those bookmarks.

To delete a bookmark, follow these steps:

1. Click on the Bookmarks button and select Edit Bookmarks.

2. If necessary, expand the folder list until you see the bookmark you want to delete.

3. Click on the bookmark's name to select it.

4. Open the Edit menu and select the Delete (Windows) or Delete Bookmark (Mac) command. (You can also right-click on the item and select the Delete Bookmark command.) The bookmark is deleted from the list.

5. Click on the OK button.

Make a mistake? If you move or delete something by mistake, you can immediately undo the change. To do so, open the Edit menu and select the Undo command. Navigator undoes the last action you took.

Renaming Bookmarks

As mentioned earlier, Navigator uses the page name for the bookmark name. Usually the name is somewhat descriptive and may work just fine. In other cases, you may get a name that is too long or not descriptive. For example, FTP sites usually have a long path name as the default bookmark name. You can change the bookmark name by following these steps:

1. Click on the Bookmarks button and select Edit Bookmarks.

2. If necessary, expand the folder list until you see the bookmark you want to rename.

3. Click on the name to select it.

4. Open the Edit menu and select the Bookmark Properties command (Windows) or the Edit Bookmark command (Mac). Windows users see the Bookmark Properties dialog box, while Mac users see the Edit Bookmark dialog box. Both list the name, location, and description of the bookmark (see Figure 11.12). This dialog box also displays the date the site was last visited and the date the site was added.

5. Edit the existing name or delete it and type a new one.

6. Click on the OK button.

Figure 11.12   Use the Bookmark Properties dialog box to enter a different name or description for a bookmark.

Adding Bookmarks Manually

The easiest way to create a bookmark, as covered in Chapter 5, is to go to a site and then use the Bookmarks I Add Bookmark command. In addition to this method, you can add a bookmark manually by typing the name and URL or address. Follow these steps:

1. Click on the Bookmarks button and select Edit Bookmarks.

2. Open the File menu and select the New Bookmark command. You see the Bookmark Properties (Windows) or New Bookmark (Mac) dialog box, which includes entry boxes for the name, address, and description.

3. Enter the bookmark's name in the Name text box.

4. Type the address in the Location (URL) text box. (Be sure to double-check the address to make sure you typed it in correctly.)

5. If you wish, enter a description for the bookmark.

6. Click on the OK button.

Sorting Bookmarks

Bookmarks are stored in the order you add them to the list. You can move the bookmark to another spot by clicking on it and dragging it to the position you want. You can also list the folders and bookmarks in alphabetical order or sort them by name, location, creation date, or last visit date. Follow these steps:

1. Click on the Bookmarks button and select Edit Bookmarks.

2. If you want to sort the items within one folder, click on that folder. To sort all bookmarks, including your subfolders, select the top-level folder (which is usually labeled with your name).

3. Open the View menu and select how you would like to sort the items: By Name, By Location, By Created On, or By Last Visited.

4. Open the View menu and select a sort order: Ascending or Descending. The items are sorted according to your selections.

Adding A Separator Line

To further divide your bookmarks, you can add a separator line to the menu. Follow these steps:

1. Click on the Bookmarks button and select Edit Bookmarks.

2. Click on the appropriate folder. The line is placed below the selected folder.

3. Open the File menu and select the New Separator command. The line is added. You see this as <separator> in the Bookmark dialog box under Windows, as a dashed line on the Mac, and as a line in the Bookmarks menu.

4. Click on the OK button.

Making Changes To Your Personal Toolbar

Earlier in this chapter, I explained how to add a site to your toolbar. But what if you want to make other toolbar changes, like deleting a button? You can make changes to the items on your Personal toolbar the same way you make changes to your bookmarks. Follow these steps:

1. Click on the Bookmarks button and select Edit Bookmarks. Notice that the top part of this list includes the items on your Personal toolbar (see Figure 11.13).

2. Make any of the following changes:

   ■ To add a folder and put buttons within the folder, select File, New Folder. Type a name for the folder and click on OK.

   ■ To delete an item, right-click on it and then select Delete Bookmark.

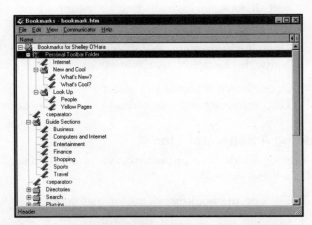

Figure 11.13   You can also edit your Personal toolbar from the Bookmarks window.

- To move an item, drag it from its current location to a new location. For example, you can set up a folder for the toolbar and then move certain sites to that folder.

- To change the name of an item, right-click on the item and then select Bookmark Properties. After making your changes, click on OK.

3. When you are finished making changes, click on the OK button.

Creating Shortcuts (Windows Users Only)

Another way you can go quickly to a particular site is by using a shortcut. In Windows 95, a *shortcut* is an icon added to your desktop. When you double-click on it, you automatically start Navigator, log on to the Internet, and then go to the site. Shortcuts provide quick access from your desktop to your favorite site.

To create a shortcut, display the page or the link to it. Then right-click on the page or link and select the Internet Shortcut command. The Create Internet Shortcut dialog box appears, with fields already filled out for Description and URL. If you want to change the description to something more helpful, do so now. The description appears in the dialog box. Then click on OK; Navigator creates a shortcut and places it on your desktop.

TIP

Navigator includes some other options to customize that are too advanced for coverage in this book. For example, you can set cache options, select to work offline, and make other changes. Consult online help for information on other customization features.

Moving On

You now have a fairly complete set of skills for working with Navigator. You know how to move among links, work with Web pages, play sounds, and download files. Now you can begin to explore other parts of the Internet, including mail and newsgroups, the topics of Chapters 12 and 13.

CHAPTER 12

Sending And Receiving Mail

You can't get by anymore with just exchanging phone numbers. Now you have to get fax numbers, cellular numbers, and of course, email addresses. With email, you can send a message from your home to your main office across the country. You can connect with someone in another country—even another continent. And what makes email so cool is that it's convenient, inexpensive, and instantaneous. You can send a message at any time from any place, and the message is sent immediately. No waiting for the mailman. No *relying* on the mailman. Also, the person on the receiving end can read and respond to that message at his or her convenience.

This chapter covers how to set up Netscape Navigator for email. You will also learn how to look up addresses, create and send email, and respond to any email you receive.

Setting Up Mail

Before you can start using the Internet's mail features, you have to set up your mail server. This simple procedure has to be done only once. Then you have to enter or confirm your email information.

Just The FAQs

What is my email address?

Your email address, which is assigned to you by your Internet Service Provider (ISP), consists of your username, the @ sign, and a domain name.

To whom can I send email?

You can send email to any other Internet user and to commercial online users—for example, to America Online users. To send email, you have to know a person's email address.

How do I get my email?

When you start Netscape Messenger, it checks for new messages and then retrieves them. You can also check for new email from the mail window using the File | Get Messages command or the Get Msg button.

How do I read my email?

Select the Inbox folder in the mail window. You see a list of message headers in the message list pane. Bold messages are new. Double-click on a message to display its contents in a new window.

What can I do with email I receive?

You have a lot of options with email you receive: Reply to it, forward it, print it, or delete it.

What is a mailing list?

A *mailing list* is a group of individuals that send email messages to each other on a certain topic. It is similar to a newsgroup, except postings are not placed on a bulletin board; rather, they are sent via email to all the subscribers.

Setting Up The Mail Server

To set up the mail server, enter a few key settings, which you get from your ISP. Follow these steps:

1. From Navigator, open the Edit menu and select the Preferences command. You see the Preferences dialog box.

2. Click on Mail & Groups to display the other items in this category.

3. Click on Mail Server to display the options shown in Figure 12.1. You need to enter the mail server username, outgoing mail Simple Mail Transport Protocol (SMTP) server, and incoming mail server. You should get these addresses/names from your Internet Service Provider (ISP).

4. In the Mail Server User Name text box, type the username assigned to you by your ISP.

5. In the Outgoing Mail (SMTP) Server text box, enter the name of your mail server for outgoing mail.

6. In the Incoming Mail Server text box, enter the name of your mail server for incoming mail.

7. Select the Mail Server Type.

8. Click on the OK button.

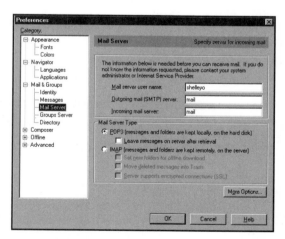

Figure 12.1   Use the Mail Server tab in the Preferences dialog box to enter the names of your mail servers.

Setting Up Your Identity

In addition to entering the appropriate email network addresses, you need to enter (or confirm) the information about yourself. Your personal data is included in your email responses and newsgroup postings.

Follow these steps to enter your information:

1. From Navigator, open the Edit menu and select the Preferences command. You see the Preferences dialog box.

2. Click on Mail & Groups, then click on Identity to display the options shown in Figure 12.2.

3. Enter how you want your name to appear in listings in the Your Name text box.

4. Enter your email address (provided to you by your ISP) in the Email Address text box. If you want users to reply to a different email address, also enter that address in the Reply-To Address text box. For example, you may prefer to send messages from your business email address and receive replies at your home email address.

5. Enter your company or organization name in the Organization text box. This field is optional.

6. If you want to include a standard closing (such as your name, company name, and title), enter the file name that stores this information in the Signature File text box. Or click on the Choose button and use the dialog box to find the file. This information will be included as the closing for all messages. This step is optional. To create a signature file, type the text you want to use and save it as a text (.TXT) file.

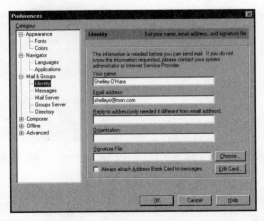

Figure 12.2   Enter your personal information on the Identity tab in the Preferences dialog box.

7. Click on the OK button.

Understanding Addresses

To send an email message to someone, you need to know that person's email address. Likewise, if you want someone to send you a message, you have to give that person your address. This section first explains your address and then tells you some strategies for finding someone's email address.

Decoding Your Address

Most email addresses consist of three parts: the username, the @ sign, and the domain name. An example of an email address is **lgodiva@iquest.net**.

The first part of the name ("lgodiva") identifies the user. When you sign up with an ISP, it assigns you a username. (You may be able to request a certain name.) The second part of the name ("iquest.net") identifies the network for the email account. This name is also given to you by the ISP and is usually the name of its network. The @ sign joins the two parts.

Like Web addresses, the last part of the domain name can tell you something about that network. Here's a brief list:

- *com*—Commercial
- *edu*—Educational
- *gov*—Government
- *mil*—Military
- *net*—Network (usually for computers whose exclusive purpose is handling Internet traffic)
- *org*—Organization

You may also see extensions that indicate the country (such as "uk" for United Kingdom).

Finding Addresses

When you know what your address is, you can give it to anyone you want, and people can then address mail to you. Receiving mail is only half the equation. To send mail to other Internet users, you have to know their email addresses. The best way is to ask and then *carefully* record the information. (Many people include their email addresses on their business cards.) When you create mail, you have to enter the email address exactly right or the mail won't be delivered.

If for some reason you can't ask someone what his or her address is, you can use any of the Web tools that are available to look up an address. For example, maybe you want to surprise your old college roommate (or beau) with a message. Follow these steps to look up an address:

1. From Navigator, click on the Lookup button and then select People. You see links to several search tools for locating people (see Figure 12.3).

2. Select the tool you want and then follow the on-screen instructions. Usually you enter the name (or partial name) and any other identifying information, such as the city, state, and country. You may also be able to select what is searched: the phone book or email addresses.

3. Click on the Search button. (The button name will vary from search tool to search tool.) The program searches its directories and displays any matches.

TIP

If you don't find a listing, try searching with a different set of criteria. For instance, enter the state, but not the city, to widen the search. Or try a different search directory.

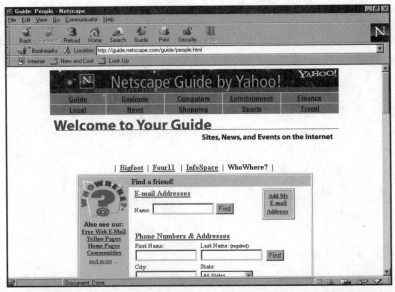

Figure 12.3 *To find an email address, you can select to use one of several search tools for finding people. (Text and artwork copyright 1998 by Netscape and YAHOO!, Inc. All rights reserved. YAHOO! and the YAHOO! logo are trademarks of YAHOO!, Inc.)*

Understanding The Mail Window

To create or receive mail, you must start Netscape Messenger. Then, use its tools to manage your email. This section explains how to start mail and how to use features of the mail window.

To start mail, follow these steps:

1. Open the Communicator menu and select the Messenger Mailbox command. Or click on the Mailbox icon in the status bar or Mailbox button in the component bar.

2. If you are prompted to enter your email password, type the password. If you select the command, you don't have to enter a password until you click on the Get Msg button. If you use the icon or button, you'll be prompted to type a password.

3. If prompted, click on the OK button. Netscape Messenger checks for mail and displays the mail window (see Figure 12.4).

The mail window consists of two panes. The top pane (called the *message header pane*) lists the message headers for any messages you have received, and the bottom pane (called the *message content pane*) displays the contents of the selected message. The section "Reading Mail," later in this chapter, explains how to select a message.

Along the top of the mail window, you see the toolbar with the buttons described in Table 12.1.

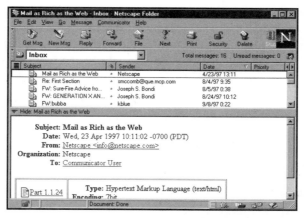

Figure 12.4 Use the mail window to review any mail you have received.

Table 12.1   The buttons in the mail window's toolbar.

Click On	To
Get Msg	Check for new mail.
New Msg	Create a new message.
Reply	Reply to the selected message. You can select to reply to the sender or to the sender and all recipients.
Forward	Forward the message.
File	File the message in a selected folder.
Next	Display the next unread message.
Print	Print the selected message.
Security	Display the security settings of the selected message.
Delete	Delete the selected message.
Stop	Stop the transmission of messages.

TIP

You can view your email folders and your newsgroups in the same window. To do so, select Communicator and then Message Center. For more information on newsgroups, see Chapter 13.

Sending Mail

The greatest thing about email is that you can be sitting in your pajamas drinking a Slurpee at 2:00 A.M. and send an email message across the globe. The person you send the message to doesn't have to be available—unlike when you make a phone call. And you don't have to worry about disturbing the recipient of your mail because he or she can read the message at any time.

When you create mail, you follow a few basic steps. The following is a quick overview, and then the rest of this section describes each step in detail. Keep in mind that although it looks like a lot of work to create a message, you don't have to complete all the steps; note that many of the steps are listed as optional. For instance, formatting the message or attaching a file are not required steps. Here are the basic steps to create mail:

1. Open a new message window.

2. Enter the recipient's address.

3. Type the message.

4. Format the message (optional).

5. Check the spelling (optional).

6. Attach a file or Web page (optional).

7. Set message options (optional).

8. Send the message.

Opening A New Message

To create a new message, click on the New Msg button in the mail window or open the Message menu and select the New Message command. You see the Composition window (see Figure 12.5).

The menu bar contains commands for creating and sending the message and the toolbar includes buttons for shortcuts to these commands. After you open this window, the insertion point is in the To text box so that you can enter the address.

Entering The Address

The most important part of an email message is the address. If you don't get the address right, the message isn't going to get there. You can use one of two methods for entering the address:

■ Type the address in the To text box. Be sure to type the address carefully. Make sure all the periods are in the right places.

■ Click on the Address button and select an address from your address book. The section "Creating Your Address Book," later in this chapter, covers how to add and manage addresses in your address book.

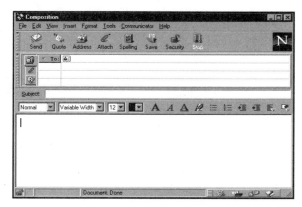

Figure 12.5   Use this form to compose a new message.

TIP

You can also add a carbon copy, blind carbon copy, follow-ups, and other fields. Click on the To button and then select the option you want from the drop-down list. Complete the field for the item.

Typing The Message

Type a subject in the Subject field; this field is required. The message header will appear in the mail window. Type a short, descriptive header that will let your recipient know what the message is about.

Then click inside the message text box and type your message. As you create your message, keep these points in mind:

- It's considered rude to type in all capitals—it's the equivalent of screaming. So use the proper capitalization.

- You can make some changes to the appearance of the text you enter—for instance, add italics for emphasis or change the color. Making this type of change is the topic of the next section, "Formatting The Message."

- Be sure to proofread your message to correct any errors and to verify that the text conveys the message you want. Keep in mind that in a one-on-one conversation, your expressions, tone of voice, and gestures help convey the tone. In a written message, you don't have these elements, so you should make sure that the message can't be misinterpreted—this is especially important with sensitive communications.

- You can use the new Spelling command to check your spelling. See the "Checking The Spelling" section later in this chapter.

- To help convey emotions, users have come up with symbols called *emoticons* that indicate a certain expression or state of mind. For example, :) is a smile. (Turn the page sideways.) Other emoticons stand for all kinds of situations—winking, mustaches, one-legged pirates, and so on. You'd be surprised what people can create out of just a few characters. I've seen an emoticon that was Abe Lincoln. As you get more experience in reading messages, you'll quickly learn to decode the most popular emoticons. You might even want to try some yourself. (These "gestures" also pop up in news messages.)

- In addition to emoticons, you may see shorthand expressions or abbreviations. Here are a few of the most common:

BTW—By the way

IMHO—In my humble opinion

LOL—Laughing out loud

As with the emoticons, you will get the hang of using shorthand expressions as you read more and more messages.

Formatting The Message

As you type your message, you can change how the text looks. The toolbar conveniently provides access to the most common changes. You can also use the commands in the Format menu. To make a change, select the text and then do any of the following:

- To apply a predefined paragraph style, display the Style drop-down list and select the style you want.

- To change the font, display the Font drop-down list and select the font you want to use.

- To change the font size, display the Size drop-down list and select a size.

- To use a different color, display the Color drop-down list and select the color you want to use.

- Click on the Bold button for bold text, the Italic for italics, or the Underline for underlining. To remove all character styles, click on the Remove All Styles button.

- Use the Bullets or Numbered List buttons to add bullets or numbers to the selected paragraph(s).

- To indent text, use the Increase Indent button. To decrease the indent, click on the Decrease Indent button.

- To change the alignment, click on the Alignment button and then select the alignment you want.

- To insert an object, click on the Insert Object button and then select what you want to insert: link, target, image, horizontal line, or table.

Checking The Spelling

Just because email seems informal doesn't mean that you don't have to worry about your spelling and grammar. You should proofread your message carefully. You can also use the new Spelling command to check for errors. Follow these steps to check spelling:

1. Click on the Spelling button. Messenger checks the words in your message and compares them to the words in its dictionary. Any words not found in the dictionary are flagged and displayed in the Check Spelling dialog box (see Figure 12.6).

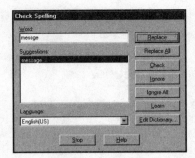

Figure 12.6　Use the options in this dialog box to correct spelling mistakes.

2. Correct each flagged word by doing one of the following:

  ■ If you see the correct spelling listed in the Suggestions list, click on it and then click on Replace to replace this occurrence or on Replace All to replace all occurrences of this word.

  ■ If the word is spelled correctly, click on the Ignore button to ignore this occurrence or click on Ignore All to skip all occurrences of this word.

  ■ If the word is misspelled, but you don't see the correct spelling listed, click in the Word text box and edit the word. Then click on Replace or Replace All.

  ■ To add this word to the Messenger dictionary so that it is not flagged again, click on the Learn button.

3. When Messenger has checked all the words, a dialog box containing a Done button will appear. Click on the button.

Adding Attachments

You can also attach something to the message: a file or a link to an Internet site. For example, you may want to send a message to your mother with a link to a new needlework site. Or you might want to send your expense report to your home office. This section describes how to attach both files and Web pages.

Attaching A File

To attach a file, follow these steps:

1. Click on the Attach button and select File from the menu. You are prompted to select the file (see Figure 12.7).

2. Display the file you want to attach. Click on the Up One Level button to move up to a higher folder. You can also double-click on any of the folders

Figure 12.7   Select the file you want to attach.

listed to display their contents. And you can use the Look In drop-down list to display the folders and files on another drive.

3. Double-click on the file or select the file and then click on the Open button. The file is now attached to the message.

Attaching A Web Page

To attach a Web page, follow these steps:

1. Click on the Attach button and select Web Page from the menu.

2. Type the address of the site in the dialog box that appears (see Figure 12.8).

3. Click on the OK button. The Web page is attached.

Setting Message Options

If needed, you can also set certain options about how the message is sent—for example, whether it is encrypted or whether you receive a return receipt. To set these options, click on the Message Sending Options button and then check any of the options you want.

Sending The Message

After you have typed the message, completed all the fields you want to include, and added any attachments, you can send the message. To do so, click on the Send button in Windows, or the Send Now button on the Mac, or open

Figure 12.8   You can also attach a Web page to a message.

the File menu and select the Send Now command (Send Mail Now for Mac users). The message is sent immediately.

If you are creating a lot of messages, you can save time by putting them in a folder and sending them all at once by selecting the File | Send Later command. This adds all messages to the Unsent Messages folder. To send mail in this folder, select File | Send Unsent Messages.

Sending Mail To A Web Site

In addition to addressing mail to other users, you may want to contact the person or Webmaster in charge of a particular Web page. Many pages include a Mail To link so you can send an email message. Perhaps you want to comment on the content of the page, request additional information, or just say hello. Click on the link to display a mail window with the Mail To address completed. Simply type your message and click on the Send button.

Receiving Mail

If you send out mail, you can expect to receive mail. You can easily tell whether you have mail and then review any messages you get. You have several options with mail you receive: You can respond to or forward a message; you can also print, mark, flag, and sort the messages, as covered in this section.

Reading Mail

You can tell whether you have mail by looking at the small icon in the lower right corner of the status bar. If you see an exclamation point, you have new messages. If you see an envelope without an exclamation point, you don't have any mail.

TIP

See a question mark? That means Netscape Messenger hasn't checked or cannot check to see whether you have new messages. Remember that you have to be set up and logged on to check for mail.

When you start Netscape Messenger, it automatically checks for mail and retrieves any messages you may have. You can also click on the Get Msg button in the mail window or open the File menu and select the Get Messages command. New messages appear in boldface in the mail window. After Netscape Messenger has found new messages, the Mailbox button displays a green dot. Netscape Messenger is set up to check for mail every 10 minutes, by default.

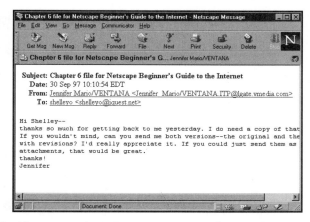

Figure 12.9   You can review the message and then reply using the buttons in the toolbar.

To read a message, double-click on it. Netscape Messenger displays the message in a separate window (see Figure 12.9). The top lines list the subject, date, sender, and recipent. The rest of the message appears below these header lines.

Handling Attachments

Some messages that you receive may have files attached. In this case, you see the file listed as part of the message (see Figure 12.10). Click on the file link to open the file. Netscape Messenger will try to launch the program appropriate for the file. For instance, if someone attaches an image file, Netscape Messenger will display the image. If someone attaches a Microsoft Word document, Netscape Messenger will attempt to start Word and display the file. If you don't have the appropriate program (Word, for instance), you may not be able to use the file. Let your correspondents know what attachment formats you can use.

Moving From Message To Message

If you have more than one message, you don't have to go back to the mail window and click on the one you want. Instead, you can use the toolbar buttons or menu commands to move from message to message:

- To display the next *unread* message, click on the Next button or open the Go menu and select the Next Unread Message command.

- To display the previous *unread* message, open the Go menu and select the Previous Unread Message command.

- To display the next message, open the Go menu and select the Next Message command.

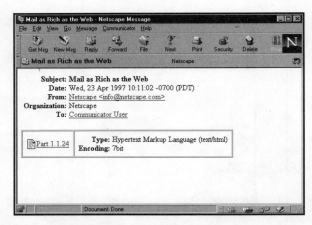

Figure 12.10   File attachments appear like this.

■ To display the previous message in the Inbox folder, open the Go menu and select Previous Message.

■ If you have flagged messages, use First Flagged Message, Next Flagged Message, and Previous Flagged Message in the Go menu to move accordingly. (The next section discusses flagged messages.)

Viewing And Marking Messages

You have a lot of control over how messages are displayed in the mail window. You can do more than just read the message. Other options include:

■ You can mark a message as read or unread. Netscape Messenger keeps track of which messages you have and haven't read. Unread messages appear in boldface. You might want to make a change from read to unread—for instance, if you started reading a message, but didn't finish. To do so, select the message in your Inbox folder. Then open the Message menu, select Mark, and then select Unread.

■ You can flag a message by selecting the message and then selecting Message | Flag. You might want to flag certain messages as a reminder to handle them.

■ You can sort messages. To do so, open the View menu, select the Sort command, and then select a sort order from the submenu. You can sort by date, flag, priority, sender, size, status, subject, thread, or whether the messages are read or unread. As a shortcut, you can also sort by clicking once on the column heading.

■ You can display all messages or just new messages. To show all, use the View I Messages I All command. To show just the unread messages, select the View I Messages I New Messages command.

Printing Messages

You can print a message using the File I Print command. If you're using Windows, you can see a preview using the File I Print Preview command. To set up the page (margins, headers, and footers), open the File menu and select the Page Setup command. Make your selections and click on the OK button.

Finding Messages

If your Inbox folder contains a lot of messages, you may want a quick way to move to a particular one. Or if a message is long, you may want to be able to quickly locate a word or phrase in that message. Netscape Messenger enables you to search any part of the message. Follow these steps:

1. Open the Edit menu and select the Search Messages command. You see the Search Messages dialog box (Figure 12.11).

2. Display the Search For Items In drop-down list and select where you want to search. You can select to search any of the mail folders.

3. Display the next drop-down list and select what you want to search for: a particular sender, subject, message text (body), date, priority, or status.

4. Display the next drop-down list and select the comparison operator. You can select to find something that contains or doesn't contain the entry, begins with the entry, and so on.

5. In the next text box, type the entry you want to find.

6. Click on the Search button. You see the results in the Search Messages dialog box. You can double-click on any message to display it. You can also use the Go To Message Folder button to go to the containing folder.

Figure 12.11   Use this dialog box to select where to search and what to look for.

Replying To Messages

Often a mail message starts a conversation. Perhaps someone requests some information from you or asks a question. Or perhaps you want to ask clarification about a message. Many times you will want to reply to a message. You can reply to just the sender or to the sender and all recipients (if the original message was sent to more than one person). You can also forward a message to another recipient, as described in this section.

Replying To The Sender

To reply to the sender of a message, follow these steps:

1. Display the message you want to reply to.

2. Click on the Reply button and select Reply To Sender or Reply To Sender And All Recipients. You can also open the Message menu, select the Reply command, and then select To Sender or To Sender And All Recipients.

   Netscape Messenger displays the Composition window with the address information completed (see Figure 12.12). The text of the original message may be included; it is indicated with a line in the left margin to distinguish it from the new message text. You can select this text and delete it if you don't want to include it.

TIP

You can change the default so that the original message is not included. Select the Edit | Preferences command. Under Mail & Groups, select Messages. Uncheck the Automatically Quote Original Message When Replying checkbox.

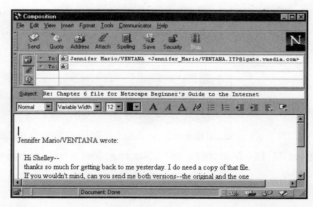

Figure 12.12   You can easily reply to any messages you receive.

3. Type your message.

4. Click on the Send button.

Forwarding Messages

Sometimes you receive a message that really should go to someone else. For example, suppose a co-worker sends you a message asking about a project, but the project is not yours. You can forward the message to the appropriate person. Or perhaps you receive a message that you think someone else should also see.

To forward a message, follow these steps:

1. Select the message you want to forward.

2. Click on the Forward button. You see a Composition window (see Figure 12.13).

3. In the To field, enter the address of the person to whom you want to forward the message. You can select a name from your address book by clicking on the Address button and then selecting the address.

4. Type the message you want included with the forwarded message.

5. Click on the Send button.

Managing Messages

To help you keep track of your messages, Netscape Messenger sets up several folders:

- An Inbox folder for new mail

- An Unsent Messages folder for mail that hasn't been sent

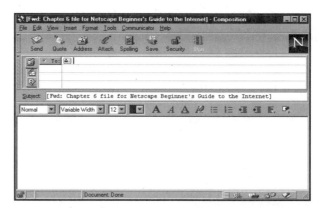

Figure 12.13   Complete the address information to forward the message.

- A Drafts folder for messages you are in the process of creating

- A Sent folder for messages you have sent

- A Trash folder for messages you have deleted

You can create other folders. For instance, you may want to keep your personal and business mail separate. You can create folders and then move or copy your messages into the appropriate ones. This section explains how to organize your messages.

Creating Folders

If you want to set up additional folders for your messages, you can do so. Follow these steps:

1. Open the File menu and select the New Folder command.

2. Type a name for the folder.

3. If you want, select which folder you want to place the new folder in.

4. Click on the OK button.

Filing Messages

After you have reviewed a message, you can easily file it to any of your folders. To do so, select the message and then select Message | File Message. Select the folder you want from the folder list you see.

You can move a message from one folder to another. Perhaps you deleted a message by mistake and want to move it from the Trash folder. Or maybe you have set up folders for different types of messages and want to move all your mail into the appropriate folders. Move a message by filing it in a different folder.

Copying Messages

You can copy a message by following these steps:

1. Select the message(s) you want to copy. You can select all messages using the Edit | Select Message | All Messages command. Or you can flag the messages you want and then use the Edit | Select Message | Flagged command to select them.

2. Open the Message menu and select the Copy Message command. You see a submenu listing the folders you have set up.

3. Select the folder in which you want to place the message(s). Netscape Messenger moves or copies them to this folder.

Deleting Messages

If you kept every message you received, your Inbox folder would eventually become unmanageable. Instead, you should delete messages you no longer need. To delete a message, select it and then click on the Delete button on the toolbar.

Deleted messages are stored in the Trash folder until you use a command to clean out the folder. To empty the Trash folder, open the File menu and select the Empty Trash Folder command.

Creating Your Address Book

You may find that you regularly send messages to certain people. Rather than retype an address each time you want to send a message, you can create an address book containing email addresses of your friends, business associates, and others that you frequently correspond with. This section explains how to create and manage an address book.

Entering Addresses Manually

To add an entry to your address book, you have to know the email address. Then you simply fill in the name and address. Follow these steps:

1. Open the Communicator menu and select the Address Book command. You see the Address Book window, which lists any addresses you have created (see Figure 12.14).

2. To add a new address, click on the New Card button or open the File menu and select the New Card command. You see the New Card dialog box, shown in Figure 12.15.

3. In the First Name text box, enter the person's name as you want it to appear on your messages.

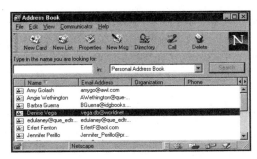

Figure 12.14   You can add names to your own personal address book.

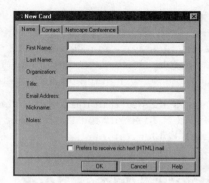

Figure 12.15 Type the email address and name of the person you want to add to your address book.

4. In the Last Name text box, type the person's last name.

5. In the Organization text box, type any company or organization for this person.

6. In the Title text box, type the person's title if appropriate.

7. In the Email Address text box, type the address.

8. In the Nickname text box, type a nickname. When you create a message, you can type this shorthand version of the name, and Netscape Messenger will use the information you enter here.

9. In the Notes text box, type any notes about this person.

10. If you want, click on the Contact tab and record other information about this person—for instance, you can enter his or her address and phone number(s).

11. Click on the OK button.

TIP

Make a mistake? Need to change someone's address? You can always edit the entries you have added. To do so, open the Address Book and click on the name you want to edit. Click on the Properties button or select the Edit | Card Properties command to display the card. Make any changes and then click on OK.

Adding Addresses From Messages

If you received an email message from someone or sent an email message to someone and want to add that person's address to your address book, you can do so easily. Select the message in your Inbox folder or display the message. Select the Message | Add To Address Book | Sender command.

Using Your Address Book

Once you've added entries to the address book, you can quickly and easily use this list to create a new message. To do so, follow these steps:

1. Click on the Address button in any Composition window (for creating new messages or forwarding messages). You see the Select Addresses dialog box (shown in Figure 12.16).

2. Select the name and then click on To, Cc, or Bcc. The bottom half of the dialog box displays the address.

3. Follow Step 2 for each person to whom you want to send the message.

4. Click on the OK button.

Joining Mailing Lists

Chapter 13 covers how to participate in newsgroups as one way of hooking up with others that have similar interests. Another way to join a group of like-minded individuals is to subscribe to a mailing list. When someone creates a message (similar to a newsgroup posting), everyone in the group receives the message via email. When someone responds, again the entire group receives mail.

You can find mailing lists ranging from the philosophy of the Middle Ages to low-fat vegetarianism, from Scottish dancing to horror movies. To subscribe

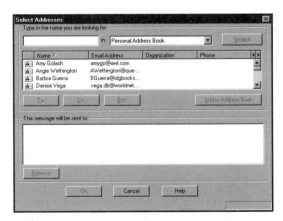

Figure 12.16   Select the person(s) you want to send a message to from your address book.

to a mailing list, you have to know the email address. (Many start with "listserv".) You can find them in some of the Internet Yellow Pages that are available. A good source is the Publicly Accessible Mailing Lists at **http://www.neosoft.com/internet/paml**. You can look through the lists by name or by subject. You can also go to **http://www.liszt.com**.

To subscribe to any mailing list, simply send a message to the mailing list's address requesting to be added. Once added, you will start receiving any mailings sent from other subscribers. You can then reply to these mailings and join in the conversation.

If you decide you don't want to subscribe, send another message requesting to drop the subscription. (You don't pay anything to subscribe to a mailing list.)

Moving On

This chapter covered how to use email to send messages to other Internet users and briefly discussed subscribing to mailing lists. Chapter 13 discusses another way to communicate with others—through newsgroups or discussion groups.

Participating In Newsgroups

For the most part, you are somewhat of a spectator when you are on the World Wide Web. You can read, save, print, and sometimes respond via email to the content, but you can't really alter the content. You don't have much influence over what appears on Web pages (except your own).

In contrast to the WWW, *Usenet* is a collection of newsgroups that are interactive; *you* create the content. Basically, a newsgroup is an online discussion group devoted to a particular topic. You and other users can read and respond to messages posted on this electronic bulletin board.

This chapter explains first what a newsgroup is. Then you learn how to set up your newsgroups and post and respond to messages. Newsgroups are a great way to connect with other users and add your two cents' worth on topics ranging from British politics to Jimmy Buffet, wind surfing to cross-stitching, the Orlando Magic to the Chicago Blackhawks.

What Is A Newsgroup?

If you think a newsgroup is about news, think again. A *newsgroup* is really a collection of opinions posted on a bulletin board set up for a specific topic. Anyone can read the messages and anyone can respond.

Several thousand newsgroups exist. When you look through the list of available newsgroups in the next section, you will probably be surprised at some

Just The FAQs

What is a newsgroup?

A *newsgroup* is an online discussion group devoted to a particular topic. The collection of all Internet newsgroups is called *Usenet*. As an Internet user, you can review messages posted on newsgroups as well as post your own messages.

How do I start the news reader?

From Netscape Navigator, open the Communicator menu and select the Collabra Discussion Groups command or click on the Discussion button in the component bar.

How do I subscribe to newsgroups?

To participate in newsgroups, you first have to set up your news server. Enter the name of the news server given to you by your Internet Service Provider (ISP). Then you can subscribe to the newsgroups you want.

To subscribe to a newsgroup, start Collabra and then click on the Subscribe button. Click on the Get Groups button to display a list of all newsgroups. To subscribe to a particular group, select the group and then click on the Subscribe button.

How do I read a message?

In the Netscape Message Center, double-click on the newsgroup you want to review. You see a list of message headers in the top window pane, which is called the *message list pane*. Double-click on the message you want to read. You see the contents of the message in a separate window.

How do I respond to a message?

You can respond to a message via the newsgroup, email, or both. To respond, click on the Reply button and then select the appropriate command. Type the content of your message and click on the Send button.

of the topics. Whatever you are interested in probably has a corresponding newsgroup. Interested in Bigfoot? Into astrology? Like cooking? Tennis? Country and western music? Do you have panic attacks? Are you a high school teacher? Computer programmer? Do you collect antiques? Like model cars? You get the idea; each of these topics probably has a newsgroup.

To keep the list of newsgroups organized, most newsgroups are divided into categories and then further divided into subcategories. An example of a newsgroup name is **rec.sport.tennis**.

As you can see from the name, each of the categories is separated by a period. The first part of the name tells you the main category. Here are some of the main category names as well as what they stand for:

- *alt*—Alternative

- *comp*—Computers

- *k12*—Education

- *misc*—Miscellaneous

- *rec*—Recreation

- *sci*—Science

- *soc*—Society

TIP

One of the greatest things about the Internet is free speech. You can say what you want without being censored, which is great. But...remember that everyone *has that same right. You may read messages that you find offensive and not be able to do much about them. If you don't like a newsgroup, just don't subscribe to it. Also, if you have children, you may want to purchase a software program that monitors and restricts access to some parts of the Internet—newsgroups in particular. Chapter 9 covers kids and the Internet.*

Messages are posted to a newsgroup. You may also hear messages referred to as *articles* or *postings*. When someone responds to a message, it starts a *thread*— a chain of responses to one message. You can follow the thread, similar to following a conversation. The "Reading And Handling Messages" section later in this chapter explains how to view and read the messages posted.

In addition to reviewing the complete list of newsgroups, you can find newsgroups mentioned in articles, in books, and on Internet sites. A good place to look up newsgroups is at **http://www.reference.com**.

Setting Up Your News Server

The first thing you have to do to participate in a newsgroup is to set up your news server. You need to know your news server name, which should have been provided by your ISP. Simply enter the name in the appropriate dialog box. Follow these steps:

1. From Navigator, open the Edit menu and select the Preferences command. You see the Preferences dialog box.

2. Click on the plus sign next to Mail & Groups to display the options within this category.

3. Click on the Groups Server option to display the options, shown in Figure 13.1.

4. In the Discussion Groups (News) Server text box, enter the name of your news server. Check with your ISP if you are not sure of the name.

5. Click on the OK button. Now that you are all set up, you can select which newsgroups you want to see.

Subscribing To Newsgroups

Initially, you may be set up to view messages for some default newsgroups, depending on your news server. In addition to the default newsgroups, you can *subscribe* to other newsgroups. Because literally thousands of newsgroups exist, you have to select which ones you want to participate in. You don't have to pay anything for these subscriptions; access to them is free.

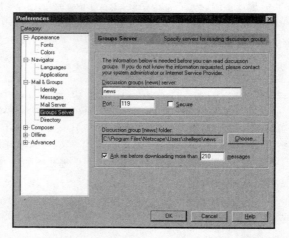

Figure 13.1   Use the Groups Server tab in the Preferences dialog box to enter the name of your news server.

To start, you may want to go through a list of all the newsgroups and select the ones you want. (Keep in mind that your news server determines which newsgroups you have access to.) You can usually guess from the name what the newsgroup is about. You can select the ones that sound interesting and try them out.

After you have worked with newsgroups for awhile, you may want to make a change. Perhaps you don't like a particular newsgroup or you want to add new ones. You can always go back and subscribe to or unsubscribe from newsgroups.

Listing All Newsgroups

You can view the list of newsgroups available from your server and select the ones you want to view. To view a complete list, follow these steps:

1. From Navigator, open the Communicator menu and select the Collabra Discussion Groups command. This step connects you to the news server. You see the default groups listed.

2. Click on the Subscribe button or open the File menu and select the Subscribe To Discussion Groups command. You see the Subscribe To Discussion Groups dialog box listing any of the newsgroups you have already downloaded. If you have yet to download any newsgroups, this list will be blank, and Collabra will automatically download the newsgroups. You can skip Step 3.

3. If you have already downloaded a list and want to update it, click on the Get Groups button. Collabra downloads the available newsgroups from your news server. This may take a while (the amount of time depends on such variables as the speed of your modem and how busy the connection is). When the list has completed downloading, you see the complete list of newsgroups provided by your news server. You can review this list to see which ones you want to add (see Figure 13.2).

You can tell a lot about a newsgroup from the list:

■ Newsgroups are divided into categories, and these categories are indicated with folder (PC) or computer (Mac) icons. Individual newsgroups are indicated with icons that look like little cartoon captions.

■ If a category contains additional subcategories, you see a plus sign next to the folder and an asterisk next to the folder name. The list also shows the number of groups within that folder. On a PC, you can expand the list to see the groups and subcategories in a folder by clicking on the plus sign. You see the groups within the selected category, and the plus sign changes to a minus sign. To collapse a list and hide the subcategories

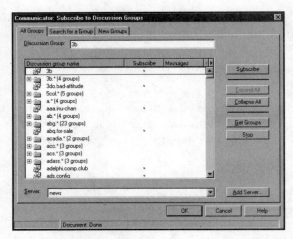

Figure 13.2   You can view a complete list of all newsgroups provided by your news server.

and groups, click on the minus sign. On a Mac, use the drop-down arrow to expand the list.

■ Newsgroups that you have subscribed to have a checkmark in the Subscribe column.

Listing New Groups

If you have already reviewed the complete list, but are interested in new groups (ones Collabra has added since the last time you clicked on the Clear New button), you can display a list of them. Click on the New Groups tab in the Subscribe To Discussion Groups dialog box. Then select from any of the listed newsgroups.

Searching For A Group

Scrolling through the entire list of newsgroups is difficult. You have to expand the list to see any subcategories, and you may miss a group of interest. A quicker way to find a newsgroup on a particular topic is to search for it. Follow these steps:

1. In the Subscribe To Discussion Groups dialog box, click on the Search For A Group tab. You see the options available for searching (see Figure 13.3).

2. In the Search For text box, type the topic you want to find.

3. Click on the Search Now button. You see a list of newsgroups that contain the word(s) you entered.

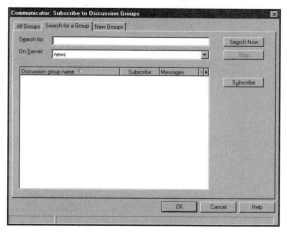

Figure 13.3 *To find a newsgroup on a particular topic, search for it from this tab.*

4. To subscribe to any of these groups, select the newsgroup from the list and then click on the Subscribe button.

5. Click on the OK button to close the dialog box.

Subscribing And Unsubscribing

Subscribing to a newsgroup is simple. Just click in the newsgroup's Subscribe column or select the newsgroup in the list and then click on the Subscribe button. You see a checkmark in the Subscribe column and the newsgroup is added to your list of newsgroups. When you are finished subscribing to newsgroups, click on the OK button. Then when you start the news reader, your news server will check this newsgroup for new messages and update the message list.

When you first start trying out newsgroups, you may subscribe to several just to see what you like and find useful. If you find one you don't really use, you can unsubscribe from it. To do so, click again in the Subscribe column or select the newsgroup and click on the Unsubscribe button.

Starting Your News Reader

To start your news reader, open the Communicator menu in Navigator and select the Collabra Discussion Groups command or click on the Discussions button in the status bar. This command sends a request to your news server to update all messages in your subscribed newsgroups. You see the Netscape Message Center, which includes the list of all the newsgroups you have subscribed to (see Figure 13.4). You also see the number of unread and total messages in

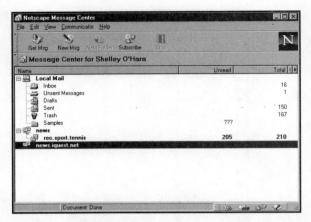

Figure 13.4   You can review the newsgroups you've subscribed to in the Netscape Message Center.

each group. (The Message Center also includes your mail folders. For more information on mail, see Chapter 12.)

The Netscape Message Center includes several tools for working with messages. You can use the menu bar to access all commands and the toolbar to access frequently used commands. Table 13.1 identifies each toolbar button and its use.

Displaying Messages

To display the messages in a newsgroup, double-click on the newsgroup in the Message Center window. Select the number of message headers to download and then click on the OK button. You see the Netscape Discussion window, which is divided into panes (see Figure 13.5). This window displays the following information about the current newsgroup:

■ The name of the newsgroup is listed in the toolbar. You can click on the down arrow next to the name to view the messages in another newsgroup.

Table 13.1   Toolbar buttons in the Netscape Message Center.

Click On	To
Get Msg	Retrieve messages from your news server.
New Msg	Create a new message.
New Folder	Create a new folder—used for the mail folders only.
Subscribe	Display a list of newsgroups so that you can subscribe to any listed.
Stop	Stop the transmission of any incoming data from the news server.

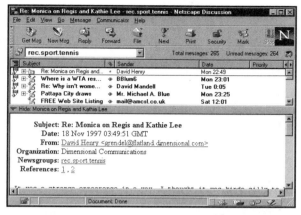

Figure 13.5   The Netscape Discussion window displays the list of messages in the selected newsgroup.

- The toolbar also displays the total number of messages and the number of unread messages.

- The top pane, the message list pane, shows the message headers within that group. You can see the subject, the sender, and the date. You can display other columns of information, such as the priority, by clicking on the scroll buttons in the column header row.

- A plus sign next to a message indicates it contains replies. You can expand the list of replies (called the *thread*) by clicking on the plus sign. Collapse the list by clicking on the minus sign.

TIP

To give yourself as much room as possible to review the header columns, maximize the Netscape Discussion window and resize the panes. Put your mouse pointer on the pane you want to resize. The pointer should look like a two-headed arrow. Click and drag to resize. You can resize columns in the same way.

- If you click on a message header, you see the contents of that message in the bottom pane, called the *message pane*.

TIP

By default, you see the Subject, Date, From, Organization, Newsgroups, and References fields. You can display more information by selecting View | Headers | All. You see the Usenet path for the message, the email address for the sender, the line length, the expiration date, and other information. To show just the Subject field, select View | Headers | Brief.

Sorting Messages

By default, messages are sorted by thread. You can select to sort by date, subject, sender, flag, priority, size, status, or whether the message is read or unread. To do so, open the View menu, select the Sort command, and then select a sort order from the submenu.

You also can control which messages are displayed. Open the View menu and select the Messages command. Select All to display all messages in the selected newsgroup, or New to display only new messages. Select Threads With New to display threads with new messages or Watched Threads With New to display threads you have marked for watching with new messages.

Using The Netscape Discussion Window Toolbar

When you are in the Netscape Discussion window, a different toolbar with buttons for working with the messages appears. Table 13.2 identifies the buttons in this toolbar.

Reading And Handling Messages

You can select which messages to read from the newsgroup, and you can easily move from one message to another within the message thread. You can also copy and paste the text when you are creating a new message. And if you want to save a copy of the message on your hard disk (the messages are stored only on the news server), you can do that as well. For instructions on all these tasks, read this section.

Table 13.2   Toolbar buttons in the Netscape Discussion window.

Click On	To
Get Msg	Retrieve messages.
New Msg	Create a new message.
Reply	Reply to an existing message.
Forward	Forward a message.
File	File the message in a folder.
Next	Display the next unread message in the thread.
Print	Print the selected message.
Security	Display the security settings for the message.
Mark	Mark the message.
Stop	Stop the transmission of messages from the news server.

Opening Messages

To open a message and see its contents, follow these steps:

1. Start the news reader.

2. Double-click on the newsgroup that contains the message(s) you want to review. You may be prompted to download the headers. You can select the number of headers to download. Make your choice and then click on OK. You see a list of all unread message headers in the Netscape Discussion window. You can tell by the Subject line what the message is about—most of the time.

3. In the message header pane, double-click on the message you want to read. You see the contents of the message in a separate window (see Figure 13.6). The top lines give you information about the message. The Subject, Date, From, Organization, and Newsgroups fields are self-explanatory. The References field tells you what message in the thread the current message refers to. For instance, if you see 1, the message you are viewing is a response to the first (1) or original message. You can go to that message by clicking on the number.

As you read messages, keep a couple of points in mind. You may feel as if you walked in on a conversation already underway—which is true. Your news server collects and updates the messages frequently. It does not—and could not—include each and every message ever posted. Instead, messages expire and are not included after a while. You may see only the tail end of a conversation, which can make it hard to follow. Use the References field to figure out where this message fits into the overall thread. When you see "Re:" in the Subject field, this is another tip that you are reviewing a conversation in progress.

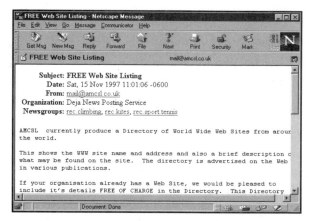

Figure 13.6   **When you double-click on a message, it is displayed in its own window.**

To help viewers follow along, many people include the text of the message they are replying to. Each line of this quoted material usually appears surrounded by angle brackets to help you distinguish it from the original message (quoted) and the reply.

Before you start posting messages, you may want to spend some time reading through different messages to get a sense of the tone. Although most newsgroups are not moderated (no one screens the messages), you are expected to follow certain rules of Net Etiquette (called *Netiquette*). Ignoring these rules can get you *flamed* (others send you angry messages). What's acceptable in one newsgroup may not be kosher in another, so read the messages to familiarize yourself with the feel of a newsgroup. They can vary wildly in content and style.

TIP

You can get pointers on Net Etiquette by opening the Help menu and selecting Net Etiquette.

Some messages may include links to a Web site. You can jump to the site by clicking on the link.

Moving From Message To Message

Many messages have responses, which you can also read. The collection of responses is called a *thread*, and you can use the toolbar buttons or the menu commands to move from message to message.

To display the next unread message in the thread, click on the Next button or open the Go menu and select the Next Unread Message command. To display the next message in the message header pane, open the Go menu and select the Next Message command.

To display the previous unread message in the thread, open the Go menu and select the Previous Unread Message command. To display the previous message in the message header pane, open the Go menu and select the Previous Message command.

To display the next group of messages, open the Go menu and select the Next Group or Next Unread Group command.

Marking Messages

Navigator keeps track of which messages you have and haven't read. Unread messages appear in boldface and with a green diamond. This distinction helps you keep track of what you've read so that the next time you visit the newsgroup, you can find your place.

In some cases, you may want to change which messages are marked as read and which aren't. For instance, you may want to mark messages you aren't interested in as read so that you can easily skip over them, or you may have read a message but want to unmark it. You can use the commands in the Message menu to mark or unmark messages. First, select the message you want to mark (or unmark). Open the Message menu, select Mark, and then select the appropriate command: As Read, As Unread, Thread Read, or All Read. You can also click on the green diamond to mark a message as read or unread.

Flagging Messages

You may want to flag certain messages. Perhaps you want to reread a message. Or maybe you don't have time to read the message now, but want to remember to read it later. Flag a message by clicking in the Flag column. (You may have to expand the list of column headers to see this column.) Click on the scroll arrows in the column header row.

To flag a message, select the message, then open the Message menu and select the Flag command.

To unflag a message, click again in the Flag column or open the Message menu and select the Unflag command.

TIP

> *You can use the Go menu to quickly display flagged messages. Use the First Flagged Message command to display the first marked message, the Next Flagged Message command to display the next marked message, and the Previous Flagged Message to display the previous marked message.*

Searching For Messages

Newsgroups can include lots of messages. You can scan through all the subjects to see whether you can find the topic you are looking for, or you can search for a particular topic. Navigator can search for text in the message headers or in the selected message. To search for text, follow these steps:

1. Open the Edit menu and select the Search Messages command. You see the Search Messages dialog box (see Figure 13.7).

2. Display the Search For Items In drop-down list and select where you want to search. You can select to search any of your newsgroups (or mail folders). For more information on mail, see Chapter 12.

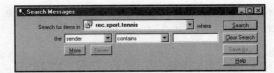

Figure 13.7 Use this dialog box to select where to search and what to look for.

3. Display the next drop-down list and select what you want to search. You can search for a particular sender or subject.

4. Display the next drop-down list and select the comparison operator. You can select to find something that contains the entry, is the entry, begins with the entry, or ends with the entry.

5. In the next text box, type the entry you want to find.

6. Click on the Search button. You see the results in the Search Messages dialog box. Double-click on any message to display it. You can also use the Go To Message Folder button to go to the containing folder.

Searching For Text In A Message

If you are reviewing a particularly long message, you can search for a word or phrase in that message. Keep in mind that the Find command (covered here) does not search all messages, only the currently selected or displayed message. Follow these steps to search a message for a certain word or phrase:

1. Select the message you want to search.

2. Open the Edit menu and select the Find In Messages command. You see the Find dialog box.

3. In the Find What text box, enter the text you want to find.

4. If you want to match the case as you have entered it, check the Match Case checkbox. On the Mac, this option is called Case Sensitive.

5. Select a search direction: Up or Down. On the Mac, you can select Find Backward.

6. Click on the Find Next button. Navigator moves to the first matching entry and highlights it.

TIP

If Navigator cannot find the text you've entered, you see an alert box. Click on the OK button to close this box. (On the Mac, you just hear a beep.) Try searching again using a different word or phrase.

Copying Message Text

If you find message text you want to keep or use in another document, you can copy and paste it. (On your system, the original text of a message is included in a reply, so if you want to refer to this text, you don't have to copy and paste.)

To copy and paste text from a message, follow these steps:

1. Select the text you want to copy by dragging across it.

2. Open the Edit menu and select the Copy command.

3. Move to the document or message where you want to paste the text.

4. Open the Edit menu and select the Paste command.

Saving Messages

By default, messages are saved on the news server only. If you want to save a copy of a message to your hard disk, you must use a command. Follow these steps:

1. Open the File menu and select the Save As command. You see the Save Messages As dialog box, shown in Figure 13.8.

2. Select a folder for the message. You can use the Save In drop-down list to select another drive. Double-click on a folder to display its contents. Use the Up One Level button to move up through the folder structure.

3. Enter a file name for the message.

4. Click on the Save button.

Deleting Messages

You cannot delete any of the messages on the news server. These messages will automatically be removed after a certain expiration date. If you don't want to

Figure 13.8   Select a folder in which to place the message.

view certain messages, mark them as read and then use the View | Messages | New command. You can also choose to ignore the thread using the Message | Ignore Thread command.

Printing Messages

Suppose that you see an important message—instructions on how to do something, an address, a recipe, or just something that you want to keep a hard copy of so that you can refer to it later. You can print a message by following these steps:

1. Open the message you want to print.

2. Click on the Print button or open the File menu and select the Print Message(s) command. You see the Print dialog box.

3. Click on the OK button. Navigator prints the message.

TIP

You can change the margins (PC only) and control other page options for the printed message. To do so, open the File menu and select the Page Setup command. Make any changes and then click on the OK button.

Getting More Messages

By default, your news server only gets a certain number of messages (the number you select when you initially display the newsgroup). If the newsgroup includes more messages and you want to get the new batch, use the File | Get Messages command. You can opt to get new messages, the next set of messages, messages selected for offline reading, or messages flagged for offline reading.

Watching For New Messages

When you post a message or even review messages, you might get involved in this "conversation." Rather than continue to check for new posted messages, you can watch a particular thread or conversation. Follow these steps:

1. Select the message thread you want to watch.

2. Open the Message menu and select the Watch Thread command.

When you mark a thread as watched, a pair of sunglasses appears to the left of the subject. When unread messages are in the thread, a small green arrow appears above the sunglasses, and the new messages are displayed in boldface.

Posting Your Own Messages

Reading messages is only half the fun of newsgroups. The other half is adding your own thoughts. You have several options for how to respond. You can respond to an existing message via the newsgroup, email, or both. And you can start your own conversation by posting a new message, as covered in this section.

Replying To Messages

When you read through the messages, you may find that you want to add your own opinion. Perhaps someone has asked for advice, and you know the answer. Or perhaps someone has expressed an opinion, and you want to agree (or disagree). You can respond to any of the posted messages, and you can respond publicly (to the newsgroup) or privately (to just the sender via an email message).

To reply to a message, follow these steps:

1. Display the message to which you want to reply.
2. Click on the Reply button.
3. Select the appropriate command:

   - To reply to the newsgroup, select the Reply To Group command.
   - To reply to just the sender (via email), select the Reply To Sender command.
   - To reply to the sender and any other listed recipients, select the Reply To Sender And All Recipients command.
   - To reply to both the Sender and the Group, select the Reply To Sender And Group command.

   You see the Composition window (see Figure 13.9). The Subject and Group entries are completed. The text of the message may also be included as quoted material. You can highlight this text and delete it if you want.

4. Type your response.
5. Click on the Send button. Navigator sends your message. You won't see your new message immediately because it is first sent to the news server and then processed as a new message.

TIP

By default, messages are sent immediately. If you are creating lots of messages, you may want to save them and then send them all at once. To do so, select the File | Send Later command. You can also save drafts using the File | Save Draft command.

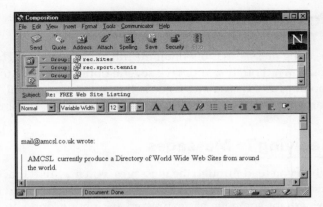

Figure 13.9   Type your response in the Composition window.

Posting New Messages

Sometimes you may want to start your own conversation. Perhaps you want to ask a question or offer an opinion. Start a new conversation by following these steps:

1. Select the newsgroup where you want to post the new message. Be sure you are in an appropriate newsgroup. Newsgroups are set up for particular topics, and it is considered rude to introduce a subject that is not related to that topic.

2. Click on the New Msg button or open the File menu and select the New | New Message command. You see the Composition window with the Group entry completed (see Figure 13.10). This window is similar to

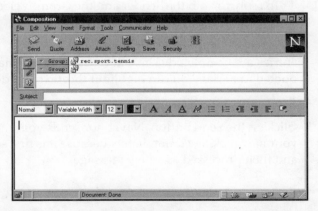

Figure 13.10   Enter a subject and the text for your new message.

the one for replying to an existing message, but the text area and the Subject field are blank.

3. In the Subject text box, type a message header. This text appears in the message header pane, so type something that will describe the content of the message.

4. Type the message.

5. Click on the Send button.

TIP

You can use the Insert menu to insert items into the message such as links, images, or lines. Use the Format menu or the toolbar buttons to make changes to the text in your message. For instance, you can change the font, use a different color, make text bold, and more. Only those with HTML-enabled news readers will be able to see the formatting features. Also, formatting is starting to be considered bad Net Etiquette because it uses up bandwidth and disk space.

Forwarding Messages

As you review the messages, you may find one that you want to share with someone else. To do so, you must know that person's email address. You can find more information about sending mail in Chapter 12.

Follow these steps to forward a message:

1. Select the message you want to forward.

2. Open the Message menu and select the Forward command or click on the Forward button. You see a Composition window.

TIP

To forward the message as a quoted message, open the Message menu and select the Forward Quoted command.

3. In the To field, enter the address of the person to whom you want to forward the message. For more information on addressing emails, see Chapter 12.

4. Type the message you want included with this forwarded message.

5. Click on the Send button.

Browsing Offline

To save connection time, you may want to browse through messages *offline*—that is, when you are not connected to the Internet. You can do so by following these steps:

1. From the Netscape Message Center, select your newsgroup server.

2. Open the File menu and select Go Offline. You see the Download dialog box (see Figure 13.11).

3. If necessary, check the Download Discussion Groups checkbox. You can also select to download mail by checking the Download Mail checkbox.

4. Click on the Select Items For Download button. You see a list of the newsgroups to which you have subscribed.

5. Select the newsgroup(s) you want to download.

6. Click on the OK button.

7. Click on the Go Offline button to download the messages and disconnect. You can still work in Collabra, reading and reviewing messages, but you will have to reconnect to upload any replies or download any new messages.

To go back online, open the File menu and select the Go Online command. Click on the Go Online button in the Download dialog box.

Moving On

Newsgroups are one form of interaction with other Internet users. This chapter explained how you can connect with a whole group of individuals. Now you have a core set of skills for doing just about everything on the Internet. Part III of this book covers some specific avenues for exploration. You can start with Chapter 14, "Shopping".

Figure 13.11   Select what you want to download.

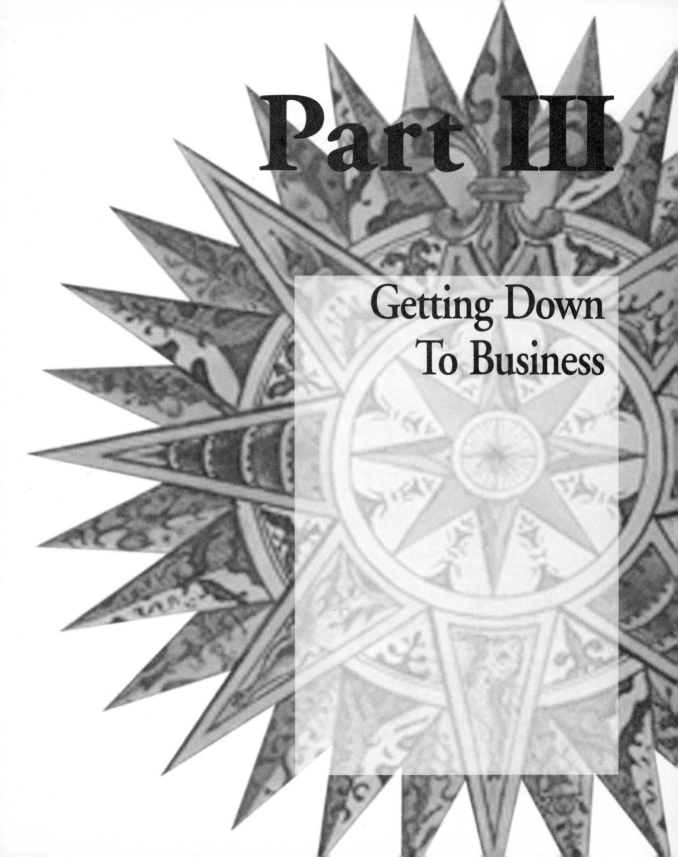

Part III

Getting Down To Business

CHAPTER 14

Shopping

Perhaps you *hate* to shop. You don't want to put yourself together, drive to a mall, fight for a parking space, try on clothes, try to find something that you like and that fits, and then wait in line to pay. Instead, you'd rather just do all your shopping from your computer—without leaving home. If so, you'll be enthused with the Internet shopping features.

Or perhaps you *love* to shop. You could shop all day, looking for the best deals, locating hard-to-find stuff, and shopping the sales. If so, you'll also enjoy the many shopping-related features on the Internet.

First, this chapter explains what you can expect from shopping on the Internet. Then, it highlights some places where you can "go" to shop. Get your credit cards ready!

Shopping On The Internet

You may be wondering exactly *how* you can shop on the Internet. What can you buy? How do you pay? Is it safe? This section discusses what you can expect on a typical shopping "trip." Keep in mind that, depending on the company, how you place an order will vary.

Shopping Sites At A Glance

All-Internet Shopping Directory at **http://www.all-internet.com**

Amazon Books at **http://www.amazon.com**

CDnow at **http://www.cdnow.com**

CDworld at **http://www.cdworld.com**

DealerNet at **http://www.dealernet.com**

DealerOnline at **http://www.dealeronline.com**

DealerSites at **http://www.dealersites.com**

Downtown Anywhere at **http://www.awa.com**

Internet Mall at **http://www.internet-mall.com**

Internet Shopping Network at **http://www.internet.net**

MALLennium at **http://www.mallenium.com**

Online Vacation Mall at **http://www.onlinevacationmall.com**

TicketMaster at **http://www.ticketmaster.com**

Trader Online at **http://www.automart.com**

TravelWeb at **http://www.travelweb.com**

What Can I Buy?

You can find companies selling everything from computer products to collectible bears, from homemade jams to pet supplies. You can book a vacation, order a new tennis racket, research a new car, purchase concert tickets, and more. This chapter provides numerous Web site addresses for shopping. If you want to buy something, you can probably purchase it over the Internet.

How Do I Order?

Some sites have an online catalog so that you can review both a text description and a picture of the item for sale. For instance, Figure 14.1 shows information about a tennis racket for sale. You can both review product information and see a picture of the racket. Order information is included in the top part of the screen.

Some sites enable you to make the purchase online, paying with a credit card. For other sites, you can call the order number or send a fax to order a product. The site should include specific instructions for placing an order. If you have questions, look for an Order Information or Contact link; use this link to get additional information.

Finally, some sites just provide product information. For example, many of the car dealer sites provide facts about the makes and models of cars, but don't enable you to purchase a car over the Internet. (But you *can* find the nearest dealer.)

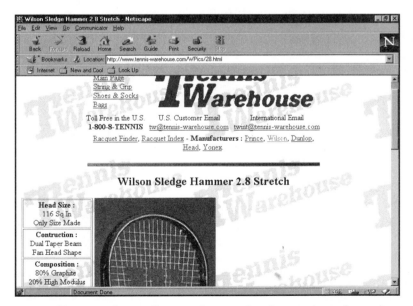

Figure 14.1   You can view online catalogs and order products from them.

How Do I Pay?

If you are making a purchase, you will most likely pay by credit card, and the site determines which credit cards are accepted. For example, Figure 14.2 shows the accepted credit cards for stores in 5th Avenue. When you place an order, you will be prompted to provide your credit card information (the name, number, and expiration date), much as you do when you order over the phone. Some sites allow COD shipping for a fee.

Your payment information is *encrypted* so that no one else can see it. Netscape Navigator has standards (*Secure Sockets Layer* or *SSL* protocol) that handle data encryption and data integrity. Netscape Navigator also requires *digital certification* for commerce servers; the certification process ensures that the company is legitimate and helps to protect against fraud. Shopping over the Internet, then, is as safe as shopping over the phone.

If you are concerned about a particular site, though, you can call the site (look for a link called Questions, Contact Us, or something similar) and ask about security for transactions. You can also check out the particular security features of a page by following these steps:

1. Display the page you want to check.

2. Click on the Security button. You see the Security features for that particular page (see Figure 14.3). For more information on security, see Chapter 7.

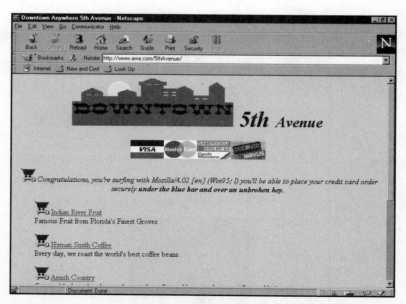

Figure 14.2   When you order a product, you usually pay by credit card.

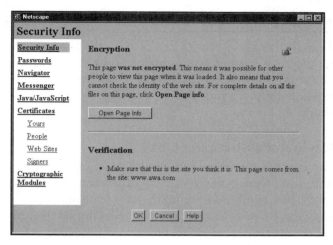

Figure 14.3   You can check out the security settings for a site.

3. Click on any of the options along the left edge to view the pertinent information for this site.

4. Click on the OK button when you are finished reviewing the security information about that page.

If you are uncomfortable for any reason, don't do business with that company.

How And When Do I Get My Order?

How the company ships the product and when you will receive your order varies from site to site. Also, any taxes and shipping charges should be spelled out somewhere on the site's Web page(s). And you should be sure you understand the return policy before you place an order.

To find out how a company gets its product to you, look for a page that covers general shipping and order information. Look for a link called Ordering (or something similar). If you can't find this information, call the company and ask.

Finding Stores

Now that you know what to expect when you go shopping on the Internet, you are ready to visit some of the several kinds of places to shop. As with "regular" shopping, you can expect to find collections of shopping sites, like shopping malls, as well as individual storefronts. This section discusses some strategies for finding shopping spots.

Visiting An Online Mall

To make it easy to find some of the shopping sites on the Internet, several places have created online malls. Some malls contain just a few key sites, whereas others have hundreds of stores. Imagine being able to visit over 100 stores without leaving your house. This section covers some of the malls and shopping directories.

Navigator's Shopping Links

You can use the Internet button in Navigator to view some categories, each with links to popular sites. One of the categories, Shopping, includes shopping links. Figure 14.4 shows the sites featured here. You can visit several sites from this directory page by simply clicking on the link you want.

Downtown Anywhere

You can find a great collection of stores and products at Downtown Anywhere, at **http://www.awa.com**.

Figure 14.5 shows the types of products from which you can select. You can visit Main Street and find an optical store, music store, clothing company, florist, and toy store. You can find companies selling computer support, Discovery Toys, tackle, videos, games, Moroccan rugs and pillows, and secretarial services. Click on the Main Street link to visit any of these sites.

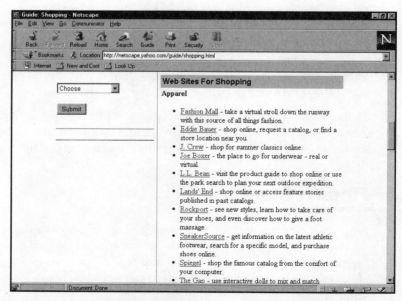

Figure 14.4   Navigator's Shopping directory includes links to some shopping sites.

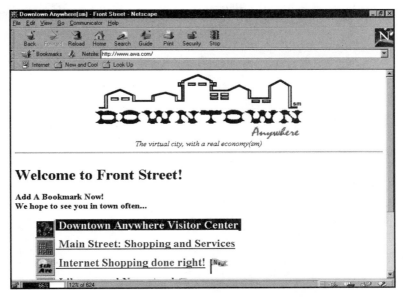

Figure 14.5   Visit Downtown Anywhere and shop its "streets."

You can also order books and news publications from the Library and Newsstand link. For travel plans, visit the Travel Center. And for sporting goods, try Sports Arena. Like art? Try the sites featured in the Museums, Galleries, and ArtNetWeb link.

MALLennium

Another place to find links to games, art, electronics, entertainment, food, music, sports, and specialty products is MALLennium. You can visit this site at **http://www.mallenium.com**.

Select the category for which you want to see links to sites. Or use the Search button to search for a particular company or product. Figure 14.6 shows the opening text page for MALLennium.

The All-Internet Shopping Directory

One of the best directories of shopping sites is the All-Internet Shopping Directory, found at **http://www.all-internet.com**.

Figure 14.7 shows the first part of the directory list. You can browse through the list and select from the categories, which are: Arts & Entertainment, Lifestyle, Malls & Such, Computing, Hobbies, Home & Garden, and Services. Each category includes links to different product types. For instance, for Arts & Entertainment, you can select: Art, Books, Records, CDs & Cassettes, and Videos & Movies.

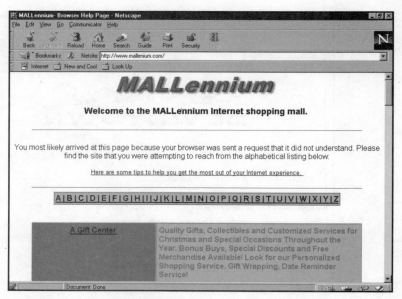

Figure 14.6   Visit MALLennium for electronics, entertainment, and other products.

When you select a particular product type, you see an alphabetical list of sites that sell that product; go to one by simply clicking on its link.

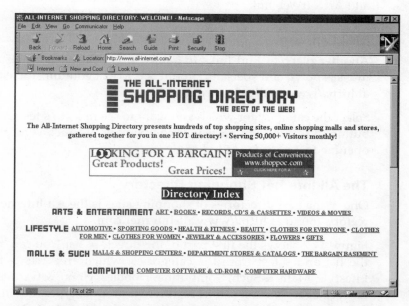

Figure 14.7   Use the All-Internet Shopping Directory to find products.

In addition to browsing, you can use the Search button to find a particular company or product. You can also view top shopping site winners and new sites using the links under Added Directions.

The Internet Mall

Another mall is the Internet Mall at **http://www.internet-mall.com**. It offers 27,000 stores. You can use any of the links, view a store index, or search the mall to find exactly what you seek. Figure 14.8 shows the home page for this comprehensive shopping site.

Searching For A Company

Many search engines also have shopping directories. Review the links on these pages to find other shopping sites. To check out these sites, follow these steps:

1. Click on the Search button.

2. Select the search engine you want to use. (Not all include shopping links, but most do.)

3. Click on the shopping link. Figure 14.9 shows some sites for Excite's shopping page.

4. Use any of the links to visit the highlighted shopping sites.

Figure 14.8   Visit this mall and find a wealth of stores.

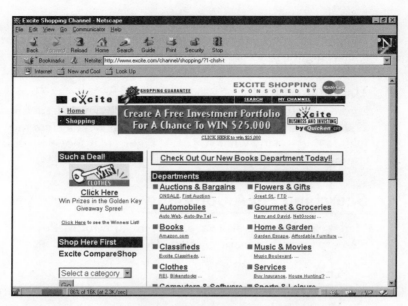

Figure 14.9   Try the shopping directories of the search tools.

Finding Other Stores

A store doesn't have to be in a mall for you to shop there. Many stores, especially catalog stores, have a Web site. You can visit these online stores and shop the "aisles." Table 14.1 lists some popular stores.

Table 14.1   Popular stores and their Web sites.

Store	Web Site
Bloomingdale's	http://www.bloomingdales.com
Dillard's	http://www.azstarnet.com/dillards
Eddie Bauer	http://www.ebauer.com
FAO Schwarz	http://www.faoschwarz.com
J. Crew	http://www.jcrew.com
Lands' End	http://www.landsend.com
L.L. Bean	http://www.llbean.com
Macy's	http://www.macys.com
May Department Stores	http://www.maycompany.com
Neiman Marcus	http://www.neimanmarcus.com
Sears	http://www.sears.com

(continued)

Table 14.1   Popular stores and their Web sites (continued).

Store	Web Site
Smith & Hawken	http://www.smith-hawken.com
Spiegel	http://www.spiegel.com
Toys "R" Us	http://www.toysrus.com
Wal-Mart Online	http://www.wal-mart.com

TIP

*If you like to shop from catalogs, go to **http://www.catalogsite.com**. You can check out the index, search for catalogs, or view a list of new catalogs. The site also highlights a catalog of the week.*

Buying A Car, Making Travel Plans, And Other Shopping

In addition to specialty stores, you can find companies selling a particular type of product, such as a car, service, or travel plans. This section covers just a few sites for buying a particular type of item.

Buying A Car

If you are in the market for a new car, you will be thrilled with the numerous car-dealer sites on the Internet. You may not actually be able to purchase a car, but you can get product information, find the dealer nearest you, research prices, and read car reviews from car-related sites. Keep in mind that this section lists only a small sampling of the many sites relating to this topic.

From DealerOnline, you can get information on dealers, preowned vehicles, and current makes and models. You can also find links to other car-related sites from this "premier Automotive Internet Provider." Visit DealerOnline at **http://www.dealeronline.com**.

You can also visit the DealerSites Virtual Auto Mall at **http://www.dealersites.com**. From this site, you can get free price quotes, look up model information, find out about auto shows, locate a dealer, research a fair price on a used car, and more (see Figure 14.10).

Yet another place for getting information on dealers, new cars, used cars, specialty vehicles, boats, and RVs is DealerNet, found at **http://www.dealernet.com**.

Figure 14.10 Visit the DealerSites Virtual Auto Mall for car-buying information.

Figure 14.11 shows the opening page with links to the various products and services provided by this site. Try the Finance & Leasing icon to get information on buying versus leasing a car.

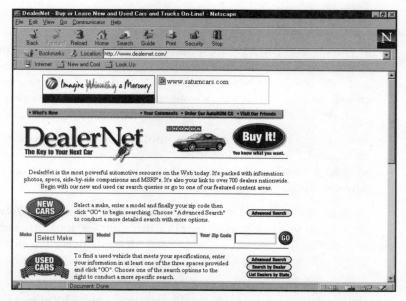

Figure 14.11 Visit DealerNet and get information on new and used cars, as well as specialty vehicles.

In addition to these sites, try any of the following:

- Cadillac at **http://www.cadillac.com**

- CarSmart at **http://www.carsmart.com**

- Chrysler at **http://www.chrysler.com**

- Ford at **http://www.ford.com**

TIP

*For new and used cars sold via classified ads, try **http://www.automart.com**.*

Buying Computer Products

Chapter 20 covers finding computer-related news, hardware, and software on the Internet. One site devoted to selling computer products is the Internet Shopping Network (ISN) at **http://www.internet.net**.

From here, you can purchase accessories, desktop computers, drives, memory, modems, monitors, and more (see Figure 14.12). Select the product you want; you can also search by product name or manufacturer.

Two other stores for computer products are the Cyberian Outpost at **http://www. cybout.com** and the Computer Discount Warehouse at **http://www.cdw.com**.

Figure 14.12   The Internet Shopping Network is a good place to buy computer products.

Making Travel Plans

In addition to car-buying sites, you can find a lot of sites devoted to making travel plans. This section mentions just four sites, but you can find many, many more related to researching and booking a vacation or business trip. Check with your own travel agency; it may have a site that you can visit.

Visit the Online Vacation Mall at **http://www.onlinevacationmall.com** (see Figure 14.13). From this site, you can look into vacation packages, sightseeing tours, and vacation merchandise. Vacation destinations include Las Vegas, Reno, Lake Tahoe, Puerto Vallarta (love it!), Jamaica, Florida, and other vacation hot spots. You can also make reservations with several tour providers and search for a vacation package.

Another place to find travel information is the TravelWeb at **http://www.travelweb.com**. You can look up a hotel in a database by using search criteria such as location, price, and amenities. You can also view choice hotels or visit the Business Travel Resource Center.

And finally, you can also visit these other highly rated travel sites:

■ Microsoft Expedia at **http://www.expedia.msn.com**

■ Travelocity at **http://www.travelocity.com**

Figure 14.13   Planning a vacation? Do your research at the Online Vacation Mall.

Buying Music

The *commerce* sites (sites that sell something) that took off the fastest on the Internet were book sites (covered later in this chapter) and CDs. If you are looking for a hard-to-find CD or if you just don't feel like going out, you can purchase your music over the Internet. Most sites let you listen to the CD, read reviews, search for a particular title, and more. If you want to buy music over the Internet, visit any of these music sites:

- CDnow at **http://www.cdnow.com**
- CDworld at **http://www.cdworld.com**
- Music Blvd. at **http://www.musicblvd.com**

Figure 14.14 shows the home page for CDnow.

Buying Event Tickets

If you are a music fan, you might want to know which concerts are coming to your area. And if you see a concert you like, you may even want to purchase your tickets. Because TicketMaster pretty much has a monopoly on concert tickets, the place for ticket information is at its Web site: **http://www.ticketmaster. com**. You can check out upcoming events, order tickets, and visit the Ticket-Master store, all from this site. You can also get the latest entertainment news.

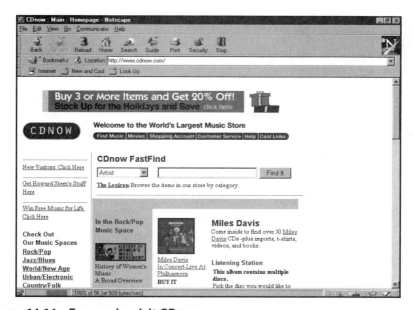

Figure 14.14   For music, visit CDnow.

Buying Books

If you are a book lover, check out amazon.com, one of the big success stories of Internet businesses. From this site, you can choose from 2.5 million book titles (see Figure 14.15). This is one of my favorite sites. You can read reviews, post your own reviews, search for books, and more. For all your book-buying needs, visit this site at **http://www.amazon.com**.

Moving On

The Internet is changing how we do business, and one area that is evolving is shopping. How and where you can purchase a product is being broadened with the entry of Internet stores. This chapter discussed how to shop on the Internet and highlighted some key shopping sites.

Chapter 15 covers keeping up to date with the Internet. You can find all the latest news at the sites highlighted in the next chapter.

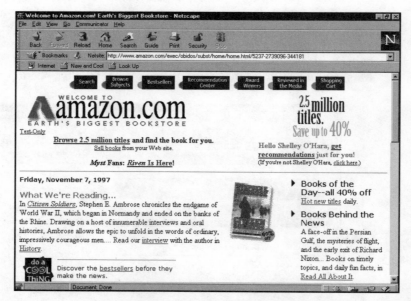

Figure 14.15   One of the best sites on the Web is amazon.com, where you can find just about any book you need.

CHAPTER 15

Reading The Latest News

Things happen so quickly that what you read in your morning paper is probably *old* news. Even stories you see on TV news may have been prepared days or weeks in advance. When you want the latest news, the best place to turn is the Internet, because it provides you with convenient access to a multitude of news sites that have continuously updated information. The Internet has no deadlines, no press time.

This chapter highlights some of the news and magazines you can find on the Internet. Some are online versions of print magazines and some are *zines*, created for the Internet only. This chapter, like the others in Part III of this book, just touches on a few of the best and most interesting sites; it is in no way a comprehensive listing of the various news sites. The sites you will read about here will get you thinking about what's available—they are a good starting point.

Getting The Latest News

Like to read the newspaper with your coffee? Then sit down at your computer (don't spill your coffee) and peruse one of the many newspapers and news sources on the Internet. This section highlights some of the best places to find the latest news.

News Sites At A Glance

Chicago Tribune at **http://www.chicago.tribune.com**

CNN at **http://www.cnn.com**

CNNfn at **http://www.cnnfn.com**

Lexis-Nexis News Service at **http://www.lexis-nexis.com**

Los Angeles Times at **http://www.latimes.com**

New York Times at **http://www.nytimes.com**

Time Warner publications (including *People, Time, Money, Sports Illustrated*, and others) at **http://www.pathfinder.com**

U.S. News & World Report at **http://www.usnews.com**

USA Today at **http://www.usatoday.com**

Wall Street Journal at **http://www.wsj.com**

Washington Post at **http://www.washingtonpost.com**

Weather at **http://www.intellicast.com**

The Weather Channel at **http://www.weather.com**

Wired at **http://www.wired.com**

USA Today

If you like *USA Today*, you don't have to go to the newsstand to purchase a copy. Instead, you can access the online version at **http://www.usatoday.com**.

The online version has categories much like the sections in the paper. You can select News, Sports, Money, Life, and Weather (see Figure 15.1). You can also click on any of the front page pictures or headlines to read the full story. Use the links along the side to view the latest scores, stocks, and news. Under Resources, you can view an index of stories and also search the site for a particular topic.

Wall Street Journal

If you are a businessperson, you may regularly read the *Wall Street Journal*. Instead of spreading out the paper on your desk, you can subscribe to and read the online version from your computer. You can find the famous journal at **http://www.wsj.com**.

Before you can access all the news stories, you have to subscribe. (The bottom of the page lists the features available to non-subscribers.) In March 1998, the subscription fees were $29 for those who had a print subscription to the *Wall Street Journal* and $49 for those who did not. The home page provides a link for subscribing and the following pages detail how to subscribe.

Figure 15.1   One news source to try is **USA** Today.

Once you've subscribed, you can read and review any of the *Wall Street Journal* stories. The Interactive Edition also provides additional in-depth background stories and is of course updated more often than the print version.

CNN

Another great source of news is CNN Interactive at **http://www.cnn.com**. From this Web site, you can read any of the headlined stories or select from any of the following categories: U.S., World, CNNfn (for financial news), Sports, ShowBiz, Weather, Health, All Politics, Sci-Tech, Style, Travel, and more (see Figure 15.2).

When you visit the CNN Interactive site, try these tips:

- You can search for a topic of interest. To do so, click on the Search button and then enter the word or phrase that describes what you want to find. Check the areas you want to search and then click on the Search CNN button.

- If your computer is slow, use the Text-Only Version link to hide the pictures. Doing so will speed up the transmission and display of the stories.

- Use the Contents button to view a table of contents.

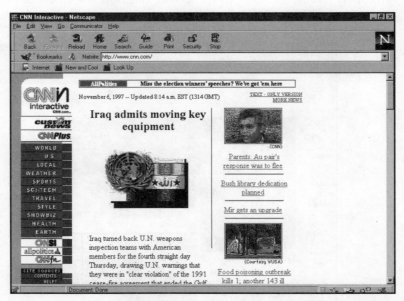

Figure 15.2   CNN Interactive gives you the latest news stories in several areas, including U.S. news.

- Want to know how current the news is? The home page lists when the information was last updated.

- Stuck? Try using the Help button to get help on the CNN Interactive features.

- For special features, try the links under Specials. You can try Quick News, Almanac, the News Quiz, and other news tidbits.

CNNfn

If your main interest is business and finance news, try a sister publication of CNN, CNNfn. You can try the financial network news service by visiting **http://www.cnnfn.com**.

The CNN financial network includes top stories as well as stories in these categories: Hot Stories, Markets, Your Money, Digital Jam, Small Business, fn Traveler, fn On-Air, Speak Up, Resources, CNN News, and others (see Figure 15.3).

Other Places To Find News

If you remember from Chapter 6, many of the search tools also include access to headlines. For example, from Infoseek (**http://www.infoseek.com**), you can view the News channel by clicking on the News button. From this page, you

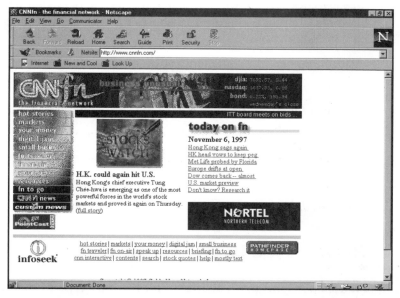

Figure 15.3   CNNfn provides current business and financial news.

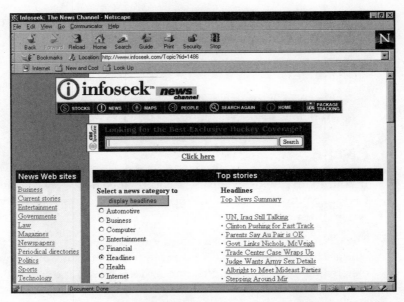

Figure 15.4   Some of the search tools also provide links to the latest news.

can review top stories, select a particular news category, visit some news sites, and more (see Figure 15.4).

You can also find other newspapers. A good way to find newspapers in your area is to use Yahoo!. You can search for newspapers. (For information on Yahoo!, see Chapter 6.) Figure 15.5 shows some of the available online newspapers in Indianapolis.

In addition, here are some other sites to try:

- **http://www.chicago.tribune.com** (*Chicago Tribune*)
- **http://www.itar-tass.com** (ITAR-TASS: The Russian News Agency)
- **http://www.latimes.com** (*Los Angeles Times*)
- **http://www.nando.net/nt** (*Nando Times*)
- **http://www.nytimes.com** (*New York Times*)
- **http://www.washingtonpost.com** (*Washington Post*)

Reading The Latest Magazines

Newspapers and news stories aren't the only type of publications you can find online. In addition, you can read some of your favorite magazines, as previewed in this section.

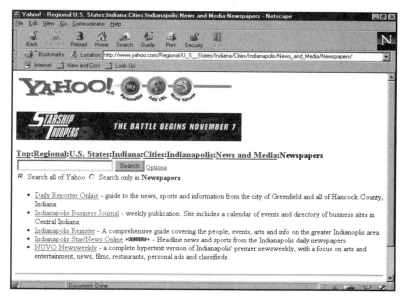

Figure 15.5 *Use Yahoo! to find newspapers from your area. (Text and artwork copyright 1998 by YAHOO!, Inc. All rights reserved. YAHOO! and the YAHOO! logo are trademarks of YAHOO!, Inc.)*

Pathfinder: The Time Warner Publications

You can find probably the largest collection of online magazines at Pathfinder: **http://www.pathfinder.com**. From this Web site, you can access one of the many Time Warner publications, including *Time, LIFE, People, CNNsi, Entertainment Weekly*, and others (see Figure 15.6). You can read these popular magazines, plus some other specialty magazines, including *Southern Living, Cooking Light, Thrive, Fortune, Money, Progressive Farmer, This Old House*, and more. Click on the name of the magazine you wish to see.

You can also try these other Pathfinder features:

■ Pathfinder highlights a few key stories on each page. You can read any of them by clicking on the story.

■ To view the available magazines and features for a particular category, click on that category's button on the page (News, Money, Business, Personalities, Entertainment, Health, Living, and Family). Figure 15.7 shows the selections for Living.

■ If you are looking for something in particular, click on the Search button. Then enter the word or phrase to search for, select what to search (Pathfinder or the entire Internet), what to look for (articles or Web sites), and choose the sort order. Then start the search.

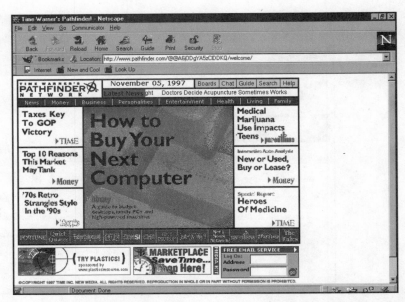

Figure 15.6   Pathfinder lets you access most of the Time Warner publications.

■ You can join bulletin-board discussion groups on several topics, including Black Culture, Games & Trivia, Celebrities, and more. Use the Bulletin Boards link to see what's available.

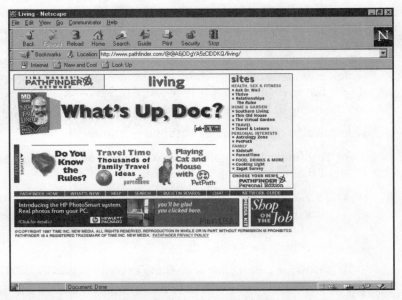

Figure 15.7   Select a category to see what sites are available.

- As an alternative to posting messages, you can chat live online with other users. Check out the Pathfinder café for chat information.

- To get help, use the Help button. You can also select Help and then select to view (and print) a site directory.

Other Magazines

Time Warner magazines aren't the only publications online. You can also find other magazines, such as *U.S. News & World Report* at **http://www.usnews.com**, *Smithsonian Magazine* at **http://www.smithsonianmag.si.edu**, *Wired* at **http://www.wired.com**, or *National Geographic* at **http://www.nationalgeographic.com**. Also try using Yahoo! (select News | Magazines) to view a list of online magazines.

A New Type Of Magazine

In addition to online versions of popular printed magazines, numerous *zines* are available, which are strictly online magazines without a printed counterpart. One of the newest zines is Slate. Figure 15.8 shows a recent cover. You can check out this latest publication of art, movies, and trendy articles at **http://www.slate.com**.

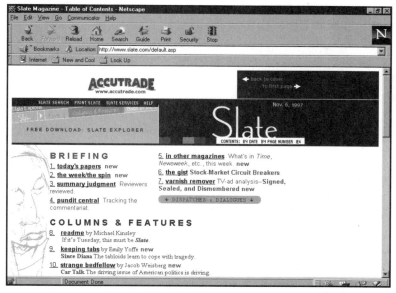

Figure 15.8 *Some of the newest magazines are created and published strictly for an online audience.*

Trying A News Service

As another alternative, you can get your news by subscribing to one of the many news services. You can use it to perform an extensive search through many, many sources. You pay a fee for the service, which varies depending on—among other factors—how often you use the service and the type of plan you select.

One of the most popular is Lexis-Nexis, which started out as a full-text legal-information service. Lexis-Nexis, according to its background page, contains more than 18,300 sources and references more than one billion documents online. You can get more information at **http://www.lexis-nexis.com**.

If you are a fan of the *Los Angeles Times* or the *Washington Post*, you may want to subscribe to their news services. You can get information on their different subscription plans at **http://www.newsservice.com**.

Prefer the *New York Times*? You can get information on its news service at **http://www.nytsyn.com**.

Weather News

If you like to know what the weather is going to be like, either in your city or a city across the globe, you can use the Web to get weather information. Try either of these weather sites:

- Weather at **http://www.intellicast.com**
- The Weather Channel at **http://www.weather.com**

News Newsgroups

Some newsgroups are actually devoted to news, rather than discussions. (For more information about newsgroups, refer to Chapter 13.) Try any of the following newsgroups (the asterisks indicate you can find many subcategories to select from):

- **clari.biz.*** (business news)
- **clari.local.*** (local news)
- **clari.news.*** (general news)
- **clari.sports.*** (sports news)

- **clari.usa.*** (U.S. news)
- **clari.world.*** (world news)

Moving On

This chapter highlighted some of the key places you can get news information on the Internet. Accessing news information is one of the primary reasons you may want to try the Internet: You can get the latest information quickly and conveniently. Another way to get information is to look it up. In Chapter 16, you will learn about some reference tools.

CHAPTER 16

Looking It Up

How would you like to have many of the resources you find at your library at your fingertips? Want to look up a word? A synonym? Need to know the area code for New York City? Or how about the ZIP code for an address in South Carolina? Want to see a map of Jamaica? Look up a fact about Ecuador? The Internet is a treasure trove of information resources. If you want to look up something, you can probably find it on the Internet. You don't even have to have a library card.

This chapter highlights some of the most popular information resources on the Internet. This list is not comprehensive; if you experiment, you can find many other resources on the Internet. This chapter will give you some good ideas of where to start looking.

Looking Up Facts

You may want to look up facts for many reasons. Perhaps you want to cheat at Jeopardy. Or perhaps you just like trivia. Maybe you have children and they have to write reports for school. In any case, you can use the Internet to research many different topics. You can access the first online encyclopedia or look up a country in the CIA's World Factbook. This section covers some of the best places to find reference tools.

Reference Sites At A Glance

AT&T Toll-Free Internet Directory at **http://www.tollfree.att.net**

Britannica Online at **http://www.eb.com**

Census Bureau at **http://www.census.gov**

CIA at **http://www.odci.gov/cia**

CityLink at **http://www.usacitylink.com**

Consumer Information Center at **http://www.pueblo.gsa.gov**

FBI at **http://www.fbi.gov**

FedWorld at **http://www.fedworld.gov**

Hoover's Online at **http://www.hoovers.com**

House of Representatives at **http://www.house.gov** and
  gopher://gopher.house.gov

IRS at **http://www.irs.ustreas.gov**

Library of Congress at **http://www.loc.gov**

Senate at **http://www.senate.gov** and **gopher://gopher.senate.gov**

White House at **http://www.whitehouse.gov**

Britannica Online

The first encyclopedia to be offered online was Britannica, which you can find out about at **http://www.eb.com**.

To use Britannica Online, you must subscribe to it. The rates vary, depending upon the plan you select. For an individual subscription, the rates were $85 in March 1998. At that time, Britannica Online was also offering a free trial subscription. The opening screen provides links that you can use to get the free trial, get subscription information, and subscribe (see Figure 16.1). You can also see a demo and search sample articles to see how Britannica Online works.

Once you subscribe, you can search Britannica and the Yearbook (which contains the primary databases) for any topics. The search results show the first 10 articles as well as the first paragraph of each encyclopedia entry. You can also look up topics in the index or use the *Merriam-Webster's Collegiate Dictionary* to look up words.

An online encyclopedia offers some obvious benefits over its printed counterpart:

- The information is updated regularly. You aren't stuck with a set of out-of-date bound encyclopedias.

- You can easily search through all the encyclopedias for a topic. This search capability helps you find information that might otherwise be overlooked.

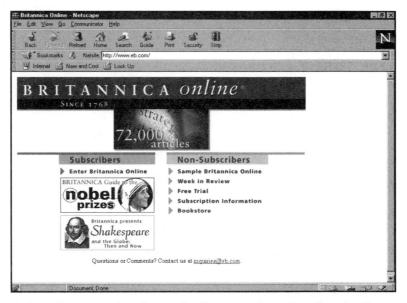

Figure 16.1   You can subscribe to the first encyclopedia offered online.

■ The entries include links to other related materials; click on these to quickly access other articles of interest.

Census Data

Another place to look up information is a government site, the Census Bureau. You can find information about the most recent census as well as economic statistics. The address for the Census Bureau is **http://www.census.gov**.

Figure 16.2 shows the home page for this government agency. The key areas of the Official Statistics page are:

■ *News*—Click on this button to read newsworthy items relating to the U.S. Census Bureau.

■ *Access Tools*—This button provides links to tools for working with census data, including the 1990 Census Lookup and a datamap.

■ *Subjects A-Z*—Use this button to look up a particular subject or topic.

■ *Search*—If you can't find the topic in the Subjects A-Z index, try using this button.

■ *CenStats CenStore*—This button provides information about products and subscriptions for sale.

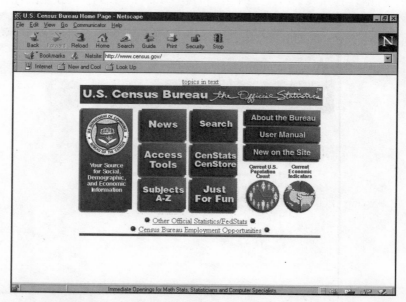

Figure 16.2   The U.S. Census Bureau is another place to look up statistical information.

- *Just For Fun*—This button contains interesting statistics.

- *About The Bureau*—This button provides information about the Census Bureau.

- *User Manual*—If you need help using the features of this Web site, try this button.

- *New On The Site*—This button lists new features added to the Web site.

- *Current U.S. Population Count icon*—Click on this icon if you want to see estimates of the current population. You can choose to see an estimate of the U.S. population or the world population. Figure 16.3 shows a recent estimate.

- *Current Economic Indicators icon*—Click on this icon to display economic indicators, such as housing starts and monthly retail sales.

The World Factbook

Another government agency, the CIA, publishes the World Factbook, which you can use to look up information about countries around the world. The address for the CIA is **http://www.odci.gov/cia**.

First, read the rules for this site (you can tell it's a *government* site) and click on the link to continue. From the home page, select Publications; from that page,

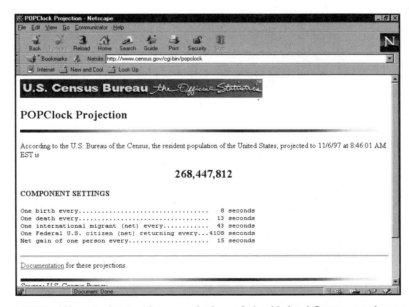

Figure 16.3   Want to know the population of the United States or the world? Try the population clock.

select the World Factbook. On the map of the different continents and regions, click on the area you want to look up. You see a list of countries; scroll through it or use the index to jump quickly to a country. Click on the country you are interested in.

When you select a country, you see a variety of information about that region. For instance, Figure 16.4 shows information about Bosnia and Herzegovina. Scroll through this page to find information about resources, climate, land use, religions, language, population, government, military, economy, transportation, and more. You can also click on the links for the graphic files to view a map or the flag.

Fast Facts From Infoseek

Infoseek, one of the search tools covered in Chapter 6, includes several reference features that you can use to look up a wealth of information. These include email addresses, stock quotes, bank and market rates, a company directory, street maps, phone numbers, words, rhyming words, synonyms using *Roget's Thesaurus*, historical documents, conversion tables, ZIP codes, and area codes. You can get to the page with links by going to **http://www.infoseek.com**.

Click on the Reference button and then select the link you want. Use People & Business to look up email, phone numbers, and toll-free numbers. Use Stocks & Companies to look up stock quotes and company information. Try Street

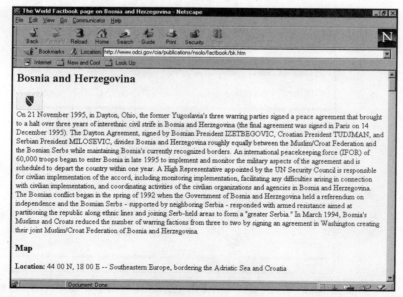

Figure 16.4   Use the CIA's World Factbook to look up information.

Maps for displaying maps and address information. Shareware & Chat lets you look up this type of information. And finally, you can use the Desk Reference, shown in Figure 16.5, to look up definitions or synonyms.

Looking Up People

When you want to get in contact with someone, you need to know his or her phone number or email address. You can use the Internet to look up both. Netscape Navigator conveniently provides a Look Up button that you can use to access some of the most popular people directories, including Bigfoot, Four11, InfoSpace, and WhoWhere? (see Figure 16.6). To display this page, click on the Look Up button and then select People.

Most of the directories for finding people work the same way. You enter the first and last name of the person you are trying to find. You can also limit the search to a particular city, state, or country. Click on the Search button to see the results of the search. For instance, Figure 16.7 shows the entry form for WhoWhere?.

When you use people-finding directories, keep the following tips in mind:

- If you can't find the person, try searching with wider parameters. For instance, if you entered the city, search again, but don't limit the search to one city.

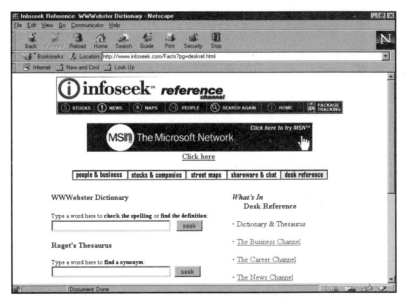

Figure 16.5 *You can look up reference information from the Reference page at Infoseek.*

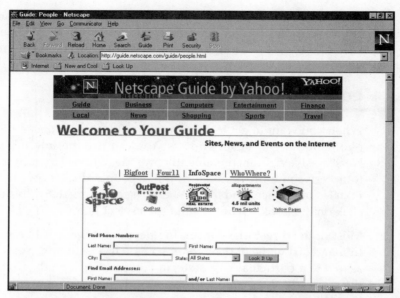

Figure 16.6 Click on the Look Up button in Navigator to access some of the search tools for locating people. (Text and artwork copyright 1998 by Netscape and YAHOO!, Inc. All rights reserved. YAHOO! and the YAHOO! logo are trademarks of YAHOO!, Inc.

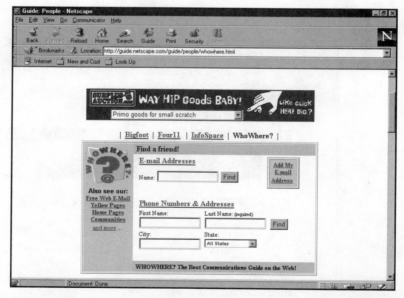

Figure 16.7 You can look up email addresses using one of several directories.

- Some of the search tools include special options for doing partial matches or for searching several cities at once. Look for a Help button or Hint link for information on using any search options.

- Most of the search tools enable you to look up either an email address or a phone number. From the search page, select what you want to look up.

- You can register your email address so it will be placed in the directory.

- Some of the search tools enable you to limit the search to a particular domain, such as America Online.

- If you can't find the person in one directory, try another one. The results may vary.

Looking Up Businesses

In addition to helping users look up people, the Internet also includes many features for locating businesses. You can look up a business in the Yellow Pages, look up toll-free numbers, see which companies do business on the Web, and do research on a company, as covered in this section.

Big Yellow

Need to know the address or phone number of a particular business? Want to see a listing of plumbers in your area? You can use Big Yellow to look up a business, just as you would use the printed version of the Yellow Pages. You can find links to Big Yellow on many pages, including several of the search pages, such as Infoseek. You can also go directly to the Big Yellow home page at **http://www.bigyellow.com**.

Figure 16.8 shows the steps you follow to complete a search. You can select a category (pizza, beauty parlor, exterminator, etc.) and/or enter a business name. You can select the city or state(s) to search. To search for multiple states, hold down the Ctrl key (Windows) or the Command key (Mac) and select the ones you want, up to five.

AT&T Toll-Free Internet Directory

If a business has a toll-free number, you can use the AT&T Toll-Free Internet Directory to look up the number. You can access the directory at **http://www.tollfree.att.net**.

Figure 16.9 shows the options for searching the directory. To search, fill in one of the fields (category, business name, city, state, or number). Figure 16.10 shows the results of a search for a particular company name.

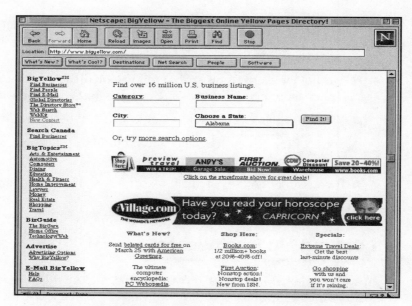

Figure 16.8   Use Big Yellow to search for a business.

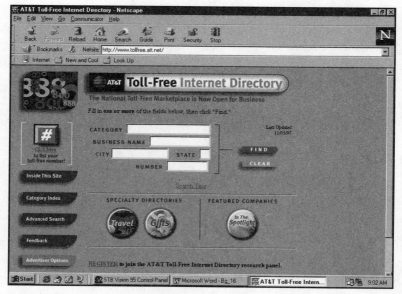

Figure 16.9   You can search for the toll-free number of a company.

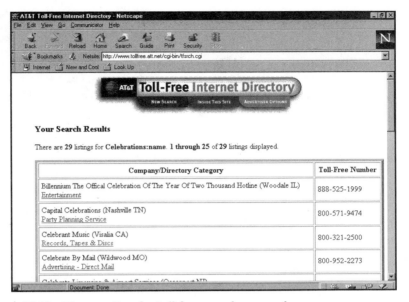

Figure 16.10   The results of a toll-free number search.

Hoover's Online Corporate Directory

Another place for corporate information, particularly financial information, is Hoover's Online. You can look up a company that you are considering doing business with. Or perhaps you are searching for a job and want to research a company. Maybe you just want to do a little digging to find out all there is to know about your competition.

Figure 16.11 shows the home page for this site, found at **http://www.hoovers.com**. You can review the latest news, do research, and look up company information. Some information is provided free. For instance, you can look up company capsules. Enter the company name, ticker symbol, or keyword and then click on the Find button. If you find more than one match, select the company you want. Then you can review pertinent company information. You can get access to more information and services by subscribing to Hoover's.

Looking Up Places

Thinking about taking a trip? Are you moving to another city? Perhaps you're just interested in geography. If any of the preceding ideas sound interesting, you will be thrilled with the many map features the Internet has to offer. This section covers some interesting map sites. Keep in mind that you can find many more sites for looking up map information.

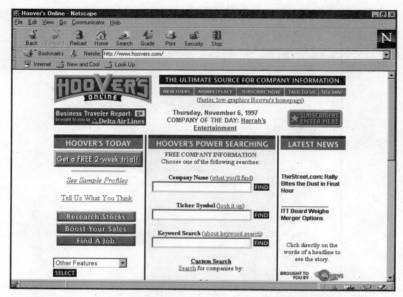

Figure 16.11   Look up company profiles using Hoover's Online Corporate Directory.

Search Sites

Many of the search sites include links to map and travel information. Both Infoseek and Excite have links called Maps. Go to the search site and then click on the appropriate map link. Figure 16.12 shows the available map links for Excite. As you can see, you can try some of the travel links, look up a map at City.Net, or look up popular U.S. and international maps. Click on the link you want.

CityLink

Another great source of information—beyond just maps—is CityLink. You can find information about educational facilities, shopping, homes for sale, government, history, and so on. The information varies because CityLink simply provides the link to a city's Web site. For example, your chamber of commerce may have created a Web site for your city, and it might be indexed on CityLink. To try CityLink, go to **http://www.usacitylink.com**.

Click on Visit A City and then use the links to find the city of interest. You see the information for that particular city. For instance, Figure 16.13 shows information for Clayton, Missouri.

Figure 16.12   Use Excite's Maps link to look up maps.

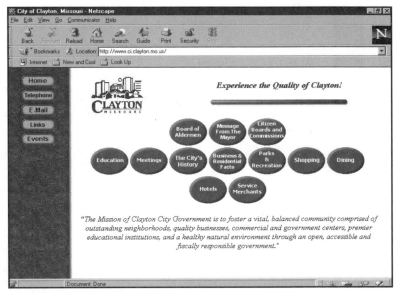

Figure 16.13   Look up city information using CityLink.

*To look up a place, driving directions, or shortcuts, try Mapquest at **http://www.mapquest.com**.*

Looking Up Government Information

The government also has several Web sites that you can use to look up information. Two sites, the CIA's and the U.S. Census Bureau's, were covered earlier in this chapter (see the sections titled "The World Factbook" and "Census Data"). In addition, you may want to try sites for the White House, the IRS, the FBI, FedWorld, the House of Representatives, the Senate, or the Consumer Information Center.

The White House

Want to take a tour of the White House? Send an email message to the president? Read about the first family's accomplishments? Peruse the latest press releases? Visit the Virtual Library stocked with White House documents, speeches, and photos? You can do all of these things by visiting the White House's Web site at **http://www.whitehouse.gov**.

Select the icon for the feature you want and then get all the latest presidential news from the White House.

The IRS

If you have a tax question or need a tax form, you can visit the IRS's Web site for information. The address is **http://www.irs.ustreas.gov**.

Figure 16.14 shows how to access a recent issue of the IRS's online magazine. You can get help, add your own comments, read articles about tax-related subjects, and order forms and publications.

The FBI

Want to keep up with the latest government investigations? Think you saw one of the 10 most-wanted fugitives and want to check out his or her picture? Want additional information about the FBI? You can get "wanted" information, read an FBI overview, learn about FBI investigations, check out FBI congressional and public affairs, and review crime statistics from the FBI's Web site. You can find links to all these features at **http://www.fbi.gov**.

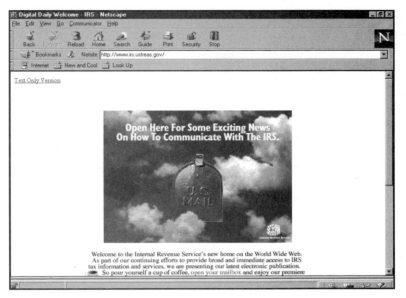

Figure 16.14   Visit the IRS's Web site for tax help.

FedWorld

Another great place to look for government information is FedWorld, at **http://www.fedworld.gov**.

You can go to the FTP site to access one of the more than 10,000 files with information about business, health and safety, and the environment. You can also search abstracts for information, check for jobs, or use the links to visit any of the other government-related sites.

The House Of Representatives And The Senate

You can also visit the Web sites of the House of Representatives and the Senate at **http://www.house.gov** and **http://www.senate.gov**.

Figure 16.15 shows the Web site for the Senate. You can look up current legislation activities, find a senator, read up on committees, and more. The House of Representatives' page is similar.

You can also try the Gopher sites for the House of Representatives and the Senate at **gopher://gopher.house.gov** and **gopher://gopher.senate.gov**.

From these sites, you can review frequently asked questions, look up members of the U.S. Senate, send email to senators, and review available documents.

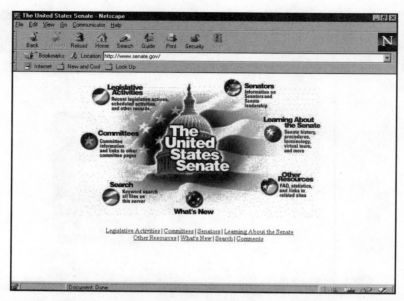

Figure 16.15   For information on the U.S. Senate, try this Web site.

The Consumer Information Center

The government publishes free information on a multitude of topics. To view the "full text versions of the best federal consumer publication available," visit the Consumer Information Center's Web site at **http://www.pueblo.gsa.gov**.

You can select a particular topic (Cars, Children, Employment, Money, Small Business, and more). You can also order a catalog, search for a particular topic, or view new catalogs using the buttons along the left-hand side of the page (see Figure 16.16).

The Library Of Congress

Another site with reference information is the Library of Congress. Here you can check out exhibitions, review articles, search the directory, read about library services, and more. The address for this government site is **http://www.loc.gov**.

Why Is The Sky Blue? And Other Questions

In addition to government sites, you can find other sites that answer questions on a variety of topics. You can look up science facts, find information on health questions, and do research. Here are some sites to try:

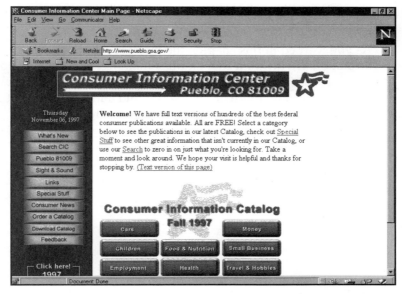

Figure 16.16   Get free publications from the Consumer Information Center.

- *Dr. Weil at **http://www.hotwired.com/drweil**—*At this site, which is part of Pathfinder (Time/Warner), you can ask the doctor a question.

- *Electric Library at **http://www.elibrary.com**—*Search magazines, newspapers, reports, and more. You have to be a subscriber, but you can get a free trial period.

- *Mayo Health Oasis at **http://www.mayo.ivi.com**—*Sponsored by the Mayo Clinic, this site has a newsstand with current articles, resources for looking up data, a place to ask questions, and more.

- *Research It at **http://www.itools.com/research-it/research-it.html**—*This is an awesome site with links to many different kinds of reference tools, including language tools (dictionary, thesaurus, translator), library tools (biographical information, quotations, biblical text), geographical tools, telephone listings, and more.

- *The Why Files at **http://whyfiles.news.wisc.edu**—*Described as "an electronic exploration of the science behind the news," this site is sponsored by the National Institute for Science Education.

Moving On

As you learned in this chapter, the Internet is a vast resource of reference information. If you want to look up something, you can probably do much of the research from the comfort of your own computer. This chapter showed you what kind of information you can find and how to look it up. Chapter 17 tells you how to get information on a specific topic: sports.

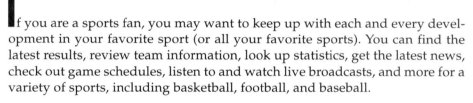

CHAPTER 17

Getting The Latest Sports News

If you are a sports fan, you may want to keep up with each and every development in your favorite sport (or all your favorite sports). You can find the latest results, review team information, look up statistics, get the latest news, check out game schedules, listen to and watch live broadcasts, and more for a variety of sports, including basketball, football, and baseball.

This chapter highlights some of the most popular places to find sports information. The major sports are covered first. Then I discuss how you can find information on other sports, like tennis, golf, and soccer. Keep in mind that even if you don't see your sport covered here, it still might have a Web site (maybe several Web sites) devoted to it; I'll discuss ways to find these sites. Finally, you can read about some places to get sporting news.

The Big Three: Basketball, Football, And Baseball

Are you plunked down in front of your TV most of the year, watching one of the three *big* sports: basketball, football, or baseball? Do you get over the excitement of the NBA finals just in time to gear up for the start of the NFL season? Do your eyes start to glaze over and your legs go numb as you watch the pre-game, game one, game two, late game, and post-game shows on Sundays during football season?

257

Sports Sites At A Glance

CNN Sports Illustrated at **http://www.cnnsi.com**

ESPN SportsZone at **http://www.espn.sportszone.com**

Fox Sports at **http://www.foxsports.com**

Major League Baseball at **http://www.majorleaguebaseball.com**

NBA at **http://www.nba.com**

NFL at **http://www.nfl.com**

NHL at **http://www.nhl.com**

Sporting News at **http://www.sportingnews.com**

USA Today Sports at **http://www.usatoday.com**

If you are a fan of major league sports, you can spend the time that you aren't watching games looking up information about them using the Internet. All three sports have official home pages where you can get a wealth of information.

The NBA

If you want information about the NBA, go to the official NBA site at **http://www.nba.com**, shown in Figure 17.1. You can expect to find the following on the NBA's home page:

- News stories about teams, games, players, and the NBA itself
- Sound clips, pictures, and video clips of games and players
- Draft information
- Game results and play-off results (during play-off time)
- TV schedule
- Game schedule
- Team and player information
- Links to scheduled chats with players as well as some email addresses
- NBA merchandise for sale

Figure 17.1   If you are a basketball fan, be sure to visit the home page for the NBA.

Click on any headline to review a story or select any of the categories along the left side of the page.

You can also visit the Women's National Basketball Association at **http://www.wnba.com**, shown in Figure 17.2. You can expect to find team, player, and game information.

The NFL

After the basketball playoffs wind down in June, you have just a few months before the football season cranks up. For all the latest information on the NFL, visit the NFL's official Web site at **http://www.nfl.com**.

This site is similar to the NBA site. You can find information about the schedule, free agents, NFL teams, locker-room chat, and news. (Unfortunately, the NFL won't let us show pictures of its Web site.) Here are a few of the things you can do from the NFL Web site:

- Click on a headlined story or player spotlight to read it.

- Look up information about your favorite team by clicking on the icon for the team you want. You can review draft picks, results, stats, news stories, and more.

- Click on the News button for columns and features, personnel reports, schedules, statistics, and NFL news.

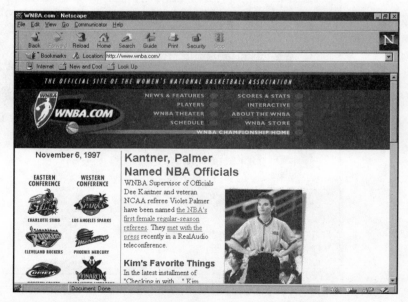

Figure 17.2 For information about the WNBA, visit its Web site.

- Use Statistics to look up stats in the record book.

- Click on Standings to view the current standings of your favorite NFL teams.

- Click on Multimedia to experience video, audio, and other graphic highlights.

- Look up players from an alphabetical list, by team, or by position from the Players page. Click on this button and then search for the player of your choice.

- Visit the NFL Store to check out available NFL books, sportswear, and other products from this page.

- Click on Play Football for polls, trivia, and questions.

- Check out the NFL schedule using the Go To Week buttons at the top of the page.

The NFL Web site also includes links to teams that have Web sites, such as the Miami Dolphins (**http://www.dolphinsendzone.com**). Figure 17.3 shows this home page.

Major League Baseball

If baseball is your favorite pastime, you can visit the official Major League Baseball site at **http://www.majorleaguebaseball.com**.

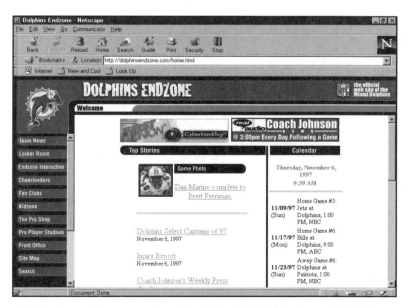

Figure 17.3   Some teams, such as the Miami Dolphins, have Web sites.

After reading the preceding sections, you can probably guess what type of information is included on this Web site, shown in Figure 17.4. You can read featured stories, look up teams, purchase MLB items at the Clubhouse, and more. For game results, click on the Scoreboard button. You see the box scores and stats for the most recent games.

Another cool feature is the Fan Forum. From here, you can go to links to many fan-related sites. For instance, click on History & Records to view the links for these topics. You can read franchise histories, review all-time leader statistics, and check out other key highlights of baseball history (see Figure 17.5).

For team information, including the roster, batting and pitching records, club schedule, playing information, franchise history, minor league affiliates, and recent game scores, look up your team of interest. Click on the American League button to look up American League teams or the National League button to look up National League teams. Then select the team you want. If the team also has a Web site, you can find a link to it on this page. For example, the Yankees have a home page.

For email addresses of the players or for information on ordering tickets, click on the Playing Info button on the team page. If email addresses or phone numbers for ordering tickets are available, you will find them here.

Figure 17.4   Baseball fans will enjoy the wealth of information available at the Major League Baseball site.

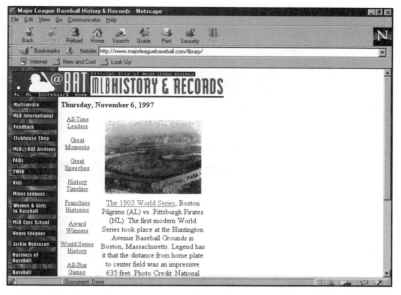

Figure 17.5   Look up history from the Fan Forum.

Other Sports

Sports beyond basketball, football, and baseball *do* exist. You can find pages relating to just about any sport you can think of—from skiing to hockey, from swimming to rugby. Most sports have at least one, if not several, sites devoted to them. The problem is that you can't always find one *official* page to start with. Instead, you have to do a little looking around.

This section highlights some strategies for finding other sports information and lists some sites for these sports.

Try Directories

To look for sports, use some of the directories that are available. For instance, you can click on the Internet button in Netscape Navigator and then select the Sports link. You see a list of some of the sports sites in the directory (see Figure 17.6). You can try the featured site(s), click on any headlined story, or select your sport of choice from the buttons at the top of the page. To go to any listed site, click on its link.

As an alternative, you can try the Nando Sports Server to find links to some sports servers for baseball, basketball, hockey, football, and the Olympics. The address for this site is **http://www.nando.net/SportsServer**.

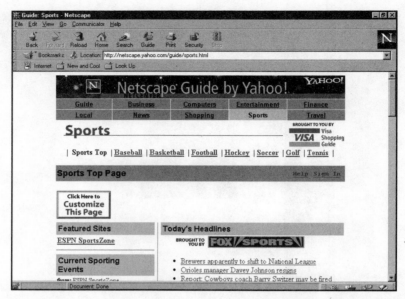

Figure 17.6 *Use Navigator's Sports link to find sports sites. (Text and artwork copyright 1998 by Netscape and YAHOO!, Inc. All rights reserved. YAHOO! and the YAHOO! logo are trademarks of YAHOO!, Inc.)*

Select the sports server you want and then use the links to find the listing of sites that interest you. For example, you can select the Hockey Server and then select National League Hockey to display a list of sites that cover the NHL (see Figure 17.7).

Try Searching

If your favorite sport isn't all that common, it may not be listed in the directories. But don't worry—chances are you can find a Web site for your sport. (This is true unless it's something *really* obscure like nude duckpin bowling. In that case, you'll have to set up your *own* Web page.)

Another way to find sites relating to your sport(s) of interest is to search. (Searching is covered in detail in Chapter 6.) Use any of the search tools you want. For example, Yahoo! lists all sports and then lets you select from the list. Follow these steps to try Yahoo! for browsing categories:

1. Click on the Search button. You see the available search tools.

2. Click on Yahoo! if it isn't already selected. You see the options for searching.

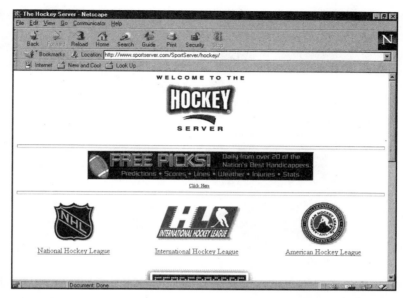

Figure 17.7 You can find an index of sports sites using the Nando Sports Server.

3. Select the Sports category. From here, you can choose to do one of the following:

   ■ Select from any of the sports links at the top of the page.

   ■ Read any of the headlined news stories.

   ■ Check out scores from recent sporting events.

   ■ View a list of Net events relating to sports.

   ■ View a list of links to other sports resources.

   ■ Search.

Figure 17.8 shows the top part of the Yahoo! sports list.

Try These Sites

Table 17.1 lists some popular sports as well as one or two representative addresses for each where you can find sports information. Keep in mind that this list is just a small representation of what's available. In most cases, only one address is included for each sport as a place to get started. Remember that you can use the preceding methods (using a directory or searching) to find additional sites.

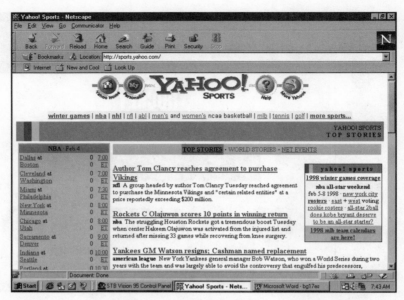

Figure 17.8 *Try searching for your sport of interest. (Text and artwork copyright 1998 by YAHOO!, Inc. All rights reserved. YAHOO! and the YAHOO! logo are trademarks of YAHOO!, Inc.)*

Table 17.1 **Some other sports sites to try.**

Sport	Site	Address
Bowling	Professional Bowling Association	http://www.pba.org
College Sports	NCAA Championships	http://www.ncaa.org
Cycling	The Global Cycling Network	http://www.cycling.org
Golf	PGA of America	http://www.pgaonline.com
	GolfWeb (Everything Golf on the World Wide Web)	http://www.golfweb.com
Gymnastics	USA Gymnastics Online	http://www.usa-gymnastics.org
Hockey	National Hockey League	http://www.nhl.com
Running	The Boston Marathon	http://www.bostonmarathon.org
Soccer	Major League Soccer	http://www.mlsnet.com
	SoccerNet	http://www.intl-soccernet.com
Swimming and Diving	United States Swimming, Inc.	http://www.usswim.org
Tennis	Men's ATP Tour	http://www.atptour.com
	Corel Women's Tour	http://www.corelwtatour.com
Volleyball	Volleyball WorldWide	http://www.volleyball.org

What you will find for each sport will vary, but you can expect to find sites for organizations, clubs, tournaments, and companies. You can find official and unofficial sites for all aspects of the sport, including rules, news stories, people of interest, governing organizations, travel information, products for sale, and just people getting together with a common interest.

Sporting News

Something is always happening in the world of sports—some game, some result, some tournament, someone getting signed or getting dropped. If you want to keep up with all the sports news, you can try some of the sports news sites on the Internet, which are covered next.

ESPN SportsZone

ESPN, probably the premier sports information network, has a Web site at **http://www.espn.sportszone.com**. You can review any of the headlined stories by clicking on them. Or select to view stories about baseball, the NBA, the NFL, soccer, tennis, or other sports using the buttons along the side of the ESPN SportsZone home page (see Figure 17.9). If you scroll further down the page, you see additional stories, plus links to Live Audio, ESPN Studios, Interact, ZoneGame, ZoneStore, Multimedia, and more.

Figure 17.9   For the latest sporting news, try ESPN SportsZone.

Fox Sports, NBC Sports, And Monday Night Football

Yet another source for news relating to sports is Fox Sports, which you can access at **http://www.foxsports.com**. As with other sports news pages, you can review headlined stories as well as opt to view scores and stats for baseball, hockey, football, and basketball (see Figure 17.10). You can also view team notebooks, post messages on bulletin boards, review past features, and get an inside look at Fox Sports TV programming.

Other television broadcasters have sports information as well. You can find NBC Sports information at **http://www.nbc.com/Sports**. And if you are a fan of Monday Night Football, visit the ABC site at **http://www.abcmnf.com**.

CNN Sports Illustrated

If you like *Sports Illustrated*, you'll enjoy the online version distributed in conjunction with CNN. The address for this premier sports site is **http://www.cnnsi.com**.

You can review articles and results, as well as participate in online events such as chats with sports celebrities. Figure 17.11 shows the home page. In addition to reading stories and checking the results of games, you can find links to events, features, and resources. You can also view pictures from the swimsuit issue. And if you have children, you can try *Sports Illustrated for Kids*.

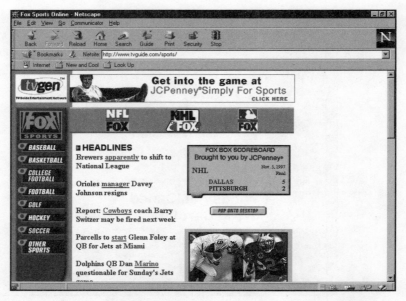

Figure 17.10   Try Fox Sports for reviewing sports stories and results.

Figure 17.11   CNN and Sports Illustrated *team up to give you this sports site.*

USA Today

Chapter 15 covers some of the main news-related features of the Internet. You can get sporting news from these sources as well. Most popular news sources have sections devoted to sports. For instance, you can access the sports pages for *USA Today* by going to **http://www.usatoday.com** and then selecting the sports page.

TIP

> *Another good site for sporting news is Sporting News at* **http://www. sportingnews.com**.

Moving On

If you are a sports fan, you'll find plenty of sports-related sites on the Internet to keep you up-to-date on the latest trades, results, news, and trends in your favorite sport. You can fill your head with trivia and look up just about anything.

Chapter 18 tells you how to use the Internet to get financial information as well as to do a little financial management. For money news, read on.

Researching Financial Information

As the saying goes, money makes the world go 'round. It should come as no surprise, then, that the World Wide Web includes many features that relate to money. You can read up on the latest financial news, look up stock quotes, do online investing, sign up for a bank account, read about credit reports, and more. This chapter focuses on some key sites for getting financial information.

Just remember that this chapter only mentions *some* of the most popular finance-related sites. The Internet is a gigantic place. In your own exploration, you can find other finance sites to help you handle your money.

Getting The Latest Financial News

Saving, investing, and spending money all require a certain knowledge of what's going on in the financial world. For instance, what a company is planning to do in the next year or so may help you decide whether or not to invest in it. The current state of the economy may help you decide where to put your savings. The more information you have, the more informed your decision will be. The Internet includes many places to find financial news, as covered in this section.

Financial Sites At A Glance

American Stock Exchange at http://www.amex.com

Bank of America at http://www.bankamerica.com

CNNfn at http://www.cnnfn.com

Equifax at http://www.equifax.com

Fortune at http://www.pathfinder.com

MasterCard at http://www.mastercard.com

Merrill Lynch at http://www.merrill-lynch.ml.com

Money at http://www.pathfinder.com

Nasdaq at http://www.nasdaq.com

Charles Schwab & Co. at http://www.schwab.com

Stock quotes at http://www.quote.com

Visa at http://www.visa.com

Wall Street Journal at http://www.wsj.com

CNNfn

CNN includes a separate financial network, CNNfn, which includes up-to-date financial information. You can visit the CNNfn Web site at **http://www.cnnfn.com**.

As you can see in Figure 18.1, you can review headlined stories or select any of the icons along the left edge of the screen to access news, market information, stories, and a resource center. Use this premier news service to find out all the latest in the financial world.

Wall Street Journal

The Bible of financial journalism is probably the *Wall Street Journal* (also mentioned in Chapter 15). You can subscribe to the interactive version by visiting **http://www.wsj.com**.

As of March 1998, subscription rates ran $29 if you had a print subscription to the *Wall Street Journal* and $49 if you did not. You can get information about subscribing on the home page (see Figure 18.2).

Like its print counterpart, the Interactive Edition includes stories and detailed background information about businesses around the world.

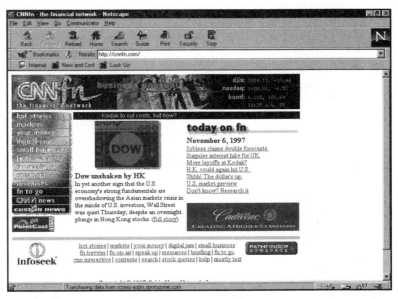

Figure 18.1   One source of financial news is CNNfn.

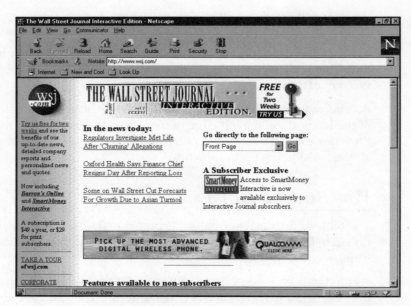

Figure 18.2   Subscribe to the Interactive Edition of the Wall Street Journal.

Money Magazine

Another source of not just financial news, but also tools for managing your finances, is the online version of *Money* magazine, which you can view at **http://www.pathfinder.com**. From this page, select *Money* to see the opening page of the publication (see Figure 18.3). You can read any of the headline stories, get reports, and check out some of the Money.com resources, including market information and hyperquotes for looking up stock quotes.

Money.com also includes links to several useful tools. Use Goals to get information on college, retirement, and other investment choices. Figure 18.4 shows some of the available tools for reaching your financial goals. Try Tools to access interactive tools for planning your financial future.

Click on the Brokerage & Financial Service Center or the Mutual Fund Center to view links to companies providing financial services. You can find links to Strong Funds Online Investor Center, Vanguard Financial Services, Merrill Lynch, and Charles Schwab.

Fortune Magazine

In addition to *Money*, you can view an online version of *Fortune* magazine from Pathfinder. Again, go to the Pathfinder site at **http://www.pathfinder.com**. Then select *Fortune*. Figure 18.5 shows the opening page for a recent issue of

Figure 18.3   You can access an online version of Money *magazine from Pathfinder.*

Fortune Online. In addition to reading stories, you can select any of the following categories: Fortune Business Rpt., Features, Columnists, Smart Managing, Small Business, Personal Fortune, Books, Fortune 500, and more. You

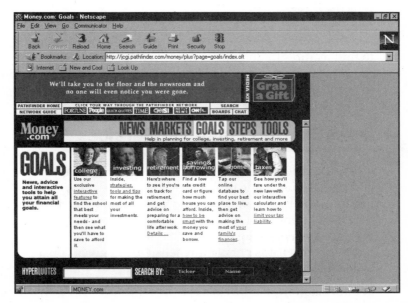

Figure 18.4   Try any of these features for help on reaching your financial goals.

Figure 18.5   Get business information from Fortune *magazine.*

can also search the archives for information from a past issue. To look up the Global 500 or the Investor's Guide, select the Special Issues/Lists link and then select the issue you want to review.

Kiplinger

Another premier source of financial information is Kiplinger. At this site, expect to find features for looking up stock quotes, calculators, advice, links to other financial sites, information about services provided by Kiplinger, and other financial information. The address for Kiplinger is **http://www.kiplinger.com**.

Investigating Financial Services

You can do more than just get financial information; you can also read about and perhaps use some of the financial services provided on the Internet. For instance, you may want to sign up for home banking from Bank of America or read about some of the financial programs provided by Visa. This section previews just a few of the financial services you'll find on the Internet. Keep in mind that this list is not comprehensive, but gives you a good idea of what's available.

For information on a special type of financial service—investing—see the section "Investing Online" later in this chapter.

Banking

Bank of America offers a slew of financial services, which you can read about and sign up for from its Web site at **http://www.bankamerica.com**.

Figure 18.6 shows the opening page. The services provided by this bank are all-encompassing. You can:

- Sign up for a home banking account.
- Get a new credit card.
- Get savings and investment information.
- Do online banking for your business.
- Look into business financing.
- Read about cash management, trade, and other corporate features.
- Review commercial real estate services.
- Get information about Bank of America, the community, and the current U.S. economy.

Simply click on the link and then review the information. To sign up for an account, just follow the on-screen directions.

Figure 18.6   For financial services, try Bank of America.

Credit Cards

If you want information about your Visa card, you can get it at the Visa Web site at **http://www.visa.com**.

The home page, shown in Figure 18.7, includes links that you can use to get additional information about Visa products and services. You can check out which events Visa sponsors, take advantage of offers and promotions, review consumer tips, look up ATM locations, request a Visa card, and more.

While most of the site is a pitch for one Visa product or another, you can try the Consumer Tips link to get information about understanding your credit card statement and better managing your credit. The New Technologies link discusses some trends in the financial world that will give you a sense of how the Internet is changing the way money is handled.

If you have a MasterCard or want information about one, try **http://www.mastercard.com**.

Credit Reports

If you have ever applied for or been denied a loan, you may wonder exactly what your credit report contains and what you can do to fix any problems.

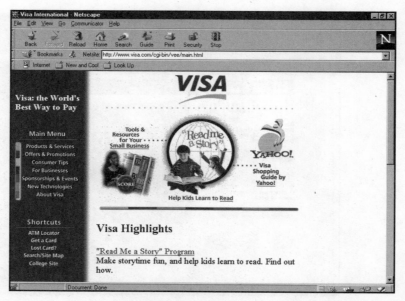

Figure 18.7 *Visit Visa's Web site for all that you want to know about Visa services. (YAHOO! and the YAHOO! logo are trademarks of YAHOO!, Inc.)*

You can get information about one of the main credit report companies, Equifax, from its Web site at **http://www.equifax.com**.

Equifax provides information and financial reporting on subjects other than just consumer credit. To get to the consumer information, select Consumer Center. You can read a description of a profile, view a list of Frequently Asked Questions, order your credit profile, and more (see Figure 18.8).

Investing Online

If you are interested in doing some investing, you can visit several sites devoted to this topic. Some sites, such as Schwab Online, let you set up an account and invest online. Other sites give you information about investing. And finally, you can look up stock quotes in numerous places. This section previews some of the key sites for online investing.

Charles Schwab

Charles Schwab has a Web site where, in addition to being able to get information, you can do online investing. If you are a current customer, you simply have to call for a password. New customers can request an application. And

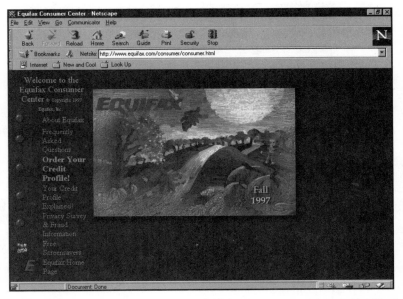

Figure 18.8 *If you have questions about your credit report, use Equifax's Web site to get answers.*

you can also try a demo if you want to see how Web trading works. You can get access to these features from Schwab Online at **http://www.schwab.com**.

Online investing offers some benefits. First, you can handle your trades at any time, 24 hours a day. Second, you can get lots of information. Third, Schwab Online (at least as of February 1998) offers a 20 percent discount for Web trading. And if you are worried about security, rest assured. Schwab is backed by the latest Internet security systems. Figure 18.9 shows the opening page of Schwab Online.

Merrill Lynch

Merrill Lynch also offers online trading. You can access its site at **http://www.merrill-lynch.ml.com**. Here you can learn about setting up an account. You can also get information on investing from the Investor Learning Center. To read up on preparing for the future (paying for college education, for instance), take a look at the Personal Finance Center. For business planning, visit the Business Planning Center. For information about Merrill Lynch services, check out the News & Research Center.

Nasdaq

If you are interested in Nasdaq stocks, visit **http://www.nasdaq.com**. Figure 18.10 shows its home page. You can look up a company's symbol, see a list of

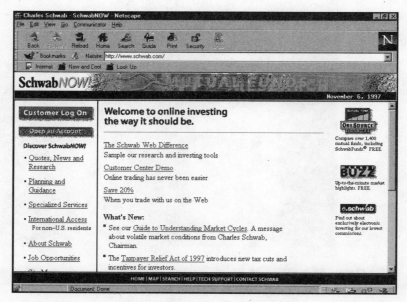

Figure 18.9   Try online trading with Schwab Online.

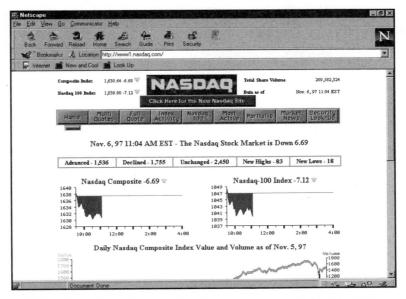

Figure 18.10   Get information on Nasdaq stocks from its home page.

the Nasdaq 100, see a full quote or multiquotes, view charts of the composite index value and volume, and contact Nasdaq, all from its site.

TIP

You can also visit the American Stock Exchange at http://www.amex.com.

Quote.com

You can find stock quotes in lots of places. You may remember from Chapter 6 that some of the search tools include icons for looking up stock information. And you may recall from Chapter 15 that some of the news sources also include stock quote lookups. Yet another site for looking up quotes is Quote.com at **http://www.quote.com**.

From this site, shown in Figure 18.11, you can get quotes on stocks, options, commodity futures, mutual funds, and bonds. You can also review finance-related stories from several news sources, including Standard & Poor's. The site also enables you to display daily and weekly charts and do research.

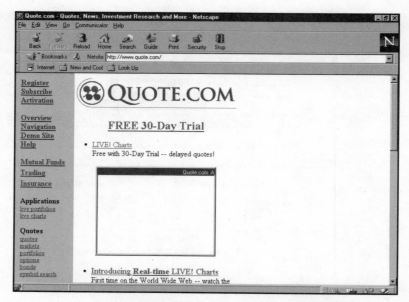

Figure 18.11 Look up quotes, charts, and news at this financial site.

Joining Some Finance Newsgroups

Web sites aren't the only source of information on the Internet. You can also share your financial wisdom with others and hear what advice they have to give. You can subscribe to one of several finance newsgroups:

- **alt.invest.penny-stocks**
- **misc.invest.*** (the asterisk indicates you can find many subcategories)
- **misc.taxes**

For complete information on subscribing to newsgroups, turn to Chapter 13.

Moving On

This chapter showed you some of the places you can read up on money on the Internet. Making good financial decisions requires lots of information, and the more information the better. You can find lots of sources on the Internet.

Chapter 19 is devoted to the topic of entertainment, which explains where you can find all the latest on books, movies, music, and TV on the Internet.

That's Entertainment

You can't spend *all* your free time playing around on the Internet. You may want to take a break and try some other form of entertainment. Go watch a movie. Read a book. See what's on TV. Listen to some music. To prepare yourself for other ways to spend your free time, you can use the Internet to look up all the entertainment information you need. Check out the latest TV schedules or see what shows are planned for the next fall lineup. Read movie reviews or get information about your favorite band or movie star. You can also purchase tickets for movies and shows using the Internet.

This chapter showcases some of the best places to get the latest gossip on the entertainment front. With all the available resources, you probably can host your own entertainment show!

Entertainment News

It seems as if most Americans are so enamored with movie stars and celebrities that they want to know each and every detail of their lives. What does Demi Moore like to eat for breakfast? Who's the best golfer out of all the band members of Hootie and the Blowfish? What scares Stephen King?

If you like to read about movies, TV, books, music, theater, and other entertainment topics, you can sample the several entertainment news spots on the Internet. This section previews three: Entertainment Weekly Online, People Online, and Mr. Showbiz.

Entertainment Sites At A Glance

ABC at http://www.abc.com

Atlantic Records at http://www.atlantic-records.com

Billboard Online at http://www.billboard-online.com

BookWire at http://www.bookwire.com

CBS at http://www.cbs.com

Disney at http://www.disney.com

Entertainment Weekly Online at http://www.pathfinder.com

FOX at http://www.fox.com

HBO at http://www.hbo.com

Hollywood Online at http://www.hollywood.com

MTV at http://www.mtv.com

NBC at http://www.nbc.com

Paramount Pictures at http://www.paramount.com

People Online at http://www.pathfinder.com

Rock and Roll Hall of Fame at http://www.rockhall.com

Sony Music at http://www.sonymusic.com

TV listings at http://ultimatetv.com

Warner Bros. at http://www.warnerbros.com

Entertainment Weekly Online

If you have read some of the other chapters in Part III of this book, you are probably familiar with Pathfinder, a collection of Time/Warner publications and features. Time/Warner publishes *Entertainment Weekly*, which is available in an online version. You can access the online magazine from Pathfinder at **http://www.pathfinder.com**.

From the Pathfinder home page, select Entertainment Weekly Online. Figure 19.1 shows a November 1997 issue. As with other online publications, you can read any of the headlined stories and featured columns. In Entertainment Weekly Online, you can also read reviews and search the archives for past stories.

People Online

Another publication that is always full of celebrity news is *People* magazine. You can access the online version from Pathfinder at **http://www.pathfinder.com**.

Select People Online. Figure 19.2 shows a November 1997 issue. As with Entertainment Weekly Online, you can read stories and featured articles. You can also check out pictures and videos in the Photos & Galleries page, read reviews on the Picks & Pans page, get the latest gossip from Celebrity Central, check out your horoscope, see what star has a birthday this week, and more. To send your own thoughts and opinions (like a letter to the editor), use the Write link.

Figure 19.1 Read up on the latest entertainment news in Entertainment Weekly Online.

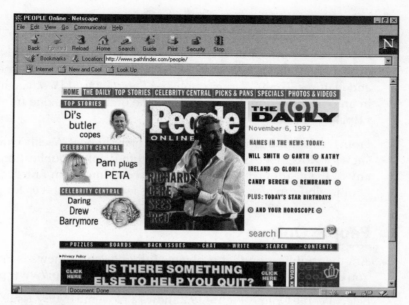

Figure 19.2   If you like People *magazine, you'll love the online version.*

Mr. Showbiz

Another source of entertainment news is Mr. Showbiz, which you can visit at **http://www.mrshowbiz.com**.

You can read the headlined news stories and reviews, as well as in-depth feature articles and interviews. Mr. Showbiz also has some fun features, such as Water Cooler Polls. Click on Games and then try Plastic Surgery Lab, where you can create a face using features from different stars. Figure 19.3 shows a remake of Nicolas Cage. Can you figure out which part goes to which star?

Movie News

Going to a movie can be expensive. Before you lay out your money, you may want to read reviews of the latest movies and hear what the critics have to say. Most movie sites offer more than a review. You can also play sound and video clips and read about the stars. This section covers some of the best places to find out all you need to know about recent movie releases.

Hollywood Online

One place to visit for all movies (not just those from a particular studio) is Hollywood Online. You can visit this site at **http://www.hollywood.com**.

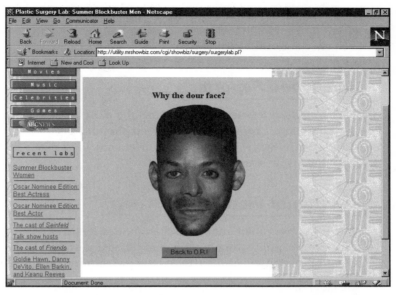

Figure 19.3   Mr. Showbiz has some fun features, such as Plastic Surgery Lab.

Figure 19.4 shows the home page for Hollywood Online. As you can see, you can access information on movies, videos, and TV movies. Look up the movie you want and see the genre, rating, synopsis, cast, notes, photos, reviews, trail-

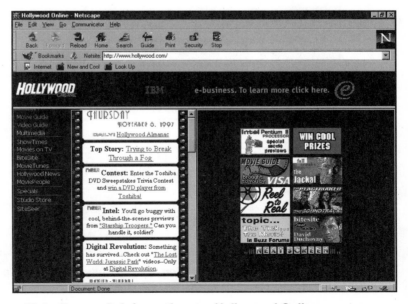

Figure 19.4   For movie information, try Hollywood Online.

ers, video clips, and related Web sites. You can also find information about movie tunes, Hollywood news, and movie people. For movie-related products, check out the Studio Store.

Hollywood Reporter

Hollywood Reporter describes itself as "the daily trade paper for the entertainment industry." You can visit its Web site and get loads of inside-industry scoop at **http://www.hollywoodreporter.com**. Figure 19.5 shows a recent page from this inside source.

Paramount Pictures

One of the big movie makers is Paramount Pictures. (This studio also owns theme parks, publishing houses, and television shows.) You can check out its recent releases by visiting **http://www.paramount.com**.

You can read up on the latest motion pictures, check out home video titles, or see what's planned for Paramount TV shows (see Figure 19.6). When you select Motion Pictures, you can jump to any of the sites set up for recent movie releases.

Figure 19.5 For insider information, try the **Hollywood Reporter.**

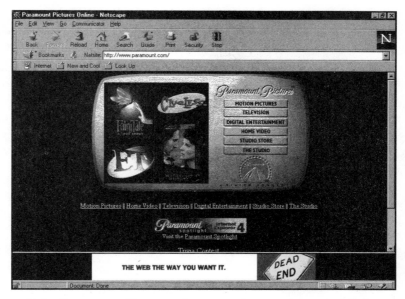

Figure 19.6   Paramount Pictures showcases its recent movie releases.

Disney

If you have children, you are probably intimately familiar with every Disney movie. For all things Disney, visit the Disney site at **http://www.disney.com**, shown in Figure 19.7.

You can read about recent movie releases. You can also check out Disney home videos, order software, see what's on the Disney TV channel, or make plans to visit Disneyland. Want some *101 Dalmatians* pajamas? Visit the Disney Store. You can find just about everything you could possibly ever want relating to Disney at this Web site.

Warner Bros.

Another popular movie maker—both for children and adults—is Warner Bros. And like most media companies, Warner Bros. operates as more than just a movie studio. In addition to movies, Warner Bros. has TV shows, videos, music companies, DC comics, and of course, stores selling products relating to its movies, TV shows, music labels, and comics. To visit Warner Bros., go to **http://warnerbros.com**.

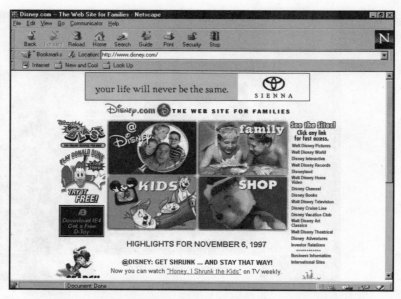

Figure 19.7   The Disney Web site provides access to all the Disney products, including movie information.

Figure 19.8 shows Warner Bros.'s home page, where you can choose which of the many Warner Bros. venues you want to explore. Select the area you want and then get all the latest information on the studio's movies, shows, and music.

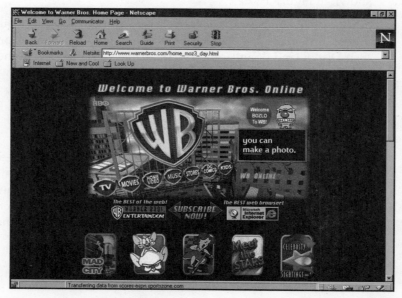

Figure 19.8   Warner Bros. makes movies as well as TV shows and comic books.

One cool thing you can do from the Warner Bros. Web site is send someone a WeB card. You have to know that person's email address. Then you select the card, write your message, enter the recipient's address and name, and enter your address and name. The card is sent as an email message. Figure 19.9 shows the current selection of birthday cards.

Music News

If you don't have time to go to the movies, you may just want to relax at home and listen to your favorite music. You can get the latest music news, such as CD releases, concert dates, and reviews, from the many music sites on the Web. This section previews just a few. Keep in mind that a lot of other music Web sites exist—you just need to look around. You can also purchase CDs on the Web. For information on shopping, see Chapter 14.

MTV

Is MTV music or TV? It used to be music, but with the addition of actual shows such as *Singled Out*, it may be more TV. Doesn't matter. It's included here in the music section. You can get information about music and TV from the site at **http://www.mtv.com**.

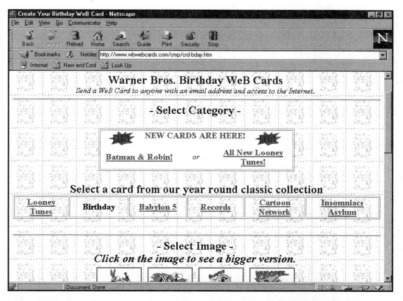

Figure 19.9   Send one of your friends a WeB card from Warner Bros.

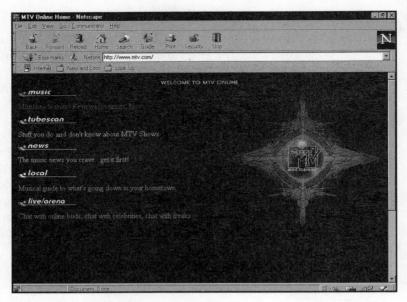

Figure 19.10   For music news, visit MTV.

You can listen to the latest music, read the headlines, check out information about the TV shows, and participate in chats (see Figure 19.10). If you are a fan of MTV, this is the place to be.

Record Companies

Many of the major record companies have Web pages, which you can visit for information about their artists. For instance, you can get information about Sony artists and bands from Sony Music Online, shown in Figure 19.11. The address for this site is **http://www.sonymusic.com**.

This site is representative of what you can expect from record companies' sites. Here's a breakdown of what you can do:

- Check out the featured artists, new albums, and links to other Web pages.

- Read up on the latest music industry news, concert dates, and video production. The Sony page for this information is called Wiretap.

- Find out when a band or artist has a new release and hear a sound clip.

- Look up an artist. From the Sony site, you can look through an alphabetical list of artists or look up artists by genre.

- Visit the Vault for catalog information. (You cannot order items from this page, but you can visit the Sony store using the link on this page.)

Figure 19.11   Check out Sony artists and bands from Sony Music Online.

- Check out sound and video clips from recent releases.

- Get tour information.

- Visit other links relating to music.

- Learn more about Sony Music. You can also find contact information using the About Us link.

Sony isn't the only record label that has a Web site. You can find similar sites for the other major record labels. Here's a list of just a few of the other labels with Web sites:

- Atlantic Records at **http://www.atlantic-records.com**

- Elektra Records at **http://www.elektra.com**

- Geffen Records at **http://www.geffen.com**

- Mammoth Records at **http://www.mammoth.com**

- Reprise Records at **http://www.repriserec.com**

- Warner Bros. at **http://www.warnerbros.com**

Rock And Roll Hall Of Fame

If you are into the history of music—in particular, rock and roll—then you'll enjoy a visit to the Rock and Roll Hall of Fame's Web site. You can visit this

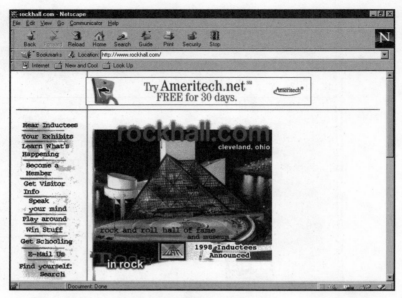

Figure 19.12   Visit the Rock and Roll Hall of Fame.

site without even stepping foot in Cleveland. Just go to **http://www.rockhall.com** (see Figure 19.12).

From the Rock and Roll Hall of Fame Web site, you can hear the music of inductees, tour exhibits, get visitor information, win merchandise, and more.

Billboard Online

For other music information, check out Billboard Online. You can get a daily music update, view the Billboard 200, check out features and sneak previews, and ask Billboard questions. Go to **http://www.billboard-online.com**.

Your Favorite Group

If you are a follower of a particular group, you can search to see whether that group has its own Web page. Many recording stars have sites with concert, record, and band information. You can also order official products. For instance, the Rolling Stones have a site at **http://www.stones.com**. You can select discography, chronology, biography, or photography. And you can visit the home page of Hootie and the Blowfish at **http://www.hootie.com** (see Figure 19.13). Find such sites by searching for them using the tools discussed in Chapter 6 or by looking for links at record-label sites.

Figure 19.13   Your favorite band may have its own Web site.

TV News

If you are a couch potato, you might enjoy sitting in front of the TV and flipping the remote. Before you get comfortable, though, look up all the TV news from the Internet sites. You can find TV listings as well as information about current shows, stars, new shows, and special events, such as chats. This section explains where to find all the TV information you need to make channel surfing as fun as Web surfing.

TV Listings

If you want to know what's on TV, don't turn to your local paper. Instead, look it up on Ultimate TV. You can access this site at **http://www.ultimatetv.com**.

In addition to finding out what's on TV, you can check out reviews, participate in scheduled chats, find job listings, take part in TV polls, and more (see Figure 19.14). You can use the Ultimate TV Show List to see links to other TV pages. For instance, you may find a link to your favorite TV show. (You can also try searching for your show or looking for a link on its TV station's page, covered next.)

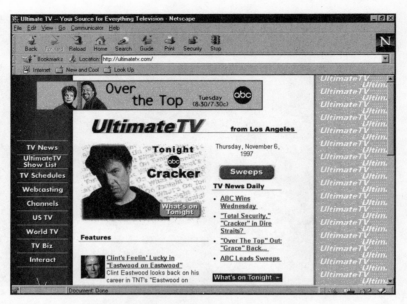

Figure 19.14   Use Ultimate TV to find out what's on TV.

TV Stations

The four major TV networks have Web sites at the following addresses:

- ABC at **http://www.abc.com**
- CBS at **http://www.cbs.com**
- FOX at **http://www.fox.com**
- NBC at **http://www.nbc.com**

Use these pages to get all the latest on the current shows, read featured articles about stars, check out listings for that network, see what that network has planned for new shows, and order products.

On these pages, you can also find links to pages for your favorite TV shows. For example, I like to look up Top Ten Lists from my favorite show, *Late Show with David Letterman* (see Figure 19.15). You can find a link to this popular show from the CBS page.

Some cable channels also have Web sites. For instance, the address for HBO's Web site is **http://www.hbo.com**.

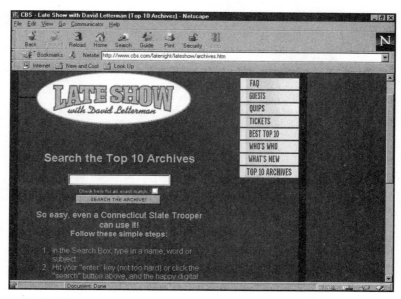

Figure 19.15   Find information about your favorite TV show(s).

Book Information

The final form of entertainment covered in this chapter is reading. If you like to read, you can visit BookWire at **http://www.bookwire.com** (see Figure 19.16). This site dubs itself as "The First Place to Look for Book Information on the World Wide Web."

While visiting this book lover's paradise, you can read reviews, review articles from *Publisher's Weekly*, learn more about the publishing industry, search for a book or author, and check out the index of over 900+ publishers and 500+ booksellers. Many publishers also have Web pages, which you can look up by clicking on the Publishers link under the BookWire Index heading. The following list of publisher types appears: General (Trade), Associations, Business, Children's, Computer, Multimedia, Mystery, Non-English, Online, Professional and Educational, Reference, Religious, Science Fiction, Sidelines, Specialty, Travel, and University. Once you select a publisher type, you see a list of all the sites within each category. For example, Figure 19.17 shows a list of some of the trade publishers with Web sites.

For book ordering, check out amazon.com at **http://www.amazon.com**. This site is covered in Chapter 14.

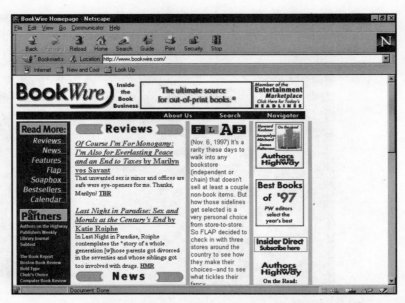

Figure 19.16   For links to most book-related sites, start at the BookWire site.

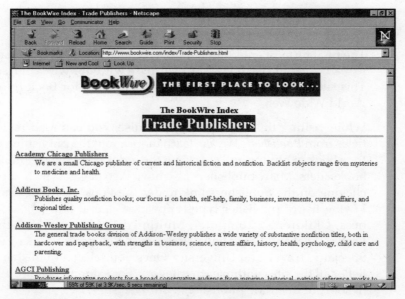

Figure 19.17   Look up publishers in the BookWire Index.

Entertainment Newsgroups

Most of the sites described so far have been places to obtain information, with not much opportunity for your input. If you want to participate—and share your own ideas—you can subscribe to any of the many newsgroups devoted to entertainment, including:

- **alt.books**
- **alt.fan.*** (the asterisk indicates you can find many subcategories)
- **alt.movies**
- **alt.rock-n-roll**
- **alt.tv**

For more information on newsgroups, see Chapter 13.

Moving On

One of the main reasons you use the Internet is to entertain yourself. And you can use it to find information about *other* ways to keep entertained. That is, you can use the Internet to find out all you need to know about movies, music, TV, and books.

Chapter 20 discusses another form of entertainment—computer games—as well as other computer-related topics, such as finding information about software and hardware on the Internet.

CHAPTER 20

Getting Computer Information And Help

It should come as no surprise to you that the Internet offers many computer resources; after all, more people are doing more things on computers these days. You can find a wealth of computer-related information on hardware, software, computer news, and products. For instance, if you are thinking of purchasing a new PC, you can visit sites like IBM and Gateway 2000 to look up specs and pricing information. If you're considering a Macintosh product, check out the Apple and Power Computing sites. You can even purchase hardware and software over the Internet. You can also get technical support. If you are having a problem with your word processing program, you can look up Frequently Asked Questions or send messages to a tech support representative.

This chapter covers hardware, software, and computer-related news. Each section describes what you can expect to find at a typical hardware or software site and then provides some specific addresses for different sites.

Computer Hardware

If you are thinking about buying a new computer or if you are having problems with your existing machine, you may want to visit the manufacturer's Web site for information and troubleshooting advice. Most of the major computer manufacturers—including Dell, Gateway 2000, Compaq, and others— have Web sites. Apple is one of the online Mac Product manufacturers. You can also visit sites for peripheral equipment. For instance, visit Iomega for

Computer Sites At A Glance

3Com at **http://www.3com.com**

Adobe at **http://www.adobe.com**

Apple Computer at **http://www.apple.com**

AST Research at **http://www.ast.com**

Berkeley Systems at **http://www.berksys.com**

Claris at **http://www.claris.com**

Compaq at **http://www.compaq.com**

Corel at **http://www.corel.com**

The Coriolis Group at **http://www.coriolis.com**

Creative Labs at **http://www.creativelabs.com**

Dell Computer at **http://www.dell.com**

Diamond Multimedia at **http://www.diamondmm.com**

Epson at **http://www.epson.com**

Gateway 2000 at **http://www.gw2k.com**

Hewlett-Packard at **http://www.hp.com**

IBM PC Direct at **http://www.pc.ibm.com/ibmhome**

Intel at **http://www.intel.com**

Iomega at **http://www.iomega.com**

La Cie Limited at **http://www.lacie.com**

Logitech at **http://www.logitech.com**

Lotus at **http://www.lotus.com**

Macromedia at **http://www.macromedia.com**

Micron at **http://www.micron.com**

Microsoft at **http://www.microsoft.com**

Power Computing at **http://www.powercc.com**

Seagate Technologies at **http://www.seagate.com**

UMAX at **http://www.umax.com**

Ziff-Davis Publications at **http://www.zdnet.com**

information on high-capacity storage, or Hewlett-Packard for information about printers. This section covers sites for computer systems as well as other hardware.

Computer Systems

You can get a wealth of information about computer systems from computer manufacturers' sites on the Internet. Here's what you can do at this type of site:

- Visit the computer showroom and see what kind of products they offer. For example, Figure 20.1 shows the home page for Gateway 2000. Use the drop-down list to select the type of product you have or are interested in.

- Review articles on hardware and software topics.

- Get product information, including specs and pricing information. You can even order a computer online from some of the sites. Figure 20.2 shows a price list for a particular line of Gateway 2000 computers.

- Research the company. Take a look at the annual report, review any awards the company has received, get employment information, and check out the press releases that describe new products.

- Visit the help desk or technical support center for online technical support. Most tech support sites include a list of common problems and

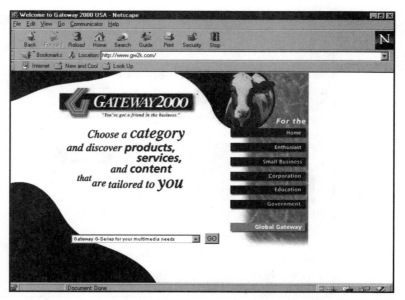

Figure 20.1   Visit computer showrooms for product information on PCs.

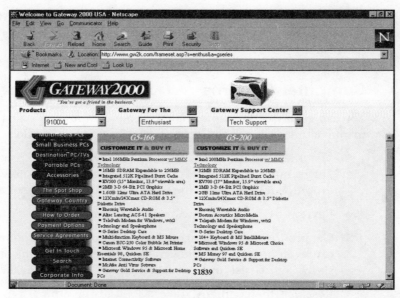

Figure 20.2   You can review specs and pricing on the different models offered.

solutions that you can review. You may also be able to send email messages to a tech support representative and download software (see Figure 20.3).

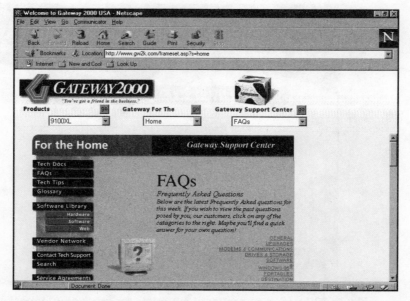

Figure 20.3   Visit the technical support center for online technical support.

Most computer manufacturers' sites include the features just listed. Here's a list of some of the most popular sites:

- Apple at **http://www.apple.com**
- AST Research at **http://www.ast.com**
- Compaq at **http://www.compaq.com**
- Dell Computer at **http://www.dell.com**
- Gateway 2000 at **http://www.gw2k.com**
- Hewlett-Packard at **http://www.hp.com**
- IBM PC Direct at **http://www.pc.ibm.com/ibmhome**
- Micron at **http://www.micron.com**
- Power Computing at **http://www.powercc.com**
- UMAX at **http://www.umax.com**

Other Equipment

Computer manufacturers aren't the only computer companies on the Internet. You can also find sites for companies that sell printers, microprocessors, mice, hard drives, removable cartridge drives, and other add-on components. At these sites, you can expect to find similar features: product information and technical support. Table 20.1 lists some add-on companies.

Table 20.1   Sites for add-on products.

Company	Address	Product(s)
3Com	**http://www.3com.com**	Modems, networking
Creative Labs	**http://www.creativelabs.com**	Multimedia equipment
Diamond Multimedia	**http://www.diamondmm.com**	Multimedia equipment
Epson	**http://www.epson.com**	Printers
Hewlett-Packard	**http://www.hp.com**	Printers
Intel	**http://www.intel.com**	Microprocessors
Iomega	**http://www.iomega.com**	Zip drives
Logitech	**http://www.logitech.com**	Mice
NEC	**http://www.nec.com**	Monitors
Quantum Corporation	**http://www.quantum.com**	Hard drives
Seagate Technologies	**http://www.seagate.com**	Hard drives

Figure 20.4   You can find add-on product information on the Internet.

Most of the companies offer more than one product; the last column in the table lists just one of the products the company is known for. Figure 20.4 shows the home page for Iomega, a manufacturer of Zip drives.

Computer Software

If you've been using your computer for any length of time, you have probably realized that you spend a lot of your money (and time) on software. Software is what makes the computer *do* something, and you may find that you are constantly adding to or upgrading your software. Or you may wonder what other products are available.

You can use the software sites on the Internet to review software products on the market. You might be interested in business software. Or perhaps you want to have some fun and would like information on the numerous games available. In addition to software that you purchase, you can also find some free (or almost free) programs called *freeware* or *shareware*. This section discusses sites devoted to finding information about software.

Productivity Software

If you use software to do some worthwhile task, it falls under the heading of *productivity software*. You can use productivity software to write a letter, set up a database, create a presentation, create a newsletter with desktop publishing, figure a budget, and more.

More and more, the trend has been to combine the four most popular program types (word processing, spreadsheet, database, and presentation) into one package and sell it as a bundle or suite. And three companies dominate the market on this type of software: Microsoft, Corel, and Lotus. In addition, you can find companies offering other types of products, such as desktop publishing programs or utility programs. Table 20.2 lists some of the sites where you can find product information.

You can expect to find information about products, support, and the company, as well as articles touting some of that company's products. For example, Figure 20.5 shows the home page for Microsoft. From this page, you can select Products to review a complete product line, then select the product on which you want information.

When you select a product, you can find articles relating to that product, product information, and support. You can also search for a topic of interest and contact the company with feedback.

Don't forget you can get information about Communicator and other Netscape products from the Netscape home page (**http://www.home.netscape.com**). Here you'll find articles about currently featured products (see Figure 20.6). You can also use the Products button to get information.

Table 20.2   Sites for software.

Company	Address	Product(s)
Adobe	**http://www.adobe.com**	PageMaker, Photoshop, PageMill, Acrobat, Illustrator
Claris	**http://www.claris.com**	FileMaker Pro, ClarisWorks, Claris Home page, Organizer
Corel	**http://www.corel.com**	Corel Office, including Corel WordPerfect, Corel Quattro Pro, Paradox, Corel Presentations, and other utility programs
Lotus	**http://www.lotus.com**	Lotus SmartSuite, including Word Pro, Lotus 1-2-3, Approach, and Freelance Graphics; also Lotus Notes
Macromedia	**http://www.macromedia.com**	Freehand, Shockwave, Director, Extreme 3D, Soundedit, x-Res
Microsoft	**http://www.microsoft.com**	Microsoft Office, including Word, Excel, Access, and PowerPoint; also Windows 95 and Windows NT

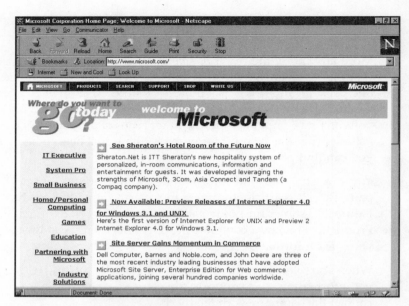

Figure 20.5   Visit Microsoft's Web site for information on all Microsoft products.

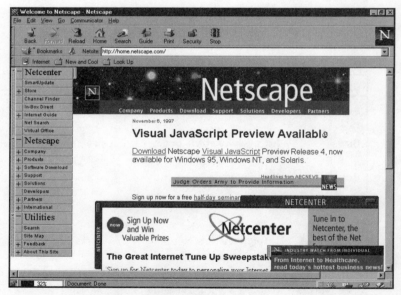

Figure 20.6   For information on Netscape products, use the links on its home page.

Games

If you like to play games, you may want to visit one of the many sites for companies that make games. Or you may want to participate in a special type of online game called multi-user dungeon (MUD), a virtual world where you can move around and interact with your surroundings and other online players.

Here are some of the best places for game information:

- Visit **gopher://gopher.micro.umn.edu**, a Gopher site with access to several MUDs.

- For links to newsgroups and games FAQs as well as game-related sites, try Games Domain at **http://www.gamesdomain.com**.

- Most popular games also have Web sites. For example, try Sierra Online at **http://www.sierra.com**.

- For free or relatively free games, visit some of the freeware and shareware sites, covered next.

Freeware And Shareware

Sometimes you may not want to shell out a lot of money for software. You may want to get something free for a change. Or try the software and if you like it, *then* pay. Most shareware programs let you try the software and then pay a small fee to register the program if you decide you want to use it. You can find freeware and shareware on the Internet. You can find one of the biggest collections at Jumbo at **http://www.jumbo.com**.

Here you can find 250,000 programs (as of March 1998). You can search through the database to find a program of interest or browse through the various channels (Kids, Utilities, Home & Hobbies, Games, Business, and more). Figure 20.7 shows the opening page for this popular shareware, games, and freeware site.

Once you find a program you want to try, you can download it to your computer. (For information on downloading, turn to Chapter 10.) Look for a Readme file with instructions on how to install and then use the program. This (or a similar) file should also tell you the registration fee for the program.

Another good collection of shareware is shareware.com at **http://www.shareware. com**. You can search the database of over 250,000 files (as of March 1998), browse through a list of new and most popular programs, or check out some of the highlighted programs (see Figure 20.8). Again, if you find a program you like, you can download it, install it, and try it out.

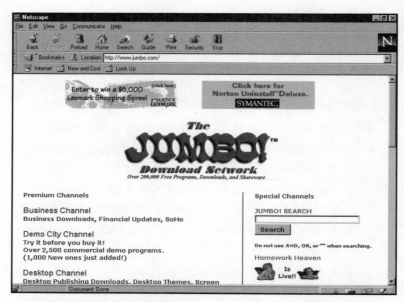

Figure 20.7   For access to some of the most popular shareware and freeware available, try Jumbo.

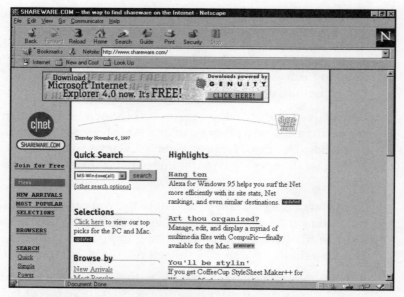

Figure 20.8   Another source of shareware is shareware.com.

Computer Publications

Keeping up with computer technology is kind of like trying to run on a tread-mill that gets faster and faster. Things change at breakneck speed. If you want to stay more current on what's happening or if you want to research a computer topic, you may want to visit some of the computer publications available on the Internet.

Computer Magazines

A good place to start when looking for publications is the Netscape Guide by Yahoo!. Click on the Internet button and then select Computers. You see links to some of the most popular computer sites on the Web. Scroll down to see the news and magazine sites, shown in Figure 20.9. You can go to any of the links by clicking on them. For instance, you can visit the IDG site to read such magazines as *Computerworld, InfoWorld, JavaWorld, Macworld, Netscape World, Network World*, and *PC World*.

Another company that publishes several magazines is Ziff-Davis. You can visit its site at **http://www.zdnet.com**. From this site, shown in Figure 20.10, you can select to review articles from several publications, check out the software library, get the latest news, and more. If you want to read one of this company's magazines—*ComputerLife, Computer Shopper, Family PC, MacUser, MacWeek, PC*

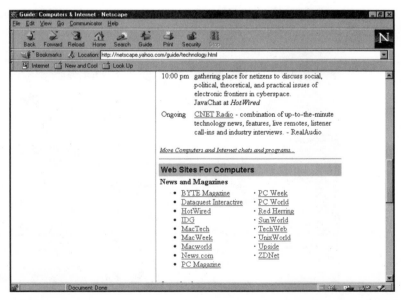

Figure 20.9   Try the links from the Computers page in the Netscape Guide.

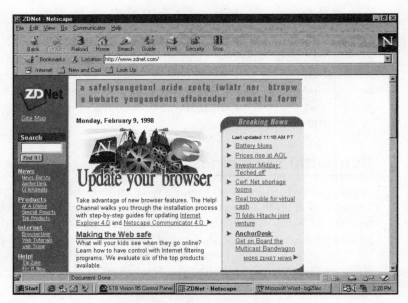

Figure 20.10   For computer news, check out ZDNet.

Computing, PC Magazine, and *PC Week,* to name a few—select the magazine link and then click on the magazine you want. Figure 20.11 shows a recent issue of *ComputerLife.*

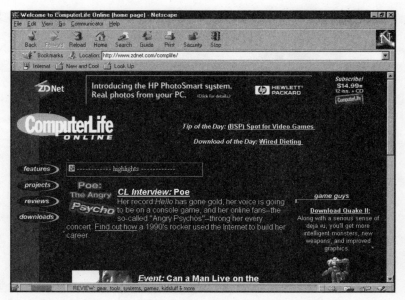

Figure 20.11   You can review any of ZDNet's magazines, including ComputerLife.

> **TIP**
>
> *For tech support help, you can look up questions in forums and newsgroups at the Tech Support site at* **http://www.supporthelp.com**.

The Coriolis Group

In addition to magazines, you can also find a lot of computer-book publishers with Web pages. For instance, if you like this book (and I hope you do), you can review other books from The Coriolis Group by visiting its Web site at **http://www.coriolis.com**.

Computer Newsgroups

Other sources of computer information are the many computer-related newsgroups. You can ask questions, answer questions, review others' opinions, post your own opinions, and more in any of the newsgroups. Here are two you may want to try:

- **alt.comp.*** (the asterisk indicates you can find many subcategories)
- **comp.answers**

Moving On

The Internet, as expected, includes many resources that relate to computers. This chapter explained what type of information you can expect to find and listed several computer-related sites. Chapter 21 tells you how to use your computer skills to find a job.

CHAPTER 21

Finding A Job

Just as the Internet is changing how we get information and how we do business, it (and computers themselves) is changing how we work. The Internet has made it possible for small businesses to access information and to sell their services as if they were "big" businesses. Computers have made it possible to work from home—to work in a *virtual* office. The Internet has also made it easier to research jobs. For instance, you may have an interview with a company and want to read up on its background. Or perhaps you don't have an interview, but want to research companies that might be interested in someone with your skills.

The Internet includes many resources not only for researching companies, but also for finding advice on searching for a job. You can review job openings or post your resume for others to see. And if you get a job in another city, you can use the Internet to find out about that city. This chapter covers some of the job-related sites on the Internet.

Researching Companies

The more you know about a particular company, the better prepared you will be to target that company for a job. If you know the company's background and products, you can then figure out how your skills match its goals. You can research companies to see what they have to offer and then send your resume

Job Sites At A Glance

Career Magazine at **http://www.careermag.com/careermag/**

Career Mosaic at **http://www.careermosaic.com**

CareerPath.com at **http://www.careerpath.com**

College Grad Job Hunter at **http://www.collegegrad.com**

Homebuyer's Fair at **http://www.homefair.com/home**

Hoover's Online at **http://www.hoovers.com**

Job Center at **http://www.jobcenter.com**

JobBank USA at **http://www.jobbankusa.com**

Monster Board at **http://www.monsterboard.com**

or contact them for an interview. Or you may already have an interview with a company and want to do your homework by researching its background.

Using A Directory

You can find information about companies by using a corporate directory. One of the best is Hoover's Online. You can use it to research more than 10,000 companies. To visit this site, go to **http://www.hoovers.com**.

You can search the corporate directory by company ticker symbol, company name, or keyword. Figure 21.1 shows the company profile for Emmis Broadcasting. You can review the addresses and names of chief employees, the number of employees, a description of the company, and more. You can also look up a stock quote and a snapshot of the company's financial data using the options at the bottom of the profile.

Visiting The Company Web Site

In addition to looking up information in a directory such as Hoover's, you can also visit a company's Web site, if it has one. If you are familiar with the company, ask for its Web address. You can also use any of the search tools covered in Chapter 6 to search for a Web address.

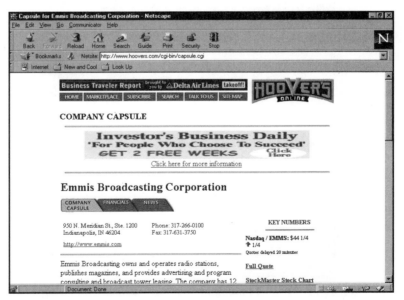

Figure 21.1   Look up a company profile using Hoover's Online.

Finding Job Openings

When you are looking for a job, you may not even know what companies to start with. Or you may find companies, but keep running into dead-ends—no jobs available. In that case, you can use one of several Internet resources for reviewing available jobs. This section first explains what you can expect to find at these sites and then highlights some of the best sites.

What Do Job Sites Offer?

Most of the job sites on the Internet offer similar features. Here are the basic things you can do from these sites:

- Search for job openings in the site's database. Almost all job sites provide a searchable database of job listings. Many let you search by location, title, salary, skills, and other criteria. Figure 21.2 shows the search page for the Career Magazine site (listed in the next section, "What Are Some Of The Best Job Sites?").

- Submit your resume. Job searching is a two-way street. You are looking for a job and companies are looking for you (you hope). The sites also offer a spot for you to place your resume. Select the link for submitting your

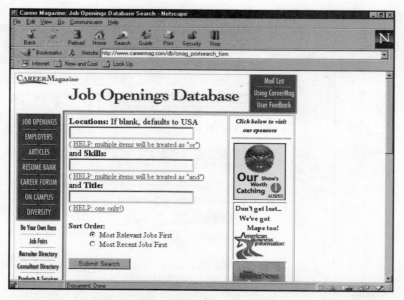

Figure 21.2   You can search for a job based on the criteria you specify.

resume and then follow the on-screen instructions. You may, for instance, submit your resume via email, or you may complete an online form listing your requirements, skills, and experience. Usually this service is free.

■ Do research on employers and look up company information. Usually information is provided just for the companies that list jobs on the site. For instance, Figure 21.3 shows just a few of the companies you can look up on Career Mosaic's Employers page.

■ If you are an employer, you can search resumes for possible matches to any openings your company has available. You can search by criteria such as skills and location to find potential employees. You may have to subscribe to the service to use this feature.

■ Get career advice, such as tips on job hunting and resume writing. Look for a career resource center or a page with articles on these topics. You may also find special features for online job fairs or for college outplacement.

■ If you are a human resources professional, you can read about the benefits of using a job site service. The site, of course, benefits from having as many companies as possible use its database.

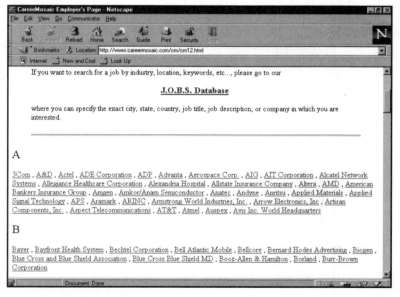

Figure 21.3   Look up employer information.

- Participate in online forums to share advice and leads with other job seekers. For instance, you can use the Career Forum feature from Career Magazine (see Figure 21.4).

- Find links to other job-related sites. For example, JobBank USA not only displays links to several other job-related sites, but you can also search these sites from the JobBank search page. You can use CareerPath.com to search employment ads from the *Boston Globe*, *Chicago Tribune*, *Los Angeles Times*, *New York Times*, *San Jose Mercury News*, and the *Washington Post* (see Figure 21.5).

- Get expert advice. You can often find columns, lists of questions, and other information. For example, at the College Grad Job Hunter at **http://www.collegegrad.com** (a site designed for recent college graduates), you can review questions submitted to Ask the Hiring Manager (see Figure 21.6). You can even submit your own question.

What Are Some Of The Best Job Sites?

Now that you know what to expect, you can visit any of the many job-related sites mentioned in this chapter. This section lists some of the best sites. What makes one site better than another is somewhat subjective. One thing that adds value is the number of job postings listed. If the site has just a few openings

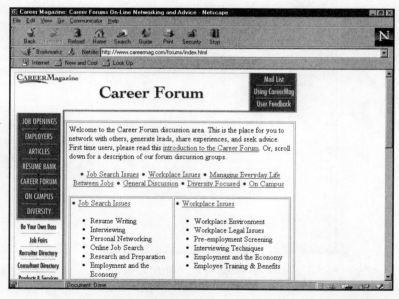

Figure 21.4   Participate in an online forum to share job advice and leads.

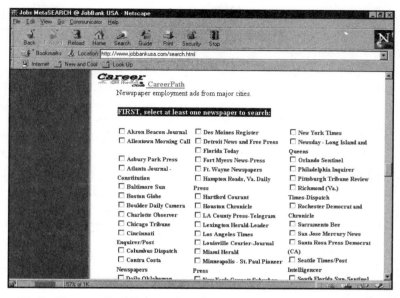

Figure 21. 5   You can find links to employment ads from several newspapers.

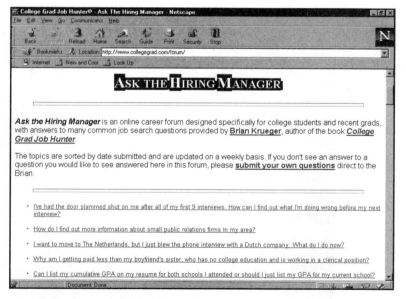

Figure 21.6   You can ask questions of experts.

listed, it's not really worth your time. The more listings, the more likely you are to find a position that might interest you. The Monster Board, shown in Figure 21.7, provides access to over 50,000 jobs.

Another factor that determines whether a site is one of the best is additional services the site provides. For instance, many sites offer job advice. Both Career Mosaic and Career Magazine have substantial job databases as well as other services. Also, you may just prefer the look and feel of one site over another. I like JobBank USA because, in addition to including some great features, the site has many links to most of the other top-rated job sites (see Figure 21.8).

The best advice I can give you is to try some of the most popular sites and see if you find something you like. If you don't find something of value, try another site. In Table 21.1, I've listed sites in the order of my preference. (You may not agree, but you probably will find at least one site you like in the list.)

Relocating To Another City

If your job search takes you to another city, you may want to do some research about that city and the area of the country in which it is located. For instance, is your salary comparable to what you are earning in your current city? For

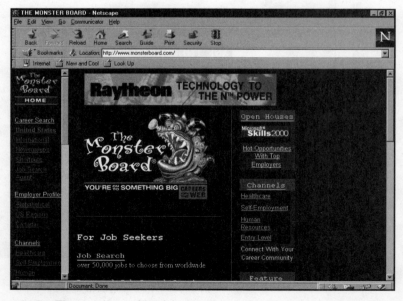

Figure 21.7   The number of jobs in the database determines the quality of a job site.

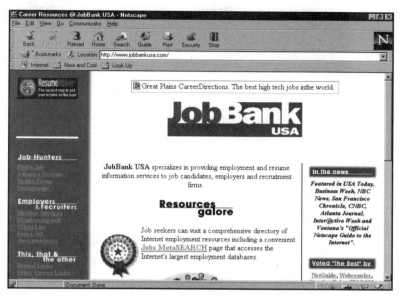

Figure 21.8   JobBank USA is a good spot for starting your job search.

relocation advice, visit the Homebuyer's Fair at **http://www.homefair.com/home**.

Select any of the links, including the Salary Calculator or Moving Calculator for calculating moving expenses. Figure 21.9 shows the entry screen for using the Salary Calculator. You can enter your present salary and then select your current location and new destination. The program will calculate what a comparable salary is at the new location.

Table 21.1   Popular job sites.

Site	Address
JobBank USA	**http://www.jobbankusa.com**
Career Mosaic	**http://www.careermosaic.com**
Career Magazine	**http://www.careermag.com**
Monster Board	**http://www.monsterboard.com**
Job Center	**http://www.jobcenter.com**
CareerPath.com	**http://www.careerpath.com**
College Grad Job Hunter	**http://www.collegegrad.com**

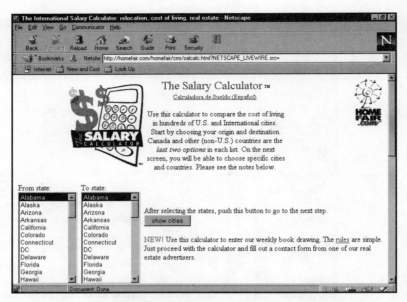

Figure 21.9   Use the Salary Calculator to figure a comparable salary in another city.

Moving On

If you are unemployed, a recent college graduate, or simply interested in a new job, you can use the Internet to explore career possibilities. This chapter explained what you can expect to find at the many career sites and listed some of the best sites to try.

Life can't be all work and no play. So the next chapter—the last chapter—covers some of the places you can visit to have some fun!

CHAPTER 22

Having Fun

So far, in Part III of this book, you have learned about some of the things you can do on the Internet, but you have really only seen the tip of the iceberg. This chapter is a hodgepodge of other things you can do and try, mostly relating to fun. You can get your horoscope, visit an electronic zoo, look for a potential mate (not at the zoo!), and more. Keep in mind that the list of sites here is not comprehensive; the Internet includes all kinds of nooks and crannies filled with everything from the useful to the bizarre.

Remember that you can find sites of interest by browsing around or trying some Internet directories, such as Netscape Navigator's New and Cool button. You can also search for a particular topic using any of the search tools discussed in Chapter 6. For example, I found the UFO site by searching. You can do the same, looking for the topic, hobby, or interest of your choice.

Looking Up Your Horoscope

If you are into astrology, you can read your latest horoscope from Astrology by Moonlight at **http://www.masterm.com/astrol.html** (see Figure 22.1). You can also find links to several other astrology resources on the Internet from this site. If you enjoy astrology, start here and then try out any of the highlighted links.

Fun Sites At A Glance

American Kennel Club at **http://www.akc.org**

Astrology by Moonlight at **http://www.masterm.com/astrol.html**

Aunt Annie's Craft Page at **http://www.auntannie.com**

CupidNet at **http://www.cupidnet.com**

The Discovery Channel at **http://www.discovery.com**

Gardening at **http://www.gardening.com**

Glamour at **http://www.swoon.com**

Hot Coupons at **http://www.hotcoupons.com**

Hot Hot Hot at **http://www.hot.presence.com**

Kodak at **http://www.kodak.com**

Mama's Cookbook at **http://www.eat.com**

Molson at **http://www.molson.com**

The Nature Conservancy at **http://www.tnc.org**

NetVet at **http://www.netvet.wustl.edu**

The Real Beer Page at **http://www.realbeer.com**

SpiritWeb's UFO Sightings Page at **http://www.spiritweb.org/Spirit/ufo.html**

The Spot at **http://www.thespot.com**

Virtual Frog Dissection Kit at **http://www-itg.lbl.gov/vfrog/**

Volition at **http://www.volition.com**

Web Personals at **http://www.webpersonals.com/date/**

World Wide Quilting Page at **http://www.ttsw.com/MainQuiltingPage**

Figure 22.1   Read your horoscope from Astrology by Moonlight.

You can visit another source for astrology, including today's stars, star bios, products for sale, and an online astrology zine, at **http://www.adze.com**.

Cooking

If you like to cook, you can find many sources of cooking information and recipes on the Web. This chapter includes two, which is just a teeny, tiny sample of what's available.

If you like Italian food, check out Mama's Cucina, sponsored by Ragu. Here you can look up recipes in Mama's Cookbook, read some of Mama's best-kept secrets, or see a list of Mama's Italian Food/Film Festival picks. You can also learn Italian. To visit this site, go to **http://www.eat.com**.

You can browse through Mama's Cookbook or search for a particular dish. The cookbook includes a cooking and pasta glossary. As Mama says, "Is there anything that makes your heart happier than a nice big bowl of pasta?" (see Figure 22.2).

Another site for cooking information can be found through Pathfinder at **http://www.pathfinder.com**. From Pathfinder, select Living; here you can find links to online versions of *Cooking Light* and *Southern Living*, where you can find other cooking information.

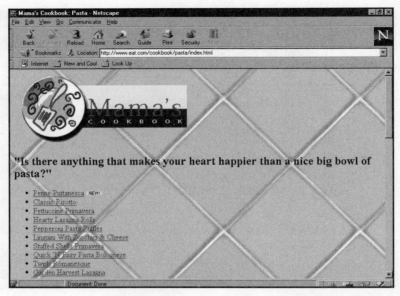

Figure 22.2   Look up recipes for pasta and other dishes from Mama's Cookbook.

If you want to share cooking information and recipes with others, try some of the cooking newsgroups such as **rec.food.cooking** and **rec.food.recipes**.

TIP

If you are a chocolate lover, visit the Chocolate Recipe Collection at ***http:// www2.godiva.com/recipes***.

Getting Into Nature

If nature interests you, you can use the Internet to read up on science topics and participate in conservation-related projects. Two sites are especially worth visiting. Check out The Nature Conservancy at **http://www.tnc.org**. Here you can read articles, view pictures, participate in chats, and learn how to get more involved.

Also, visit Discovery Channel Online at **http://www.discovery.com**. Discovery Channel Online has several general subject areas (History, Technology, Nature, Exploration, and Science). Figure 22.3 shows its home page. Click on a button to view the related features for a particular subject. You can also use the links along the left edge of the page to take a look at Discovery Channel, Learning Channel, Animal Planet, Discovery Travel, Live Events, and other topics.

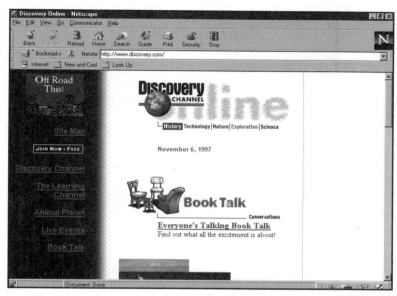

Figure 22.3 *You can get all kinds of science and nature information from Discovery Channel Online.*

Being Fashionable

If you are into fashion, you may want to take a look at Swoon's magazine rack at **http://www.swoon.com** (see Figure 22.4). You can check out articles from online versions of *Mademoiselle, GQ, Details,* and *Glamour*—some of the most fashionable fashion rags. From Swoon, you can also get advice on dating, mating, and relating.

Or try painting your "e-nails" at the Gap's site, **http://www.gap.com** (see Figure 22.5).

Table 22.1 lists these and other sites for fashion news.

Dissecting A Frog

From fashion to frogs—see, the Internet *does* have something for everyone. You can use the virtual frog dissection kit to practice your surgery skills (see Figure 22.6). To get started, read the Help page, which provides complete instructions. Even if you are past high school biology, you will enjoy trying this site at **http://www-itg.lbl.gov/vfrog/**.

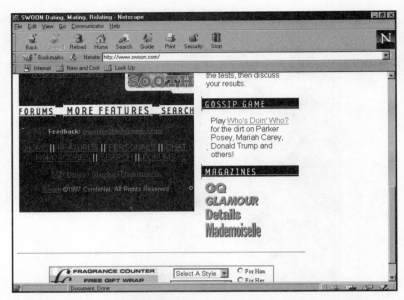

Figure 22.4 *Read some online versions of popular fashion magazines from Swoon.*

Figure 22.5 *Have some fun painting your "e-nails."*

Table 22.1 Fashion sites.

Site	Address
Avon	http://www.avon.com
Carole Little	http://www.carolelittle.com
Clinique	http://www.clinique.com
Cover Girl	http://www.covergirl.com
Esprit	http://www.esprit.com
Fashion Icon	http://www.fashion-icon.com
The Gap	http://www.gap.com
Joe Boxer	http://www.joeboxer.com
Revlon	http://www.revlon.com
Supermodel.com	http://www.supermodel.com
Swoon	http://www.swoon.com

TIP

To visit the Froggy Page, containing all things froggy, go to **http://www.frog. simplenet.com/froggy**.

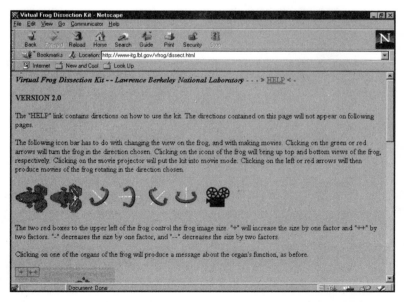

Figure 22.6 Practice frog dissection at the Lawrence Berkeley National Laboratory site.

Getting Free Samples

Do you enjoy a good bargain? Are you a coupon-clipping fanatic? If so, you will love the two sites in this section. Volition (shown in Figure 22.7) includes links to information about free stuff and products. You can try the links at this site to order all the free stuff your mail carrier can handle. The address is **http://www.volition.com**.

Another site you can use to look up available coupons and learn how to get them is the Hot Coupons site at **http://www.hotcoupons.com**.

Growing A Garden

Look at your thumb. Is it green? If so, you can add to your gardening skills by trying some of the gardening sites on the Internet. Keep in mind that this section mentions just one site (a good one!); you can find many others related to this topic.

Visit Gardening.com at **http://www.gardening.com**. You can find a plant encyclopedia with over 1,500 plants, a problem solver, and a site directory (see Figure 22.8).

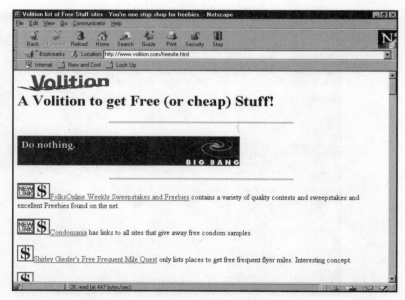

Figure 22.7   Get free products from the links at Volition.

Figure 22.8   Look up all the plant information you need from this gardening site.

Taking A Picture

You can learn more about Kodak and its products, view some great high-resolution photographs, get information about digital imaging, and more from the Kodak Web site at **http://www.kodak.com**.

Having A Drink

When you come home from the office, do you like to relax with a cocktail? If so, check out some of the drink sites on the Internet. You can get all the information you could ever want about microbreweries from **http://www.realbeer.com**.

Figure 22.9 shows the Real Beer Page and all its features, including Brew Tour, Brew Travels, Brew Zines, and Burp Me.

You can also try the Molson and Budweiser sites at **http://www.molson.com** and **http://www.budweiser.com**.

And if it's wine you like to drink, visit the Grapevine at **http://www.winery.com**.

Figure 22.9   The Real Beer Page includes everything you could ever want to know about microbreweries.

Finding Romance

If you are single and having a hard time meeting someone, you may want to try some of the personal romance services on the Internet. You can use these matchmaking services to find a potential beau or get information about travel, news, and shopping for single adults. Here are a few places to try:

- **http://www.cupidnet.com**
- **http://www.flirt.com**
- **http://www.webpersonals.com/date/**

And if the romance doesn't work out, you can send a Dear John letter via email. Try this site for all your love letters and not-so-love letter needs: **http://www.nando.net/toys/cyrano.html**.

If you don't feel like getting involved yourself, but need some form of romantic diversion, visit the Spot, a cybersoap shown in Figure 22.10. You can keep up to date with the cyberstars and their romances at **http://www.thespot.com**.

If you don't like this soap, try the East Village at **http://www.eastvillage.com**.

Figure 22.10   Like soap operas? Then try the Spot, a cybersoap.

Learning About Pets And Animals

If you like animals, one of the best places to find not only a wealth of information about veterinary medicine and animals, but also numerous links to other animal-related sites, is NetVet at **http://www.netvet.wustl.edu**.

From this site, you can also visit an electronic zoo, shown in Figure 22.11. From the zoo, select the type of animal you want information about: amphibians, birds, cats, cows, dogs, ferrets, fish, horses, marine mammals, pigs, primates, rabbits, reptiles, rodents, wildlife, zoo animals, and others. When you select the type of animal, you see all the related links you can visit.

If you like dogs, you can get information about breeds, read advice on buying a pet, and see a list of some breeders by visiting the American Kennel Club site at **http://www.akc.org**.

Figure 22.12 shows the breed standard for Bulldog. (As I mentioned earlier in the book, I have an English Bulldog named Jelly Roll.)

Finally, visit the Pet Channel for all your pet needs, including pet horoscopes, at **http://www.thepetchannel.com**.

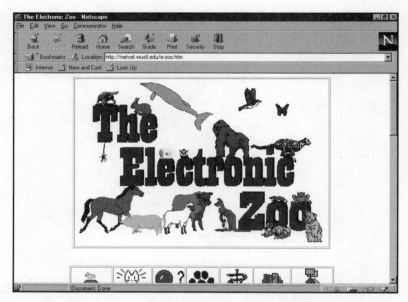

Figure 22.11   Visit animals and get information from the electronic zoo.

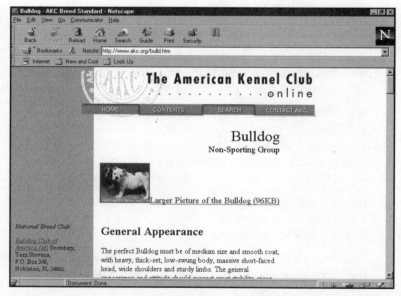

Figure 22.12   Look up breed information from the American Kennel Club site.

Being Crafty

Arts and crafts your thing? You can find many craft-related sites on the Internet, including Aunt Annie's Craft Page with projects such as making Dracula's blood. Visit this site at **http://www.auntannie.com**.

If you like quilting, visit the World Wide Quilting Page at **http://www.ttsw.com/ MainQuiltingPage**.

These are just two sites with information about crafts. You can find a wealth of other sites by searching. And you can find a lot of newsgroups relating to crafts, including **rec.crafts.metalworking**, **rec.crafts.quilting**, **rec.crafts.textiles. needlework**, and **rec.crafts.textiles.sewing**.

Visiting An Art Museum

If you enjoy art, you can visit **http://www.metmuseum.org** for an overview of collections on display at the Metropolitan Museum of Art.

As another resource, try the World Wide Arts Resources, the "biggest gateway to the arts on the Internet." This site's address is **http://www.wwar.com**.

Finally, you can find links to other museums at **http://www.comlab.ox.ac.uk/ archive/other/museums**.

And More . . .

You can't really begin to imagine some of the sites you can find on the Web. Here are some other fun (bizarre? interesting?) sites that should give you an idea that there indeed is something for everyone.

If you want to keep up on the latest Elvis sightings, visit the Elvis Spotter's Web page at **http://www.nwlink.com/~timelvis/news1.html**.

On a "related" topic, you can get a lot of information on UFOs, such as pictures of UFO sightings, at **http://www.spiritweb.org**. Figure 22.13 shows the UFO Sightings page of SpiritWeb.

Do a little armchair psychology by taking the Briggs-Meyer's personality test. You answer around 60 or so questions, your answers are tallied, and you see the type of person you are. You can try this test at **http://www.sunsite.unc.edu/ personality/keirsey.html**.

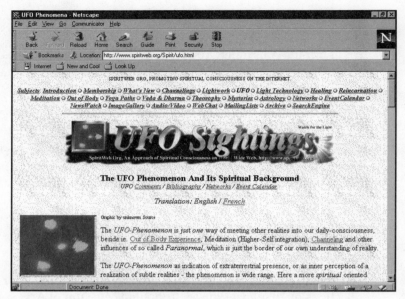

Figure 22.13   Check out information about UFOs.

Want to enjoy a short trance? Try **http://www.hypnosis.com**. Want to explore your past life? Talk to Madame Celeste at **http://www.madameceleste.com**.

Moving On

This chapter gives you some ideas of the other topics and areas of interest you can find on the Internet. The chapter is in no way a comprehensive look at the wealth and variety of sites—it's just a small peek. If you can't find a site that suits your interests, see Appendix B for brief instructions on creating your own Web page. And if you run into any problems while using any aspect of the Internet, consult the troubleshooting guide in Appendix A.

Part IV

Appendices

Troubleshooting Guide

Having a problem? If so, use this handy troubleshooting guide, which is organized into the following categories: problems with startup, with the World Wide Web, with news, with mail, and with file transfers. Each section lists common problems and solutions.

Problems With Startup

I can't log on to the Internet.

If you can't log on to the Internet, you could have one of several problems. Check the following:

- Is your modem set up and connected? To use the Internet, your modem must be set up and connected to your computer. Check your connections.

- Have you signed up with a company that provides Internet access? You need an account with an Internet Service Provider (ISP) or a commercial online service such as America Online. You can find out more about these companies in Chapters 2 and 3.

- Did you follow the proper logon procedures? Depending on your ISP, you follow different steps to log on. Usually, you enter your password and username. You must also enter the right phone number. If you still have problems, call your ISP for technical support.

I can't remember my password.

Most ISPs provide you with a password for logging on to the Internet. The password ensures that only you have access to your Internet account. If you forget the password, call the ISP to get a new one.

When I start Navigator, I see a message that says Netscape is unable to locate the server.

To access the Internet, you must first log on to your ISP. If you aren't logged on, you see this message and then Navigator displays the Dial-Up Connection dialog box so that you can get connected. Be sure you follow the steps to get connected to your ISP.

Problems With The World Wide Web

I can't access a site.

If you try to go to a particular site and can't access it, the problem could be one of the following:

- First, be sure that you are connected to your ISP. You can't access any of the sites unless you are connected.

- Second, if you entered an address, check that you entered it correctly. Some addresses are tricky. Be sure you typed the address exactly as it appears and did not insert any spaces. All the symbols (periods, tildes, and so on) must be in the right spots. Also, some addresses are case sensitive. Try typing the address again.

- Third, if you are sure you typed the address correctly, then the address may have changed or the site may have moved. Sometimes you see a message telling you the new address. Or you may see an error message.

- Fourth, the server may be busy or down. When you access a Web page, you are accessing the files on another network. If that network is too busy (some times are busier than others) or down for some reason, you won't be able to access the files. In that case, try again at a later time.

I used the Find command, but it didn't find any sites.

The Find command does not search for Internet sites; it searches for text on the current Web page. To search for a site, you must use a search engine. See Chapter 6 for more information on searching.

I can't find the site I want.

If you are looking for a particular site, you can use one of several search tools. You can view and use some of the most common search tools by clicking on the Search button in Netscape Navigator. Chapter 6 covers how to use some of these tools.

If you use a search tool and can't find the site, try using a different search tool. Each one usually provides different results.

If you have no luck using different search tools, try searching for the site using a different word or phrase.

My screens look different from those shown in this book.

Most of the content of the Web is updated frequently. The Web pages you see in the figures in this book have most likely changed. You shouldn't worry if you see something different.

I clicked on a link, but nothing happened.

Are you sure nothing happened? You can tell whether Navigator is busy by looking at the Netscape icon in the upper-right corner of the screen. If you see shooting stars, Navigator is busy. You can also check the progress of an action by looking at the status bar. Sometimes moving to another site takes awhile. (You can stop the move by clicking on the Stop button.)

If you don't see any shooting stars, you may not have clicked on the link. Try clicking on it again. Also, be sure what you are clicking *is* a link. Links usually appear in a different color and are underlined. You can tell when the pointer is over a link because the pointer looks like a hand and the address for that link appears in the status bar.

I can't play a sound or movie.

Sounds and movies are stored in different file formats; to play them, you need a program or plug-in that can handle that particular file format. For example, Communicator comes with several plug-ins, and you can play back sounds and movies. Also, you can use Windows 95 Media Player or Apple's MoviePlayer to play back some movies. Other sounds and movies may require different software, and if you don't have the software, you can't play the sound or movie.

I don't want my children to visit certain sites.

You can block certain sites so that children do not have access to sites with adult or questionable content. Several programs for monitoring the Web are available. See Chapter 9 for more information.

I don't have all the plug-ins.

A *plug-in* is a small program that adds some special function or feature to your Web browser. Netscape Communicator includes a SmartUpdate feature, which you can use to update your plug-ins. See Chapter 8 for more information.

I am not sure whether a page is secure.

If you are worried about the security of a particular page, you can check the settings by clicking on the Security button or clicking on the lock icon in the status bar. You can view several different security settings for the page.

Problems With News

I get an error message when I try to use Collabra.

Before you can use your news reader, you must set up your news server, as covered in Chapter 13. Basically, you enter the server name given to you by your ISP. After you set up the news server, you can then access the news reader.

I see only a few newsgroups listed in my news window.

Initially, you are signed up to receive only the default newsgroups. To participate in additional newsgroups, you must subscribe to them. To display a list of all newsgroups, start the news reader. Then click on the File | Subscribe to Discussion Groups command or click on the Subscribe button. Select the newsgroup you want to subscribe to and then click on the Subscribe button.

I don't have the same newsgroups as someone else that I know.

Your news server determines which newsgroups you have access to. You may not have the same newsgroups as someone else who uses a different news server.

Remember that the list of newsgroups is organized into folders. You can expand the list by clicking on a folder with a plus sign. You may need to do this to find the newsgroup you want.

I find a newsgroup's content offensive.

One of the greatest things about the Internet is free speech—anyone can say anything. Unfortunately, that means that you may come across ideas and content you find offensive. If this is the case, the best thing to do is to quit reading the newsgroup. You can unsubscribe to a newsgroup by clicking in the Subscribed column next to its name.

I can't find a message I saw earlier.

Messages are periodically purged from the newsgroup after a certain expiration date. If you don't see a message listed, it may have been deleted.

To save a message, you can print a copy using the File | Print command. Or you can save a copy to your hard disk using the File | Save Message(s) As command.

I posted a message, but I didn't see it listed.

When you post a message, it is first sent to the news server and then routed with the other incoming messages to the newsgroups. That means you won't see it listed immediately.

If you replied via email, you won't see the message listed at all; instead, it is sent via email to the sender.

Problems With Mail

I can't check my mail.

To check your mail, you first have to set up your mail servers, as described in Chapter 12. Also, when you start Netscape Messenger, you must type your password. Check with your ISP if you don't know your password.

I sent a message, but it wasn't delivered.

To send an email message to someone, you must know that person's email address, and you must type it exactly. First, verify the address, then be sure you have entered it correctly.

I don't want to send a message I've created.

If you have not clicked on the Send button, you can cancel a message by clicking on the Close box for the window. You are asked whether you want to close without sending the message. Click on the Yes button. If you have already clicked on the Send button, you cannot get your message back.

I don't know my email address.

Your email address is usually your username, the @ sign, and a domain name. You need to check with your ISP to find out what your exact address is. Most of the time you can request a certain username unless someone else is already using it.

Problems With File Transfers

I downloaded a program, but nothing happened.

When you download a program, you usually have to follow a few additional steps to get the program to work. Many times you have to decompress the files and then you have to install the program. Look for a Readme file with specific instructions on how to complete the program setup.

I downloaded a file, but I can't find it.

When you download a file, you can specify a folder to put it in. If you forget which folder you used, try the default folder (usually the Netscape folder). Also, try searching your hard disk for the file. With Windows 95, for example, you can click on the Start button and use the Find | Files Or Folders command to search your hard disk. Mac users can press Command+F and use the Find utility to locate the file.

I downloaded a file, but the entire file did not download.

If the download was interrupted for some reason, you may not have received the entire file. You may not even have received an error message telling you there was a problem. If you think the transmission was halted, try download-ing the file again. You may have to sit at the computer and watch to verify that the entire file was downloaded.

I can't access an FTP site.

Some FTP sites are anonymous and anyone can download files. You may have to type a username and password, but the opening screen tells you what to type. Other FTP sites are restricted—you can't use a "generic" password. To get access to these files, you must have permission. Check with the site ad-ministrator.

I can't upload a file.

Depending on the FTP site, you may not be able to upload files. Check with the site administrator.

More About Netscape Communicator

This book covered the main things you can do on the Internet—browse using Netscape Navigator, send email with Messenger, and participate in newsgroup discussions with Collabra. As you get more and more comfortable with the Internet, you may want to explore other avenues. Netscape Communicator includes some other components that you can use in your Internet exploration, including Netcaster, Composer, and Conference. This appendix briefly introduces each of these Communicator components so that you have an idea of what they do.

Using Netscape Netcaster

Netscape describes Netcaster as a "dynamic information-delivery tool for Intranet and Internet users." What does that mean? It means a new method for delivering content via the Internet. Rather than actively going to a site and getting information, you can subscribe to a particular site and have content delivered to your desktop. This technology is sometimes referred to as *push technology*. This section reviews this particular component.

Understanding What You Can Do With Netcaster

What can you do with Netcaster and what are its advantages? Read the following list for a summary:

■ You can subscribe to particular channels of content, including ABC News, CNNfn, CBS SportsLine, Disney, Thrive, and more.

■ You can find channels on the Internet. Netcaster provides access to Channel Finder.

■ You select how often you want information delivered to you. The information is downloaded at the interval you specify, and you can work offline to review the information.

■ You can create a *Webtop* —a channel on your desktop that provides constant information, such as a stock ticker.

Taking A Look At Netcaster

To start Netcaster, open the Communicator menu and select Netcaster. You can also click on the Channel Finder link on the Netscape home page. You see the preview with the Channel Finder displayed (see Figure B.1). You can review and then subscribe to any of the channels listed.

Using Netscape Composer

As you explore the Internet, you may become so enamored that you decide to create your own Web page. You might create a Web page for your business or

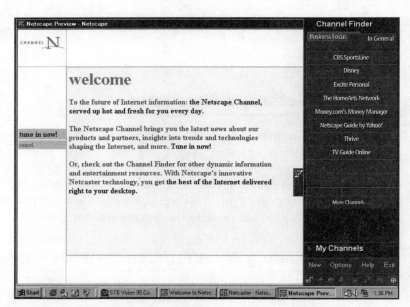

Figure B.1   Use Netscape Netcaster to have content delivered to your desktop.

your own personal use. Netscape Communicator includes a Web-authoring component called Composer that you can use to design, create, and edit Web pages. This section gives a brief overview of this process.

Step 1: Find A Web Hosting Service

The first step is to find a network that will publish your page. Most of the "big" sites and companies on the Web have their own server (a networked computer that stores the data, programs, and Web pages for that site). When you visit a site, you access the files on the computer that acts as its server. Setting up this type of site can cost *a lot* of money and is best suited for businesses. Before you leap into this venture, you need to do a lot of research.

Don't despair, though. If you represent a small business or are just a hobbyist, you don't have to set up an entire network server. Instead, you can use a Web hosting service. With this type of arrangement, you publish your Web pages on the service's networked server. You create the files, which are then placed on the network for others to access.

Finding Services

To find a Web hosting service, start with your Internet Service Provider (ISP), which may also include Web hosting services. You can expect the cost for this service to range from free to $85 a month or higher. Ask your ISP for specific information; if it doesn't offer Web publishing, you can try one of the dedicated Web hosting services, such as InfoStreet. Again, the cost varies, starting from around $22 a month. Check local computer magazines or use the Internet to search for a Web hosting service.

Comparing Services

Not all services are the same, so when you are considering which service to use, you should ask a lot of questions. Use the following list of questions to compare different service providers:

- How much does the service cost? Be sure to take into account any subscription fees you are paying.

- Are you charged any setup fees? Some providers charge nothing. Some may charge $10 or more to set up your page.

- How much storage space is provided? The data and images from your Web page take up disk space on the network. The service provider may have a set limit.

- Are additional fees charged if your Web page is larger than the limit? If your document size is larger than the limit, you may have to pay for additional storage space. Also, some providers charge a traffic fee—that is, if the site generates more than a certain level of traffic (or *hits*), there might be additional fees.

■ Are you charged each time you update your page? Some service providers charge a fee; some don't. If you plan on making changes frequently, look for a service that lets you update for free.

■ Does the service provide programs for creating a Web page? Some services provide programs that lead you step-by-step through the process of creating a Web page. Such programs are obviously the best way for beginners to get started. On the other hand, you might not have as much control over the look of the document if you can use only a set program and its options.

■ How fast is the connection? You want the visitors to your page to be able to view your page quickly, so pick a service that provides fast connections. (Look for one with a T1 connection.)

Step 2: Create Your Web Page

Once you find a service provider, you can start to put your creativity to work—you can create your own personal Web page. And that's where Composer comes in. Netscape describes Composer as a "fully integrated, Web document-authoring tool." What does that mean? It means you can use this component to quickly and easily create HTML documents (Web pages). Rather than type complex formatting commands, you can use this menu-driven program to format the text, insert graphics, add links, and more. Figure B.2 shows Composer.

You can also find other Web features in programs such as Word for Windows or PageMaker. And you can purchase standalone Web authoring programs.

When you design your Web page(s), keep these guidelines in mind:

■ Keep the design simple. As you expand your skills, you may want to get a little more creative, but at first stick with a simple design.

■ Consider using some graphic images to liven up the page, but remember that too many images or images that are really complex take a lot of time to display. Balance the two factors.

■ Proofread your text. Be sure your information is clear and concise. Make sure you don't have any embarrassing errors, such as spelling mistakes.

■ Visit other Web pages that you like and note how they are designed. You can view the source code of a page by opening the View menu and selecting the Page Source command to see how the page is set up.

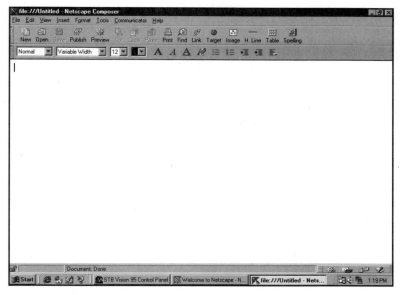

Figure B.2 ***You can use Composer to create Web pages.***

- Remember to include links to other sites of interest. If you don't include related links, your site is somewhat of a dead-end. Instead, include links to sites you like or think will be of use to the visitors to your page.

Step 3: Publish And Test Your Page

After your page is complete, you can test it by viewing your pages using Netscape. Evaluate the page to see how it looks. Does it look how you intended it to look? Do you see any mistakes? What changes would you make? You might want to make notes for changes you plan to make in the future.

Then you are ready to publish it—that is, put it on the server for others to visit. How you publish depends on the hosting service you are using. For instance, you might send the files to the server's FTP site. Ask your publishing service what to do.

Next, publicize your page. Tell your friends, family, co-workers, and so on about your page. Ask for their feedback. Also, look for places to advertise your Web page. For example, visit some of the search services and directory sites and look for links on how to get your site listed.

Using Netscape Conference

The final component in Communicator is Netscape Conference. You can use this program to talk "live" with other Internet users. You can hold conference calls, including video conferencing, or send live text messages. You can also send files and even browse the Web with someone else. You can connect with other users that have Conference or a similar realtime communication program. For more information on this component, review the features in Netscape's online help.

Glossary

America Online—A commercial online service that is owned and operated by one company. America Online (often called AOL) provides content, mail, bulletin board systems, and file transfers for its members. It also offers limited access to the Internet. Commercial online services differ from the Internet in that the Internet is not owned or operated by one company.

anonymous FTP site—A file transfer site that anyone can access.

applet—A small program that is written in the Java programming language and can be distributed as an attachment in a Web document. See also **Java**.

BBS (Bulletin Board System)—Manages electronic posting of messages. As a user, you can post new messages, read messages, and respond to messages. You can also chat with other users and download files from most BBSes.

bookmark—The stored address and label of a site you've visited. You can go quickly to any of the sites saved in your bookmark list.

browser—A program you use to display and navigate among Internet documents. Netscape Navigator 4 is a browser.

cable modem—A type of modem that enables you to use your current TV cable connection to connect to the Internet. This type of service is becoming more available as cable companies expand their Internet service.

cache—A temporary storage place in memory for sites you have visited in the current session. For instance, Navigator keeps recently visited pages in the cache. If you want to return to one of these pages, Navigator can pull the page from the cache rather than download it again from the network, which would take longer.

CGI (Common Gateway Interface)—An Internet standard for handling forms and other interactive tasks.

channel—A content source on the Internet. Content is "published" to your PC, where you can then browse it offline.

chat—A method for communicating with other online users live and in realtime. When you type your comments, they appear on screen in the chat room. Others online can then respond. See also **IRC (Internet Relay Chat)**.

client—One part of a client-server computer system. The client connects with the server and then can access information or use services from the server. Netscape Navigator is a client program. See also **server**.

Component bar—A row of icons you can use to select which Communicator component you want to work with.

CompuServe—A popular commercial online service. CompuServe used to provide content, mail, bulletin board systems, file transfers, and some Internet access for its members. CompuServe was purchased by America Online.

download—Copy a file from another computer system to your computer system.

email—Short for electronic mail. A method for sending messages to other online users.

encryption—A method for scrambling a message so that others cannot read it. Encryption enables you to perform secure transactions—such as send your credit card number—over the Internet.

FAQs (Frequently Asked Questions)—A list of questions commonly asked by users. This list is a good way to familiarize yourself with a topic.

frame—A division of a Web page. Netscape Navigator version 2.0 and higher enables Web authors to divide the content of a page into frames. Each frame is independent and has its own address.

freeware—Software that is publicly distributed and can be used free of charge.

FTP (File Transfer Protocol)—The Internet standard for transferring files from one computer to another.

GIF (Graphics Interchange Format)—A type of graphic file format. GIF files are often used on the Internet.

Gopher—A service you can use to navigate information on the Internet, specifically information in text format. Information on Gopher sites is presented in text only—no graphics—unlike on World Wide Web sites.

home page—The first page you see when you visit a Web site. Also, the first page that your browser displays when you log on to the Internet.

HTML (Hypertext Markup Language)—A type of formatting language that controls how a Web page is displayed.

HTTP (Hypertext Transfer Protocol)—The standard used for transferring documents on the Web.

hypertext—A document that contains links to other documents. You can jump to and display the other documents by clicking on a link (which is usually underlined and in a different color).

image map—A picture on a Web page that you can use to link to other sites. Each part of the picture is a link.

intranet—A network used internally by companies. The network works similarly to the Internet: Those connected to the local network can browse the intranet, access files, and send messages.

IRC (Internet Relay Chat)—A protocol you can use to chat online over the Internet. See also **chat**.

ISDN (Integrated Services Digital Network)—A special type of phone line that enables you to have both voice and digital data on the same phone line. ISDN lines and modems offer a huge advantage in speed, but are more expensive and are most commonly used by large businesses. They are becoming more viable for the home as new, inexpensive ISDN lines are developed by the phone companies.

ISP (Internet Service Provider)—A company that provides your connection to the Internet. Unlike a commercial online service, an ISP provides complete access to the Internet; it also does not package and publish its own content.

Java—A popular programming language used to develop applications for Web browsers. Java apps are transferred "live" over the Internet. See also **applet**.

JPEG (Joint Photographic Experts Group)—A type of graphics file commonly used to store images on the Internet.

listserv—A program used to handle mailing lists on the Internet.

Location toolbar—Part of the Navigator program window. You can use the text box to type an address. Also includes the Bookmarks folder.

modem—The hardware device you use with your computer to communicate over the phone lines.

Mosaic—The first Web browser and, at one time, the most popular. (Netscape Navigator, created by Marc Andreessen, the creator of Mosaic, is now one of the more popular browsers.)

MPEG (Motion Picture Experts Group)— A standard for compressed video files.

multimedia—The presentation of information in many different media—sounds, graphics, text, and video.

Navigation toolbar—Part of the Navigator program window. You can use the buttons in this toolbar to navigate from page to page.

Netiquette—An informal set of rules or manners that Internet users are expected to follow.

Netscape Collabra—Part of Netscape Communicator. You can use this program to participate in newsgroups.

Netscape Communicator—A suite of Internet programs, including Netscape Collabra, Netscape Composer, Netscape Conference, Netscape Netcaster, and Netscape Navigator.

Netscape Composer—Part of Netscape Communicator. You can use this program to create Web pages.

Netscape Conference—Part of Netscape Communicator. You can use this program for realtime conversation (like a telephone conference call).

Netscape Navigator—One of the most popular browsers used to view Web pages. You can also use Navigator to send email, participate in newsgroups, and download files.

Netscape Netcaster—Part of Netscape Communicator. You can use this program to subscribe to a channel and have that content delivered to your PC. You can then browse the content offline.

news reader—A program that enables you to read the messages in a newsgroup.

newsgroup—An Internet discussion group dedicated to a specific topic. You post and review messages on this electronic bulletin board.

page—A document displayed on the World Wide Web. The page may be one screen or more and may contain text, images, sounds, animations, videos, and links to other pages. The page is formatted using HTML.

plug-ins—Add-on programs for Netscape Navigator that enable you to display different types of documents. For example, Shockwave is a plug-in program created by Macromedia. You can use it to play some types of movie files.

POP (Point of Presence)—The local connection you use to get Internet access.

PPP (Point-to-Point Protocol)—A method for connecting directly to the Internet. Most Internet Service Providers offer this type of connection.

protocol—A set of rules for how to handle communication on the Internet. For example, FTP (file transfer protocol) handles how files are downloaded from the Internet.

push technology—A method of delivering content from the Internet. You subscribe to the channels of your choice, and these channel providers send content to your PC on the schedule you specify. You can then browse the information offline.

search engine—A tool you use to find particular sites on the Internet. You can use one of several search engines, including Yahoo!, Infoseek, Lycos, Excite, and others.

server—One part of a client-server computer system. The server is the software on a host computer that fulfills the requests from other computer programs (called clients) for files, information, and services stored on the server host computer. See also **client**.

shareware—Software that you can copy and try. If you want to continue using the software, you pay a small fee to register it.

SLIP (Serial Line Internet Protocol)—A method for connecting directly with the Internet. Most Internet Service Providers offer this type of connection.

spider—A program used by many search engines to collect information from Web pages for indexes.

SSL (Secure Sockets Layer)—A protocol used for data security. Data is encrypted so that sensitive information (like your credit card number) can be transmitted safely across the Internet.

tags—The formatting codes used in an HTML document. See also **HTML (Hypertext Markup Language)**.

TCP/IP (Transmission Control Protocol/Internet Protocol)—TCP is the standard used on the Internet to work with packets to ensure that data is sent without errors. IP is the standard used to transmit information over the Internet and to define Internet addresses. TCP is usually used with IP.

Unix—An operating system used on computers. Many Internet networks use Unix.

upload—To copy a file from your computer to another site.

URL (Uniform Resource Locator)—The specific address for an Internet site.

Usenet—The collection of Internet newsgroups.

Winsock—The standard Microsoft Windows programs used to connect with the Internet and other TCP/IP networks.

World Wide Web—An Internet service that displays pages of information graphically. The pages may include pictures, sounds, animations, and video clips, and are usually linked to other pages.

Index

C

F

G

H

M

N